MOSELEY 1850–1900

Space, place and people in a middle-class Birmingham suburb

Janet Berry

West Midlands Publications
an imprint of
University of Hertfordshire Press

First published in Great Britain in 2023 by
West Midlands Publications
an imprint of
University of Hertfordshire Press
College Lane
Hatfield
Hertfordshire
AL10 9AB

British Library Cataloguing in Publication Data

A catalogue record for this book is available from the British Library

ISBN 978-1-912260-64-5

Design by Arthouse Publishing Solutions
Printed in Great Britain by Henry Ling Ltd

MOSELEY
1850–1900

Contents

Figures

Abbreviations

BCT	Barrow Cadbury Trust
CRL	Cadbury Research Library, University of Birmingham
LBA	Library of Birmingham Archives
LBLH	Library of Birmingham Local History
MSHGC	The Moseley Society History Group, 'The Collection'
PC	private collections
PCFA	F. Adams, secretary, The Moseley Society
PCRB	R. Brown, volunteer archivist, St Mary's Church, Moseley
PCRC	R. Cockel, committee member, The Moseley Society History Group
SMCA	St Mary's Church Archive, Moseley

1

Introduction

Over the course of the fifty years between 1850 and 1900 Moseley developed from a tiny hamlet just south of Birmingham to a flourishing middle-class suburb. This book explores when, why and how Moseley developed as a middle-class suburb, the people instrumental in its development, its houses, architecture, gardens, residents, interiors and lifestyles, and its residents' involvement in volunteerism and philanthropy. It interweaves the personal experiences of people who lived in the suburb, bringing to life what it was like to be surrounded by change, in a new residential area, in new homes with new neighbours, charting new codes and experiences and joining new institutions. It considers how its residents lived in all their diversity – as individuals, in groups and via networks – examining their everyday lived experiences, reactions and responses. It exposes residents' assumptions, values and virtues behind the façade, as well as 'hidden' areas: their vices, misfortunes, problems and insecurities. It threads the impact of class, gender and new technology through the chapters. Living through such change was an exciting challenge of modernity for some, but others reacted against the losses, disruptions and pollution that occurred. Moseley was more than a collection of buildings where people lived: it was a physical, social, cultural and psychological space where people conveyed messages about who they were and how they wanted to be seen for themselves and by others.

Two images of the village green illuminate the radical change to Moseley village wrought by suburbanisation. In the first, from 1858, a lone mother and child populate the village green, an edged but uneven triangular space of mud and rough grass left when the old road was drained and the new turnpike road was formed in 1801 (Fig. 1.1). The row of low-roofed buildings includes the Bull's Head public house, the oldest pub in Moseley, dating back to 1700, 'a no-frills alehouse for working villagers' and, nearby, the village blacksmith's forge.[1] Rising above these is the stone tower added in the sixteenth century to St Mary's, founded as a 'chapel of ease' in 1405. Timber-framed houses run around St Mary's Row on the left along a road that is rough and cobbled but pavemented. This road was an ancient route that followed a track linking the River Rea at Cannon Hill with the River Cole at Yardley Wood by way of Moseley and Wake Green. It led to Elmhurst, the large house almost hidden

1 C. Gilbert, *The Moseley trail* (Birmingham, 1986), p. 9.

Figure 1.1. Moseley village green, 1858. Moseley Society History Group, 'The Collection' (MSHGC), Clive Gilbert Photographs (MC/D1/F16/7).

by trees on the right of the image. Beyond was a road junction, the highest point of the old village, where Ladypool Lane (now Church Road) forked off left from Wake Green Road. This junction, a dry bench of land close to a good spring, was probably the focal point of the original settlement. The timber-framed Elizabethan farmstead that once stood on the site was called 'Village Green House'. A little further on, Lett Lane (now School Road) forked off right towards King's Heath.

In 1900, remembering his regular visits to Moseley in the 1840s, Thomas Anderton recalled this scene:

> As for Moseley … it was a pretty little village in those days. The old village green, the rustic country inns … and some low-roofed, old-fashioned houses, backed by the parish church tower, made up a picture which still remains in my mind's eye.
>
> Beyond Moseley Church was a pretty road to Moseley Wake Green, in which were, if I remember rightly, one or two timbered houses and some old-fashioned residences, surrounded by high trees … . In another direction from the church was a country road running to Sparkbrook, and near which were an important house and lands belonging to the wealthy Misses Anderton.[2]

2 Thomas Anderton, *A tale of one city: the new Birmingham* (Birmingham, 1900), p. 116.

Figure 1.2. Moseley village green, 1895. Personal collection Roy Cockel (PCRC).

Such rural scenes appealed to the urban middle classes because they represented a seemingly idyllic rural environment, peaceful and innocent-looking in contrast to busy, competitive Birmingham.

In the second image, from 1895, the cottages have been replaced by tall shops (Fig. 1.2). St Mary's church tower still stands proud, but the Bull's Head has been rebuilt and the village green is now manicured and enclosed by iron railings. There are superior pavements and streetlights, tram rails are visible in the foreground and 'growlers' await passengers alongside a cabmen's hut. Horse transport suggests the 'carriage class' and a local commercial scene. This image celebrates suburbanisation and civic pride, newness, modernity and civilisation. It reflects the desire of the middle class for a peaceful, well-ordered and well-appointed environment and feeds into ideas about a shared universe of like-minded middle-class people centred around a village green.

The changes were celebrated by some: in 1900 William Spurrier, a Moseley resident, local historian and Birmingham silversmith and electroplater, described Moseley enthusiastically as 'one of the most beautiful residential districts in the Kingdom … . Now we have good and well-lighted roads, three churches, Railway Station etc., etc., with a population of some 5,000 residents in upwards of 1,100 houses.'[3] This use of the language of the town rather

3 SMCA, *Canon Colmore's log book*, W.J. Spurrier, *Moseley of today and a look into the past*, p. 447. The Reverend William Harrison Colmore, vicar of St Mary's church from 1876 to 1907, cut pages out of St Mary's parish magazines and pasted them into a log book between 1877 and 1892.

than that of the country was typical of attitudes to 'improvement' in the late nineteenth century.

There was nostalgic sadness too, though. Thomas Anderton wrote in the same year:

> The prevailing colour of the old village green is now red brick, and the modern colour does not agree so well with my vision as the more rustic tones of a bygone day; whilst the noise and bustle of tram cars, the swarms of suburban residents that emerge from the railway station (especially at certain times in the day), are fast wiping out the peaceful, pretty Moseley of my youthful days.[4]

H.W. Nutter's ode *Moseley as it was and as it is* also lamented the passing of the old village:

> For forty years and more, this village green
> To me has been a sweet familiar scene
> Nor can the changes that are passed o'er
> Each long-loved tree and many a cottage door
> Erase the thought of every well-known spot,
> So loved of old and ne'er to be forgot …
> But oh! How changed! The townsman's red-brick pile
> With palisades, all in the newest style-
> And rows of terraces and villas trim,
> Of every kind to please the builder's whim.
> And cockney houses line the pleasant road,
> Of different houses and of various mode.
> Whilst through the fields, where bloomed the sweet woodbine
> The steaming engine thunders down the line.
> How green the hedgerows then! How still the way!
> Save sound of rural wain with fragrant hay,
> Or rustic villager, with basket stored,
> To market plodded with his precious hoard.[5]

Moseley grew slowly before 1850, from around 191 households and a population of around 400 in 1811 to some 380 households in 1840 and a population in the district of around 1,000 in 1841.[6]

---

4 Anderton, *A tale of one city*, p. 116.

5 Gilbert, *The Moseley trail*, pp. 4 and 5.

6 N. Hewston, *The history of Moseley village* (Stroud, 2009), p. 29; A. Fairn, *A history of Moseley* (Halesowen, 1973), p. 42; Gilbert, *The Moseley trail*, p. 2; F. Price, *The Moseley Church of England National School: a history 1828–1969* (Birmingham, 1998), p. 1.

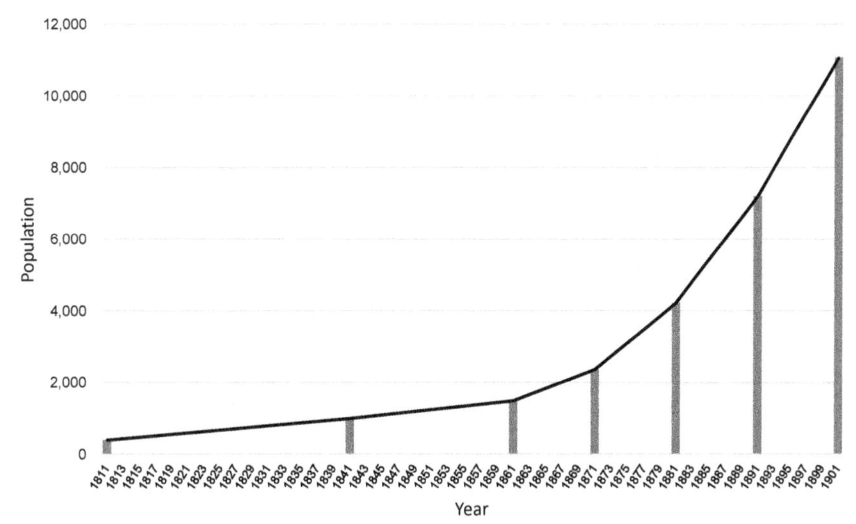

Figure 1.3. Moseley's population, 1811–1901. Ian Berry.

In the second half of the nineteenth century, however, Moseley grew exponentially, from approximately 1,500 residents in 1861 to 11,100 in 1901 (Fig. 1.3). Each decade saw more new residents, with the last decade of the century a peak period of growth. Moseley was one of several villages surrounding Birmingham that developed as suburbs over the nineteenth century. The population of some, such as Moseley, Handsworth and Northfield, peaked in the 1890s, whereas others within walking distance of the city centre and easily accessed by private transport and later by public transport, such as Aston, Balsall Heath and Edgbaston, peaked earlier – between 1871 and 1881. During the second half of the nineteenth century Moseley's growth was controlled by its landowners and subsequently it remained smaller than most other Birmingham suburbs except for Acocks Green. Acocks Green was much further out than Moseley and developed more intensively later, when served by a railway. Suburban development of this kind was also happening around other cities, such as Manchester.

Moseley's boundaries fluctuated in the nineteenth century (Fig. 1.4). Moseley was situated in the parish of King's Norton, Worcestershire, before 1911, and was within the Moseley Yield for tax purposes, along with King's Heath, Balsall Heath and Brandwood End. The church, St Mary's, achieved parish status from 1755 but had no defined boundary until confirmed as a District Chapelry in 1853. In 1863 the southern part of this parish was separated into a consolidated chapelry of All Saints, King's Heath. In 1875 another District Chapelry, St Anne's Church, Park Hill, was created to the north and in 1879 Wake Green was added to St Mary's parish. This was typical of what was happening across the country.

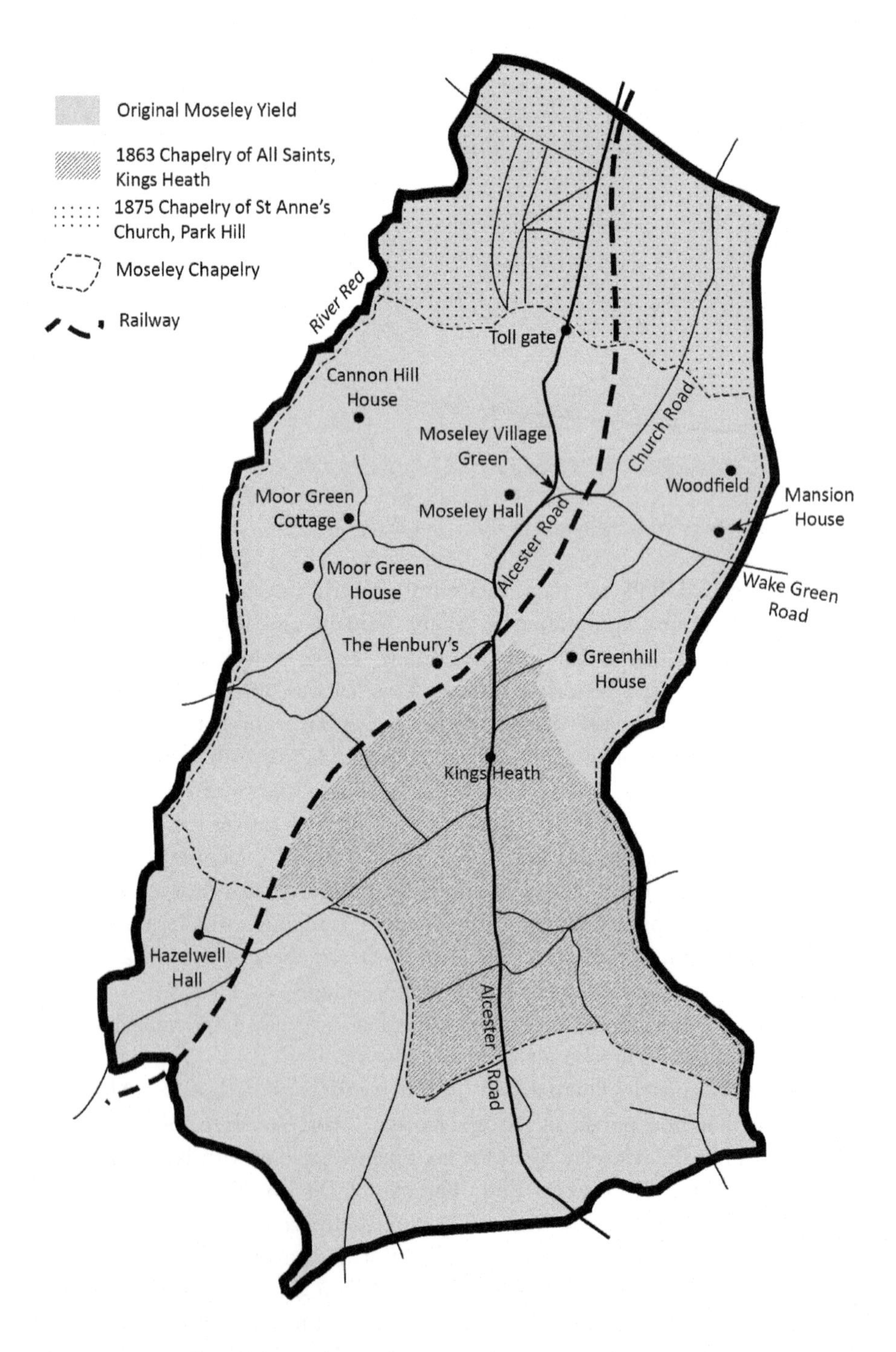

Figure 1.4. The Moseley tithe map, 1838, illustrating Moseley Parish and King's Heath Parish. St Mary's Church Archive (SMCA). Redrawn by Sarah Elvins.

The first half of the nineteenth century was a proto-suburban phase for Moseley during which factors came into play that made the village ripe for suburban development from mid-century. These were both general developments – the formation and expansion of the middle classes and the growth and industrialisation of Birmingham – and specific factors both physical and personal, including transport developments – a railway line through the village and the introduction of an omnibus service.

The growth of Birmingham and its industrial and commercial success were significant factors in Moseley's suburbanisation. Conditions and events in the city prompted many members of the middle classes to look for a safer, healthier and more salubrious environment in which to live, generating a 'flight to the suburbs'.[7] Between 1801 and 1851 Birmingham's population increased dramatically, from nearly 74,000 to around 300,000. By 1901 it had increased to 750,000. People were attracted to the city as industry expanded and Birmingham became the world's leading manufacturer of metalware, including goods such as buckles, buttons, screws, nails, pens, pins, jewellery, coins, medals and guns, produced largely in small, cramped, badly lit, poorly ventilated workshops. Considerable numbers of people also came into the town from the country for work following poor harvests. Little planning or housing legislation and no environmental control resulted in piecemeal, high-density housing, insanitary slum conditions, overcrowding, pollution and disease. The large number of young people in the population led to an increase in crime and the cultural, moral and physical impoverishment of the working classes were both visible and alarming to many Victorians. Disturbances reinforced perceptions of the city as a dangerous place. For example, in 1839 the Moseley yeomanry was called 'to assemble at Moor Green, in consequence of the disturbances at Birmingham' – the Birmingham Bull Ring Riots, which followed the rejection of a Chartist petition presented to parliament by Thomas Attwood.[8]

The development and growth of a middle class, or middle classes, was a crucial factor in the suburbanisation of Moseley. The size of this middle class increased across Britain in the nineteenth century, enhancing its sense of cohesion and significance as a group. Middle-class people's sense of themselves as members of a separate class within society, with a different ethos, was reinforced by other factors. Middle-class money was derived from business, whereas the aristocracy was supported by land and agricultural rents, while the

7 F.M.L. Thompson (ed.), *The rise of suburbia* (Leicester, 1982), p. 13; H.J. Dyos, *Victorian suburb: a study of the growth of Camberwell* (London, 1966), p. 8.

8 MSHGC, Extracts from the diary of Matthew Boulton (1807–41). Born in Turvey, Bedfordshire, Matthew Boulton went to live early on with a distant relative, Joseph Dyott (1755–1837), who was a wealthy landowner of Wake Green Road. Dyott left Boulton his fortune when he died.

widening gap between the middle and working classes was marked by differing mores and a turn away from manual labour on the part of the middle classes.[9] The desire for social recognition and pride in business prowess grew, sharpening ideas of social place.[10] The 1832 Reform Act incorporated heads of middle-class households politically for the first time and the interests of the middle classes were reflected in the 1834 Poor Law Amendment Act and the 1835 Reform of Municipal Government, the latter, along with the 1829 repeal of the Test and Corporation Acts, removing civil disabilities from nonconformists.[11] The middle classes were 'at the heart of the revivals which swept through all denominations' and ideas about home as 'havens of comfort, stability and morality' emerged.[12] Birmingham's industrial and commercial success meant that many achieved a level of financial success that elevated them economically into the middle classes, enabling them not only to fund a move to Moseley but also to pursue the values and lifestyles that the middle classes came to represent.

The middle classes, though, incorporated a range of differences in matters such as occupation, income, religion and politics. By the middle of the nineteenth century 'these disparate elements had been welded together in a powerful unified culture' that provided a clear sense of middle-class identity in Britain and an effective pressure group for suburban development.[13] In practice, as intimated above, it was not a unified group: the middle classes consisted of a hierarchy, encompassing an elite, who might be wealthier than some members of the aristocracy, down to those just above the skilled artisan level. This impacted on the cultural life of Moseley, particularly after 1850, and created a wide spectrum of experience that was manifested in the homes, gardens and lifestyles of its various residents, their position in suburban society and the power and control they exerted.

At the top of the pyramid of society in Moseley were the super elite such as Joseph Chamberlain (1836–1914) of Highbury, Moor Green, and Richard Cadbury (1835–99) of Moseley Hall and Uffculme, Moor Green. Below them were wealthy men such as John Avins (1816–91) of Highfield House, Church Road, who retired to Moseley in 1858 having made his fortune in Birmingham. Slightly further down the hierarchy were well-to-do employers – for example, Althans Blackwell (1850–1929) of Brackley Dene, 30 Chantry Road, who was a partner with his brother-in-law, Nathaniel Cracknell

9 L. Davidoff and C. Hall, *Family fortunes: men and women of the English middle class 1780–1850* (Abingdon, 2002), pp. 18–22.

10 *Ibid.*, pp. 19 and 20.

11 *Ibid.*

12 *Ibid.*, pp. 21 and 22.

13 *Ibid.*, p. 23.

Reading (1849–1924) of Inglewood, Wake Green Road, in a silversmithing and jewellery factory at 186–7 Warstone Lane in the Jewellery Quarter, Birmingham – and independent professionals such as Edward Holmes, an architect living in School Road. Below these were workers such as commercial travellers, including William Crompton, living in 1901 at Maycroft, a modest semi-detached house in middle-status Ascot Road, and James Barston, living in the lower-status Queenswood Road in 1881. The middle classes were well aware of the nuances that separated the different social layers of the social and economic hierarchy and, as Moseley expanded in the later part of the second half of the nineteenth century and more lower-middle-class residents moved to the suburb, these differences became more evident.

The sense of the middle classes as a separate social group promoted their members' desire to live alongside their own group in socially exclusive areas and proclaim their new financial and social status. The formation of a suburb such as Moseley was part of this process. Living in Moseley presented opportunities for the middle classes to fulfil social aspirations and live as 'gentlemen' in the style of upper-class country-house living. It reflected nostalgia for a rural idyll of yesteryear, a 'Golden Age' where a social hierarchy that had been 'lost' in the process of urbanisation and industrialisation still existed. It was nostalgia, though, for a time when their own social class had not existed in any substantial form.

The middle classes began not only to look to live alongside others of the same social standing but also to live in single-family houses with gardens. Ways of satisfying these notions emerged in the first half of the nineteenth century. In 1810 the Regent's Park development by John Nash (1752–1835) in London placed houses in a rural setting that gave residents the illusion that they looked out on their own country park. In 1824 he added Park Villages East and West, in which each rustic cottage was different and each was in its own garden. Such developments were also taking place in the provinces. In 1836 the Victoria Park Manchester Company established a residential area approximately two miles south of Manchester city centre, an estate of substantial houses in spacious grounds intended for the families of the prosperous business and professional middle classes. Development by the building lease system, used extensively in Moseley after 1850, became easier from the 1840s because the number of landowners legally able to grant building leases was increased by changes in the law relating to settled estates and charity and ecclesiastical land, by General Acts that clarified the law relating to building development and by a string of judicial decisions. Various improvement acts in the late 1840s enabled the raising of rates for improvements. The Towns Improvement Clauses Act 1847, for example, included drainage, sewerage, gas and water pipes, numbering houses and the lighting, naming, paving, maintaining and cleaning of streets.

The middle classes, then, increasingly had the financial means, the ideology and the desire, backed by the example of villa-building and wider legal regulations, to create an effective demand underpinning suburbanisation. Moseley, of course, was not exclusively middle class: servants and services were needed to enable the middle classes to function in their new environment and demonstrate their elevated social position, which brought some working-class people to the suburbs. Servants, though, mostly lived in, making them often invisible in the built landscape, and there was little physical and social evidence of their presence.

Moseley had specific advantages that attracted the middle classes. It was the kind of settlement that appealed to their nostalgic view of the countryside – a picturesque established nucleus that included an old church, St Mary's, a manor with an extensive country estate, Moseley Hall, a village green and a few cottages. It was a settlement with a long history. Moseley developed in the Saxon period and is mentioned in the 1086 Domesday Book as 'Museleie', but its first name was probably 'mus(a)-leage' meaning 'field-mouse clearing'.[14] It was set in a rural environment that included Hall Farm and Fleetwoods, near today's Park Hill and Anderton Park Road, farmsteads in Lett Lane (later School Road), Moor Green Lane, Springfield Road and Low Lane (later Stoney Lane), and cottages in Cotton, Bully (later Billesley) and Lett Lanes. Writing in the 1894 *Moseley Society Journal* Edward Holmes, a Moseley architect, remembered how, when he walked to Birmingham's Free Grammar School in about 1844, School Road was a 'narrow bye road' 'bounded by holly hedge' and 'innocently rustic', and that 'the houses then were few and far between on Alcester and Moseley Roads'.[15] At the same time shops and services began to develop – important to people moving from a city. In 1841 there were timber merchants in the Cotton Lane area, George Johns, builder and carpenter, William Phillips, hatter, Thomas Averill, tailor, John Smallwood, boot and shoemaker of Wake Green, and a blacksmith, Thomas Maydew.[16]

Moseley's proximity to Birmingham made easy access to the city possible, but at the same time it was sufficiently far away to pre-empt fears of encroachment, to engender a sense of distance from the city's problems and to preserve a sense of a country retreat. The village was on an ancient highway, the Alcester–Birmingham turnpike road. This road had been levelled where necessary, and drained and straightened in 1801, and was wide enough for two coaches to pass each other. These improvements ensured a passable surface and a direct route to Birmingham that facilitated travel to the city for work, shopping and entertainment. Attending cultural events was important to the status and

14 Fairn, *History of Moseley*, p. 9.

15 MSHGC, C3/D2/F1/36, *Moseley Society Journal*, 1/10 (November 1894).

16 *Bentley's directory of Worcestershire*, 1841; Fairn, *History of Moseley*, p. 42.

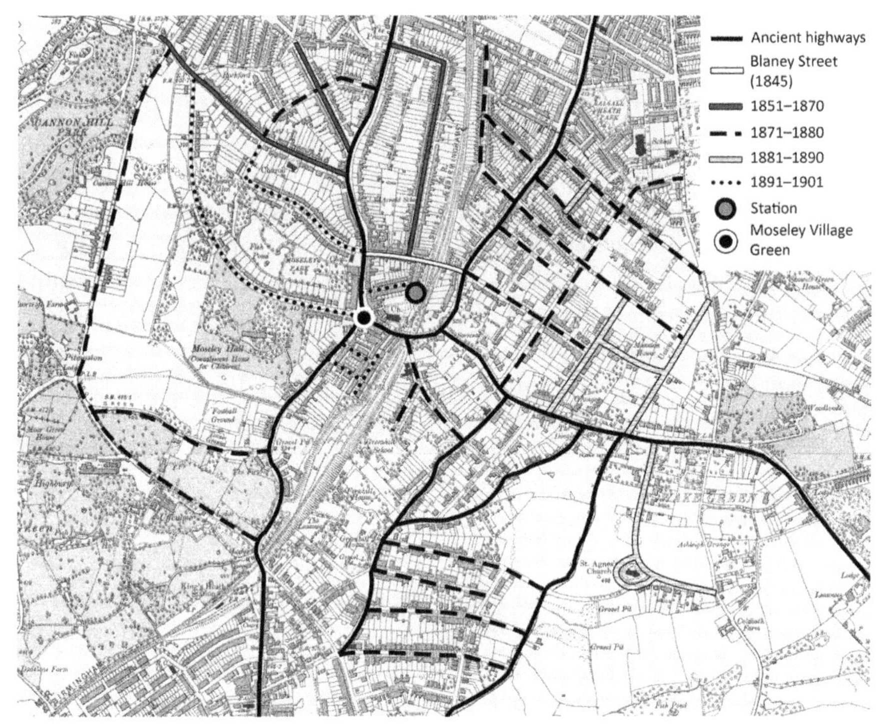

Figure 1.5. Road development, Moseley. Map constructed by Janet Berry (https://digimap.edina.ac.uk, 'Digimap', 'Historic', 'Historic Roam'. Accessed 2015). Redrawn by Sarah Elvins.

lifestyle of the Moseley middle classes. Matthew Boulton, a Moseley resident (not the more famous Handsworth industrialist), wrote of events he attended in Birmingham in his 1838–41 diary.[17] He enjoyed the ball at Birmingham County Hall on 5 October 1838 – 'certainly the most splendid Ball I was ever at. No expense spared, about 600 present.'[18] There were bazaars, such as the one at the Shakespearean Rooms on 28 September 1840, and flower shows, such as 'the Flower Show of the Society of Arts' on 18 May 1837. On 19 September 1837 there was 'a new oratorio by Mr Mendelsohn [*sic*] called "St Paul", to the delight and gratification of all present' at a very full town hall, Birmingham.[19] The next day the town hall was again crowded, this time for the *Messiah*, and on 22 September 1837 for a performance that 'commenced with an organ prelude by Mr Mendelsohn'.

In the early years of the century, access to Birmingham from Moseley meant travelling by private horse or carriage, on foot or by public coach. Public

17 MSHGC, Extracts from Matthew Boulton's diary.

18 *Ibid.*

19 Birmingham Town Hall was specially built in 1834 for Birmingham Music Festival.

coaches were relatively frequent. In 1815 a coach departed from the Fighting Cocks on Moseley village green to Birmingham on Mondays, Thursdays and Saturdays at 10am and 4pm.[20] Fares were high, 1s 6d to 2s in the 1820s to ride inside – too expensive for the mass of the population (a skilled tradesman earned around 3s 4d per day) – and the timings were too infrequent as a commuter transport system. Stagecoaches, smartly turned-out and punctual, lasted longer on this turnpike than on others, because there was no railway to Alcester until the 1840s. Owning a horse or a private carriage was affordable only for the better off, which meant that newcomers buying or renting property in Moseley were the well-to-do middle-classes. Carriage ownership generally grew rapidly, to four per 1,000 inhabitants in 1840, reflecting this group.[21] This transport scenario set Moseley on its way to becoming a middle-class commuter enclave. Six other ancient highways centred on Moseley provided easy access to other areas, and together the ancient highways formed a basic framework for future road and public-transport developments (Fig. 1.5).

The increasing road traffic meant Moseley became a crucial stopping place for stagecoaches and other vehicles on their way to and from Birmingham, which brought more trade and alerted visitors to the advantages of the village. It helped establish Moseley inns as places to be visited both en route and as destinations in their own right. The Fighting Cocks was on a site where there had been a pub since 1750. It had developed out of the Red Lion, once owned by Richard Grevis of Moseley Hall, and was a meeting place for the local gentry and Conservatives.[22] Commercial travellers were also attracted to the village. Joseph Dixon, a haberdasher and travelling salesmen with a shop in Birmingham, wrote in his journal of 17 October 1827 that, after journeying to Henley, he breakfasted with his father at Mr Frederick Shore's near Moseley Wake Green and there 'sold some of my goods', which included pearl buttons.[23]

Moseley was also attractive because of its healthy environment and suitable geology for building. Its location south-east of Birmingham meant the prevailing south-westerly winds carried away the smells and smogs of the city. It was elevated, and height both was considered healthy and meant splendid views over the surrounding countryside at a time when 'a prospect' was sought after. From Greenhill House, School Road, the Shorthouse family could see the Abergavenny Sugar Loaf and Brecon Beacons in Wales on a fine day. William Spurrier described the village as 'perfectly healthy and salubrious,

20 Fairn, *History of Moseley*, p. 43.

21 M.J. Freeman and D.H. Aldcroft (eds), *Transport in Victorian Britain* (Manchester, 1988), p. 142.

22 Gilbert, *The Moseley trail*, p. 9; R. Cockel, *Moseley village walks from the dovecote* (Birmingham, 2006), p. 10; *Listed buildings of Moseley* (Birmingham, 1989), p. 23.

23 CRL, MS/14/3, *The journal of Joseph Dixon, 1822–1828*, p. 93.

Figure 1.6. Moseley Hall, 1831. Author's own collection.

being on the top of a considerable elevation' with 'plenty of natural fall for drainage' and gravel subsoils that ensured good drainage, factors that were 'very advantageous to house-building'.[24] He also pointed to the good clean water in springs, deep wells and the natural watercourses of the Rivers Rea and Cole, an important health consideration.

Birmingham businessmen and manufacturers were already moving out to Moseley before 1850, setting a precedent and paving the way for future incomers. John Taylor, a wealthy Birmingham manufacturer of metal products such as buttons and small gilded or japanned objects such as snuff boxes, bought Moseley Hall from the Grevis (or Greaves) family along with the 938-acre estate for £9,000 in 1764.[25] His son, also John Taylor, a banker who founded Taylor's and Lloyd's Bank, the predecessor of Lloyds TSB, rebuilt the hall in brick and stone for £6,000 in 1776, and again in 1792–6 after it was burned down in the 1791 Birmingham Priestley Riots, extending it to either side and adding a porticoed entrance (Fig. 1.6).[26] Humphry Repton, the first person to call himself a landscape gardener, advised on the grounds in 1792 and many of his suggestions were adopted over time, notably the enlargement of the lake, tree planting and the positioning of the entrance drive to give a more imposing

24 SMCA, *Canon Colmore's Diary*, Spurrier, *Moseley of today*, p. 447.

25 Fairn, *History of Moseley*, p. 29.

26 *Ibid.*

Figure 1.7. The Mansion House. MSHGC (MC/D1/11/7).

approach to the house.[27] This rebuilding and enhancing of Moseley Hall gave Moseley a status manor house and squirearchy that attracted newcomers into the second half of the nineteenth century. After John Taylor II died in 1814, his widow remained at the hall and James Taylor, his second son, succeeded him. During the Taylors' ownership Moseley Hall was the centre of village life; the family was uppermost in organising and supporting village traditions, such as the yeomanry and the hunt, and the hall and its residents remained at the heart of Moseley life during the nineteenth century, an attraction to those wishing to associate themselves with the elite middle classes.[28]

More wealthy Birmingham industrialists moved out to Moseley in the first half of the nineteenth century, building or adapting large houses set in estates and grounds. The Andertons, city ironmongers and slum landlords, lived at Mansion House, a large, gracious dwelling on the 596-acre Wake Green Estate, inherited by Isaac Anderton from his father in 1833 (Fig. 1.7). In 1801, William Shorthouse moved to the twenty-roomed South Hill House at Greenhill, with its 120 acres of grounds and farmland. He was the founder of Shadwell Vitriol Works, manufacturing chemists of oil of vitriol and aqua-fortis manufacturers, at 64 Shadwell Street and 9 New Market Street, Birmingham. He immediately

27 <http://moseley-society.org.uk/wp-content/uploads/2015/11/HoD-2015-Moseley-Hall-leaflet.pdf>, accessed 15 March 2023.

28 MSHGC, Extracts from Matthew Boulton's diary; the Yeomanry were volunteer cavalry regiments raised from small farmers who owned land, with officers from the more well-to-do section of society.

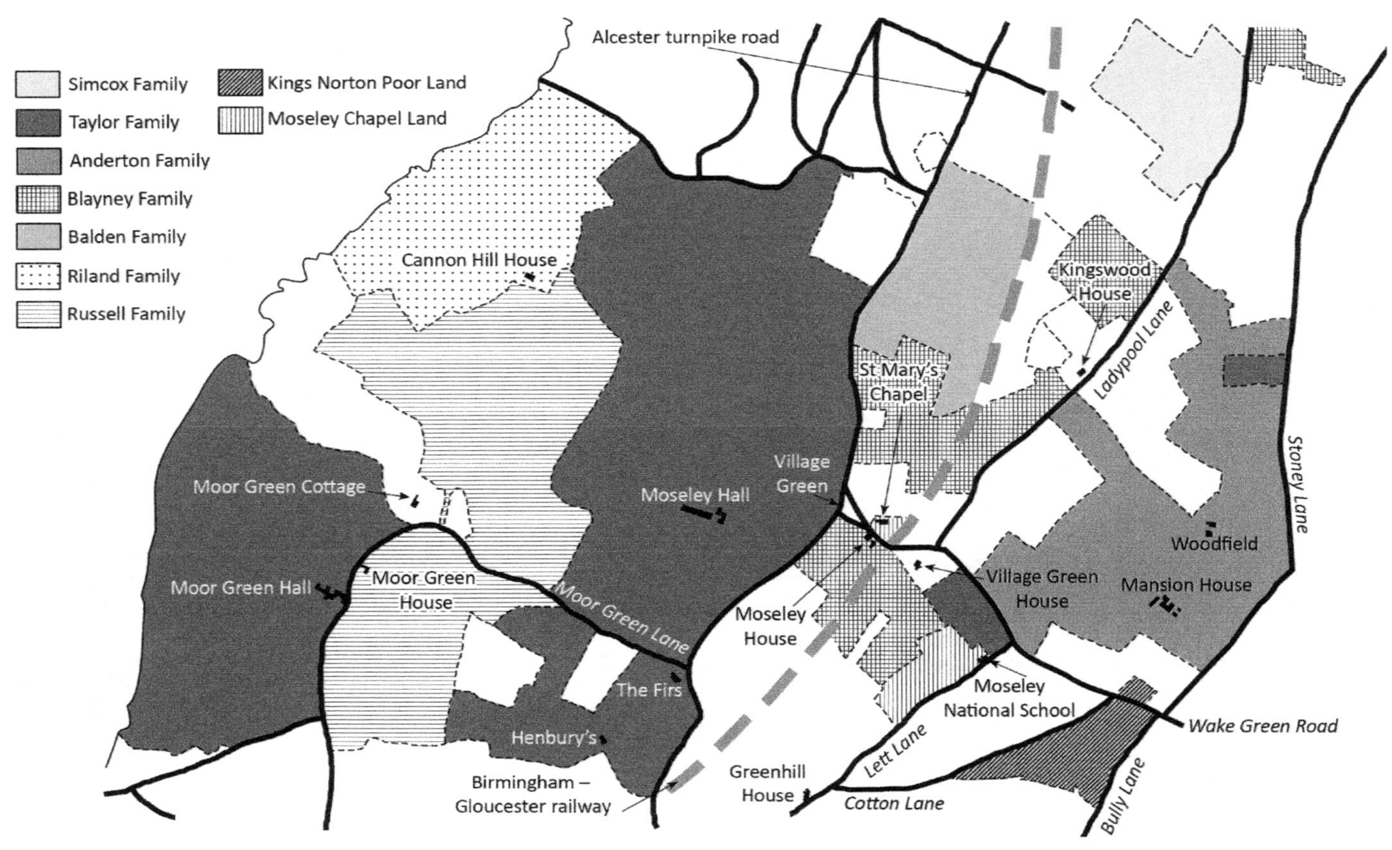

Figure 1.8. Moseley tithe map, 1840. Fairn, A., *A history of Moseley* (Halesowen, 1973). Redrawn by Sarah Elvins.

Figure 1.9. St Mary's chapel, 1812. Library of Birmingham, Local History Department (LBLH), WPS/WK/M6/144, by permission of the Library of Birmingham.

Figure 1.10. Moseley National School. MSHGC (C2/D3/F7/21).

enlarged the old house and his wife developed gardens remarkable for their size and quality. Joseph Purden, metal merchant, took over the Henburys, an estate of forty-five acres on Alcester Road.[29] The tithe map of 1840 locates these and other large establishments and shows that land in Moseley was concentrated in the hands of a small number of locally based families, a pattern that was important later in enabling a cohesive and ordered approach to development that preserved the village for the middle classes (Fig. 1.8).

No evidence has been located to indicate any middle-class snobbery against people like Shorthouse and Purden, who had made their fortunes in Birmingham's 'dirty' industries. Indeed, an active middle-class social and cultural life in Moseley during the first half of the nineteenth century was an attraction to potential residents. For example, Mr Palmer of Cannon Hill held a large evening party on 7 February 1839. Various local cultural clubs flourished, such as the Moseley Book Club, where, on 5 July 1839, Mathew Boulton 'dined … and bought lots of books'. He attended 'a Committee Meeting of the Natural History Society' on 11 May 1838 and on 28 October 1839 a lecture by Messrs St Croix on a new method of taking landscapes by Daguerreotype. The village celebrated the coronation of Queen Victoria and Matthew Boulton wrote: 'This day her majesty the Queen was crowned. I put on my military uniform for the first time. Our Squadron met upon the common in Review Order and went through the exercise, then drank to the queen in a glass of wine.' Afterwards they sat down to a substantial lunch provided by the lieutenants of the cornet.

St Mary's chapel was the only religious site in Moseley in the first half of the nineteenth century. It was the focus of much imagery as a picturesque device. An 1812 image shows a rural scene – the chapel on a rise, ancient cottages in front of the church that remained there until after 1871 and, down the roadway to the left, the village green, the grounds of Moseley Hall and rural views beyond (Fig. 1.9). In 1823 the chapel was enlarged and redesigned along Gothic lines, with a gallery replacing an earlier loft with room for the organ, the choir, 150 of the congregation and an additional 362 seats (274 free).[30] The chapel was very active. It held vestry meetings, such as the one on 16 November 1840 'respecting the repairs to be done to the Tower' and Mr Taylor of Moseley Hall mounted a petition 'against abolishing Church rates' in 1837.[31]

St Mary's brought attention and status to Moseley by establishing the first National School in Birmingham, which opened in 1828 in Lett Lane (School Road) and comprised two rooms, one downstairs for boys and the other upstairs for girls, and a small house for staff (Fig. 1.10). The local middle classes were at

29 Gilbert, *The Moseley trail*, pp. 2–3 and 5.

30 *St Mary's, Moseley guidebook and history* (Moseley, 2018), pp. 7 and 25.

31 MSHGC, Extracts from Matthew Boulton's diary.

the forefront of this initiative. Reverend Walter Farquhar Hook, appointed as curate-in-charge at Moseley Chapel in 1826, set up a committee of local men in 1827 with himself as secretary and James Taylor of Moseley Hall as treasurer. Fifty or so local upper-middle-class persons became subscribers, including the Taylor families, Joseph Dyott, the Andertons and William Congreve Russell. The National School was intended for the children of estate servants, its cost of 2d weekly excluding the children of the poor. It was stimulated by faith and optimism in the transformative capacity of schooling and was intended to encourage good habits, such as church attendance, economy, decency and cleanliness, and ultimately to reduce drinking, crime, strikes and riots. As such, it was a means of producing a peaceful and cooperative working class and workforce, an important element given Moseley's proximity to a nearby industrial city and the many Moseley residents and donors who were businessmen and manufacturers. Those giving a guinea subscription also had the power to hand out one ticket for one pupil for a year, demonstrating the paternalistic power of the middle classes in the local community. On the opening day, Easter Day 1828, ninety-seven boys and eighty-two girls marched to Moseley Chapel for a church service followed by a lunch of roast beef and plum pudding – numbers that suggest a substantial working-class population in the Moseley area.

Moseley's middle-class children did not attend Moseley National School. They attended private schools, of which there were several in Moseley. Mr J.T. Sansome, for example, ran Moseley Classical and Commercial School in Alcester Road from 1825, which was inherited on his death in 1837 by Mr and Mrs G. Sansome. The Misses Charlotte and Mary Ann Thrupp had a boarding school on the south side of School Road, Moseley, which opened in 1824 and continued until 1847. Lavinia Bartlett, a well-to-do middle-class lady from north Birmingham whose son attended the Thrupps' school, wrote in her travel diary of 1843–51 of visiting 'my dear boy at Moseley' on 20 May 1843.[32] Charles Augustus had suffered a virulent attack of croup in the night, but he met his mother at the door in good health. Lavinia Bartlett was about to embark on a trip abroad and on finding her son well was able to start her journey to France.

The period from the 1770s to the 1830s was the 'Golden Age' of canals. No canals were built near Moseley – an advantage to the middle classes moving to the village, as canals frequently brought industry to the rural environment. Moseley residents were, though, involved in canal development. Matthew Boulton dealt in Old Birmingham Canal shares and attended meetings 'of the proprietors of the Old Canal in Paradise Street' on, for example, 11 May 1838. Between 15 October and 2 November 1838, he 'sold twelve shares in the Old Birmingham Canal at £148 each'. On 19 December 1838 he attended a

32 CRL, MS/447, *Travel diary of Lavinia Bartlett, 1843–1851.*

Figure 1.11. The railway tunnel and cutting, Moseley, 1890. PCRC.

meeting of the Old Canal Proprietors at Paradise Street to consider a petition to parliament regarding the making of a canal from West Bromwich to the Fazeley Canal at the Aston Junction.

In 1840 a railway was built through Moseley – a key development that paved the way for later suburbanisation. Isambard Kingdom Brunel surveyed a line in 1829–30, but his route was too expensive. The 1833 route of the engineer Captain Moorsom was accepted and authorised by parliament in 1836. The plan went some way to protecting the village from damage. The proposed line was kept away from Moseley Hall and ran to the east of Moseley chapel in a deep cutting – over a mile in length, with a maximum depth of 85 feet, and included a tunnel to protect the chapel from vibration and noise. The railway company, though, pressed ahead with a cutting to save £1,500 rather than the proposed tunnel, which angered local people, who took the case to the Court of Chancery. The company was compelled to cover part of the cutting to form a tunnel, a move they described as 'forced' on them by 'local opponents in parliament' and by 'objectors'.[33] The tunnel brought Moseley acclaim, because it was among the first and greatest railway works in the Birmingham area; the Gothic-arched tunnel portals were unique. Figure 1.11 shows the cutting's depth and the stylish tunnel entrance, and celebrates the construction prowess and technical advances involved. The neat slopes, bright green in the colour image, and trees offset concerns that railways destroyed the idyllic rural landscape.

33 P.J. Long and the Rev. W.V. Audrey, *The Birmingham and Gloucester Railway* (Gloucester, 1987), p. 14.

Local landowners were affected, including St Mary's church, represented by the Rev. William Morrell Lawson, James Taylor, Thomas Blaney, William Shorthouse, William Congreve Russell and William Spurrier.[34] They variously gave up houses, offices, carriage drives, gardens, pleasure gardens, walks, paddocks, plantations and pastures. Part of the church's glebe land was appropriated for the line and tenants' houses were demolished, including that of Edward Dickenson, who moved to St Mary's Row and later became the church beadle. There were detailed provisions for compensation for the landowners, but not for tenants. Four men died working on the track in the parish in 1840, some of whom had come a good distance to work in Moseley – Richard Child of Moseley Street, aged thirty-three, Henry Blackwell of Kimble, Wiltshire, aged eighteen, Robert Hawkins of King's Heath, aged forty-two, and Charles Hesketh of Barton, Lancashire, aged thirty-one.[35]

The Moseley railway line brought both financial gain and infrastructure. William Anderton directed in his 1835 will that land sales should be postponed for up to two years, citing the probability of a railway line – the Birmingham–Gloucester line – over his land that would probably bring a larger profit.[36] In the late 1830s William Shorthouse received £6,000 from the Midland Railway for two or three fields through which the company drove their deep cutting. The amount was just about what the whole estate had cost in 1801.[37] In 1839 Samuel Lloyd conveyed part of the freehold estate Balsall Heath House to the Birmingham and Gloucester Railway for £3,755 plus £500 paid by the same railway company in lieu of building a bridge connecting the lands severed by the railway.[38] A wooden trestle bridge was built over the line in 1849, extending Blaney Street and connecting it with Church Road, which opened up access east of the village green to the main Alcester Road and transport facilities there (Fig. 1.12). Blaney Street was renamed Woodbridge Road in consequence. This was the only road development prior to 1850, but it was a signal of future development.[39]

The disturbance caused by the huge engineering works must have been tremendous, both exciting and frightening. Local people and others visited the site to follow progress and view the navvies at work and then the first trains. Thomas Anderton wrote in 1900 of perceptions of Moseley tunnel in the 1840s: 'The railway tunnel which is now looked upon as only a long bridge, was then

34 The *Birmingham to Gloucester Railway Act 1836, Section 8*, courtesy of PCRB.

35 LBA, EP/77/2/4/1, St Mary's Church Burials, 1813–50.

36 LBA, MS/39/26/6, Will of William Anderton.

37 *Some Moseley personalities*, Vol. III (Birmingham, 2014), pp. 13–14.

38 LBA, MS/39/26/21–2 a/3/273/17, Conveyance of Samuel Lloyd.

39 LBA, H.J. Everson, 'Directory of Moseley', 1896.

Figure 1.12. The old wooden bridge, Woodbridge Road. MSHGC, Clive Gilbert Photographs (MC/D1/F12/16).

regarded as something large in its way, and, perhaps, slightly dangerous, almost justifying a little something strong to sustain courage when travelling through it.'[40]

Many feared railways would bring dirt, fumes and noise, as well as industry and the hoi polloi, and the health hazards of train travel were much debated by doctors.[41] Others, such as Matthew Boulton, found the prospect of the new railways exciting. On 17 July 1837 he 'went to see the trains come in on the railway to Liverpool … . It is an animating sight to see the trains moving so easily and swiftly along.' On 6 May 1840 he 'went with Mr Bramah in his carriage to Smethwick to see his extensive works for making railway carriages', a works that was established in 1839 in Cranford Street. Thomas Cook began organising occasional day excursions at a cheap rate for the less well-off in 1841, viewing these as contributing to moral improvement for the lower orders.[42] He negotiated with the Midland Railway Company for special trains for private outings for organisations such as temperance clubs, trades union galas and Sunday schools.

The railway, though, had little effect initially on Moseley because 'Moseley Station' was not in the village centre but at King's Heath, which meant

40 Anderton, *Tale of one city*, p. 116.

41 MSHGC, C2/D1/F4/17, William Dargue, *Moseley*.

42 J. Paxman, *The Victorians: Britain through the paintings of the age* (Reading, 2009), p. 19.

residents walked, or used private or hired transport, to get to the station. The location of the station in King's Heath suggests that Moseley people did not want their village disturbed by rail passengers.

The introduction of the horse-bus helped lay the foundation for the future development of Moseley as a suburb. In 1846 Hughes ran a horse omnibus service with six omnibuses daily and four on Sundays along the Alcester Road between Moseley and New Street, Birmingham.[43] However, at first fares were high, there were no early morning or late evening buses to suit some work hours and the lack of late buses meant those attending evening events in Birmingham needed private or hired transport. On the other hand, the omnibuses were larger and faster than coaches, were covered, and had a rear entry for easy access and increasingly more comfortable seating. The daily services and journey times became more convenient and fares decreased over time. These early omnibuses, then, only suited the better-off middle classes and those in occupations where starting times were later or a matter of choice, which again helped secure the suburb for the middle classes. They did, though, widen the opportunity to those members of the middle classes who could not fund private carriages. Omnibuses were crucial to Moseley's later development and continued to serve the suburb for some time.

Omnibuses were also important in developing Moseley's postal service, an important asset for the middle classes given their social and business involvements and the fact that many were at a remove from family and friends. Post initially came to Moseley by stagecoach or mail coach. From 1849 omnibuses brought post to Moseley, including parcels. Parcels under 14lbs cost 2d by omnibus; above 14lbs (but under 28lbs) they cost 3d, which had to be prepaid. The 'Penny Black', which went on sale from 6 May 1840, was the world's first adhesive postage stamp used in a public postal system. A total of 82 million letters was posted in 1839 and 169 million in 1840 – a huge increase.[44] A letter weighing up to half an ounce (14g) could be sent to any destination in the country for 1d. Before this, communications had been complex and expensive, with the recipient usually required to pay on delivery.

Moseley, then, had a range of advantages that, along with the growth of Birmingham and the middle classes, and transport developments in the decades between 1800 and 1850, paved the way for suburbanisation. Many of the factors involved continued to influence the growth of Moseley after 1850 and will be traced in subsequent chapters. Chapter 2 explores the phases of development in the second half of the nineteenth century, tracing the story of how, why and when Moseley grew, spread and developed as a flourishing middle-class enclave.

---

43 A.G. Jenson, *Early omnibus services in Birmingham 1834–1905* (Biggleswade, 1963), p. 4.

44 *Bath Postal Museum guidebook.*

2

Moseley's suburbanisation, 1850–1900

Moseley developed in four phases over the second half of the nineteenth century. From 1851 to 1871 suburbanisation gathered pace. In the next two decades it took off and intensified, and in the decade 1891–1901 it became a mature suburb. The pace of development fluctuated, slowed by the control of landowners and economic circumstances and stimulated by transport developments. Change also brought regrets, concerns and controversies and the slow erosion of the rural landscape.

1851–71: suburbanisation gathering pace

At first there was minimal change to the village: the increase in population between 1841 and 1861 averaged only twenty-five people per year. Between 1861 and 1871 Moseley's population increased more markedly – by approximately 940, from 1,500 to 2,440, an average of ninety-four new residents per year. Moseley was fortunate in that land was concentrated in the hands of a small number of families, which enabled a more consolidated approach to development, but also suggests the ongoing influence of the landed gentry rather than a radical new social structure shaping the area. These families were largely locally based, which gave them a personal interest in how the village developed. They released land slowly and in small blocks with covenants that stipulated the type and cost of houses; such covenants excluded the less well-off, thereby protecting the village from rampant development and helping preserve Moseley for the middle classes. The Blayney family sold their land off in small tracts from 1843 to 1886 and modest plots of land came up for sale in 1853 and 1858, the latter among the first from the Shorthouses' Greenhill estate.[1] In 1865 a field of freehold land in Church Road next to Highfield House, John Avins' home, was offered for sale following the death of the owner, Mr William Nutt.[2] It was described as 'well-adapted for erecting a villa residence'. The death of a landowner, particularly those with numerous inheritors, often prompted such sales. In 1868, two-acre plots of the Grange Farm estate and land between Cotton, Billesley and Greenhill Lanes were put up for auction.[3] The potential for development was clearly there and being

1 LBA, MS/179416, Bham/Sc, Birmingham: a collection of auctioneers' bills, Vol. 1.

2 *Ibid.*

3 LBA, MS/183, Grange Farm building estate brochure.

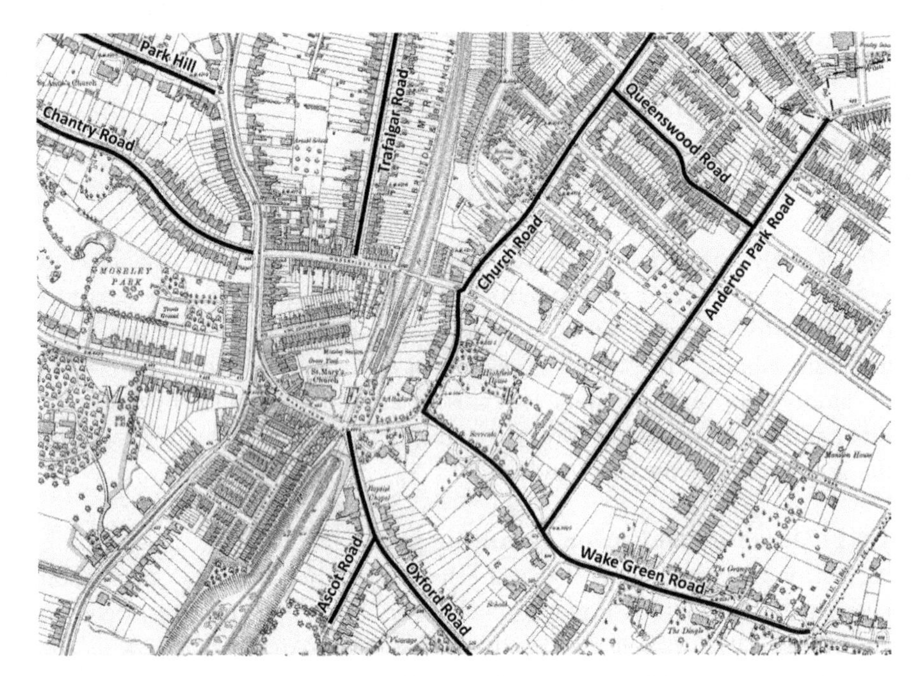

Figure 2.1. Key roads. Map constructed by Janet Berry (https://digimap.edina.ac.uk, 'Digimap', 'Historic', 'Historic Roam'. Accessed 2015). Redrawn by Sarah Elvins.

noticed, but development was controlled and small-scale, a decided advantage in determining the kind of suburb Moseley would become.

Road formation was modest between 1851 and 1871. H.J. Everson, a Moseley resident and local historian, listed thirty-six roads built in Moseley between 1850 and 1900.[4] Three of these were formed in this period: Park Road (1850), Trafalgar Road (1852) and Park Hill (1868), all off the village centre (Figs 1.5 and 2.1). A total of 102 new houses was built between 1861 and 1871 in seven roads. Fifty of these were in Trafalgar Road, leaving fifty-two built in the other six roads, an average of just over eight new houses in these roads. Houses were often built before roads were formed or rapidly thereafter. Ascot Road and Oxford Road (to School Road) were new roads proposed in 1871 on part of a 'very attractive' freehold estate, 'eminently suitable for the erection of first-rate suburban villas'.[5] Thirteen houses were built in Ascot Road in the same year as the plan and seven in Oxford Road. Coppice, Forest and Woodstock Roads, all formed in 1870, had twenty-two houses by 1871.

A crucial event that spurred Moseley's development was the building of the station in the heart of the village behind St Mary's church, which opened on

4 LBA, H.J. Everson.

5 LBA, Bham/Sc 1368.

Figure 2.2. Moseley station, late nineteenth century. PCRC.

1 November 1867, some twenty-seven years after the Moseley section of the railway was completed. Thomas Lewis, writing in *Birmingham Faces and Places* in 1890, thought there was 'no prettier station or one more picturesquely situated than that which was opened at Moseley'.[6] Figure 2.2 shows a station with a terrace of neat buildings, litter-free platforms, gas lighting, the wooden bridge and, celebrating the locomotive, an oncoming train. A report in the *Birmingham Daily Post* on 31 October 1867 stressed the convenient siting of the station, the short eleven-minute journey to Birmingham and the frequent and advantageous services offered:

> The station is formed immediately on the town side of the Moseley tunnel, and at the back of the old church. Access is gained to the station both from the upper or old part of Moseley, and also from the newly built district in the vicinity of the wooden bridge which spans the line some 200 yards below. The station is built on the Moseley side of the railway. According to present arrangements, six trains leaving New Street will stop at Moseley, and seven leaving Moseley for town each weekday. A dinner train leaving New Street at the convenient hour of one p.m. arrives at Moseley at 1.11, and an equally convenient train picks up the after-dinner passengers at 2.48, and deposits them on New Street Station platform at 3.5. After business hours Moseley may be reached by trains leaving town at 5.20 and 6.30, or later still, at 7.00 p.m.

6 M. Baxter and P. Drake, *Moseley, Balsall Heath and Highgate, the archive photographs series* (Chalford, 1996), p. 74.

The dinner train was a significant attraction to the elite employers of Moseley's middle classes, who were in a position to take a two-hour lunch break, and an indicator of a lifestyle many desired. In 1864 a Moseley resident signing himself 'S. Niak' had asked the *Birmingham Daily Post* to press for a station at Moseley, complaining that Moseley residents working in Birmingham were unable to go home for lunch because the Moseley omnibus journey took forty minutes due to 'frequent stoppages, in many cases prolonged by passengers not tendering the exact amount of fare' – perhaps an exaggeration reflecting middle-class attitudes to omnibus travel. For Moseley's middle classes commuting to and from the city by train meant an attractive and convenient station, a short journey time, a frequent, comfortable and convenient service and carriages that were differentiated by class.

The station also enabled easier access to other lines and made travelling greater distances more convenient. Saturday half-days became normal practice in the 1860s, which, along with Bank Holidays, made outings more possible. Crowds could travel to parks, public buildings, places of interest, exhibitions and resorts. Six million went to the Great Exhibition in 1851.[7] Holidays away from home had not been possible below the social level of the middle-middle classes before, but day excursions and weekend trips came within the means of all but the poorest and family holidays became popular, leading to the growth of resorts. However, very few families with children and an income below £100 per year would have gone together for more than a day excursion to the seaside.[8]

Finally, a station in the village centre allowed the delivery of fresh produce, catalogue purchases, garden plants and building materials from all over the country, easing the conduct of a middle-class lifestyle.

However, there was a significant anti-railway lobby generally across the country which may have influenced some Moseley residents. Doctors claimed that tunnels caused colds, catarrhs and consumption, that plunging into the darkness of a tunnel and then emerging into the light damaged the eyes, that the deafening noise, gloom and glare of the engine fire had a bad effect on nerves and that being moved through the air at high speed was 'gravely injurious to the lungs' and, for those with high blood pressure, would cause apoplexy.[9] Pro-rail doctors said the opposite: that the speed and swing of the train would 'equalise the circulation', promote digestion, tranquillise the nerves and ensure good sleep.[10] There were also fears that railways would attract ribbons of terraces, but few such houses were built in Moseley.

7 Freeman and Aldcroft, *Transport in Victorian Britain*, p. 48.

8 G. Best, *Mid-Victorian Britain 1851–1875* (St Albans, 1973), p. 226.

9 T. Burke, *Travel in England* (London, 1945–6), p. 116.

10 *Ibid.*

During this phase improvements were made to the omnibuses that serviced Moseley, stimulating its development. By 1857 a low longitudinal roof seat increased passenger accommodation. Later, forward-facing benches on the upper deck took capacity to twenty-four. New omnibus services came to Moseley in 1869, attracted by the potential of an expanding market. Two Liverpool brothers, William and Daniel Busby, formed the Birmingham Omnibus Company with ten luxurious new green omnibuses accommodating thirty-three passengers.[11] They ran half-hourly from 8.45am until 7.45pm from the outer termini and half an hour later from the city, and were cheap, at 3d inside and 2d on top. The service was enhanced by 10 per cent discount tickets for regular travel and the possibility of booking through-journeys. These omnibuses and the services on offer competed with the railway for passengers, but also offered an effective alternative means of transport for the less well-off.

Horse-drawn trams were introduced to the suburb in 1869, stimulating further development and opening up Moseley to a wider range of the middle classes. Their introduction indicated that Moseley was thriving – tramways were built only on potentially profitable routes, following the 'established traffic flows of a wealthy clientele' from the city to the suburbs.[12] Made of the new mass-produced steel, horse-drawn trams could carry more people faster and more cheaply and gave a smoother ride in more comfortable interiors, making them more attractive to the better-off. These trams were not necessarily readily accepted: the press was critical, as tram lines and 'industrialised transport' were considered a threat to 'existing patterns of movement' and an 'intrusion into an essential public space'.[13] Moseley residents must have found the installation of tram lines disruptive, but there were advantages: roads were widened and gutters, drains, kerbs and footpaths provided. Although fares never became low enough for the working classes they decreased over time, making them affordable to the less well-off; thus, like omnibuses, tramway penetration brought less-well-off new residents to Moseley, changing its character in the longer term.

Omnibuses, trams and trains brought various problems. Buses and trams could feature aggressive competition for passengers, overcrowding and furious driving. Passengers came into close proximity with strangers from different social strata. Some had different standards of behaviour, including drunkenness, stone-throwing, fighting and men having 'ladies on their knees' – all activities likely to deter the middle classes and make train travel, with

11 Jenson, *Early omnibus services.*

12 B. Schmucki, 'The machine in the city: public appropriation of the tramway in Britain and Germany, 1870–1915', *Journal of Urban History*, 38/6 (2012), p. 1066.

13 *Ibid.*, pp. 1062–3.

Figure 2.3. The Fighting Cocks, trade card, 1864. MSHGC, Clive Gilbert Photographs (MC/D1/F12/23).

its hierarchical carriages, more attractive.[14] Rules prohibited 'smoking in the interior', 'drunkenness' and 'using obscene or offensive language', suggesting the need to regulate such behaviour and the desire to attract the respectable. Women had to find new ways of behaving to safeguard their privacy, signal decency and manage relationships with men. They found themselves in new situations, such as queueing in the street or on railway platforms and possibly jostling for a seat or even standing until a seat became vacant. Women's respectability was demonstrated by their dress and manner. Etiquette books advised middle-class women about getting on and off transport, fare paying and how to deal with fellow passengers. That there was a need for such advice confirms women were taking advantage of public transport and were out in the public sphere regularly.

Reports of accidents and crime related to public transport in Moseley were few. However, in 1868 an imposter represented herself as a servant from Leamington who had been robbed of her return ticket to town and all her money while on a Moseley omnibus.[15] She appealed to her fellow passengers for 1s 10d, the fare home, and promised to go home by the next train and send the amount in stamps. She seemed so earnest that she managed to get the sum from the chapel-keeper of Newhall Street.

The improvements to transport and the building of the station opened Moseley up to more visitors and travellers, prompting developments in the village's hospitality sector. In about 1860 the Fighting Cocks was partially rebuilt as an imposing commercial hotel and in 1870 the Trafalgar Hotel, a new commercial and posting hotel, was built in Woodbridge Road. The Fighting Cocks and the Trafalgar Hotel were large enough to accommodate rooms where commercial travellers could write up their order books and dine. Both hotels developed features designed to attract a wider custom – pleasure gardens and sporting facilities, such as a bowling green, and, in the case of the Trafalgar Hotel from 1875, a purpose-built roller-skating rink that could be used throughout the year and was also a venue for bands and concerts. They advertised their services and facilities regularly in Birmingham newspapers and through trade cards (Fig. 2.3). These hotels also functioned as local civic buildings and community centres. The Trafalgar was used for legal sessions and for meetings of Moseley's Liberal element. The Fighting Cocks was the meeting place for Tory sympathisers and the Moseley Book Club.

Suburban development was not just about residential accommodation. Shops offered an important service to residents. Three traders named in

14 Freeman and Aldcroft, *Transport in Victorian Britain*, p. 143; Jenson, *Early omnibus services*, p. 4.

15 *Birmingham Daily Post*, 11 December 1868.

Bentley's Directory of 1841 survived into the 1850s and an 1858 trade directory listed eight shops, mostly in Woodbridge Road.[16] Twelve shops were listed in 1867, but only one, Thomas Hadley, grocer and tea dealer, was still there from 1858, suggesting shops changed hands frequently as the suburb expanded. Moseley had a post office and its services improved: dispatches increased to two in 1868 and arrivals to two daily in 1871. In 1871 Moseley Post Office also became a Post and Money Order Office and Post Office Savings Bank under Thomas Hadley, who was not only a grocer but also a spirit merchant. These services were an important support to commercial, business and social communication.

An important attraction of Moseley was that it was crime-free and safe, a perception reinforced by a police presence. The 1856 County and Borough Police Act made it compulsory for all towns and counties in England and Wales to set up a proper full-time paid police force with one policeman to every 1,000 people.[17] The government paid some of the costs of any police force that met with the approval of Inspectors of Constabulary, with the rest paid by local taxation. George Lear was the county police officer based in Blaney Street in 1858.[18] Press reports of crime in Moseley are few, but the prestigious homes of Moseley were tempting to criminals. In 1852 Mr Tarleton's house, Lime Grove House, was robbed of silver worth £40.[19]

One issue for constables was the enforcement of pub opening hours. At the time, 'bona-fide travellers' were legitimately allowed to be served outside of normal trading hours, but confusion abounded about what constituted a bona-fide traveller. On Sunday 17 April 1864 at 11.20am Constable Place found the Bull's Head open and thirty-two people drinking and smoking and the Fighting Cocks very full, including one or two drunks and people using bad language.[20] He claimed the drinkers were strangers, making them bona-fide travellers, presumably to protect villagers, but he was not believed. The proprietors, John Taylor of the Bull's Head and William Shipton of the Fighting Cocks, were fined £2 and £5 respectively by magistrates.

However, the rural ambience and attractiveness of the village to the middle classes suffered little between 1851 and 1871. The 1850 *Post Office Directory* described Moseley as 'a pleasant and romantic village' and, according to

16 *W. Kelly & Co.'s Directory of Birmingham with Staffordshire and Worcestershire* (London, 1850); *Isaac Slater's General and Classified Directory of Birmingham and its vicinities* (Manchester, 1852–3); *Dix & Co.'s General and Commercial Directory of the Borough of Birmingham and 6 miles around* (Birmingham, 1858). These traders were George Johns (builder), Thomas Averill (tailor) and Thomas Maydew (blacksmith).

17 <https://www.bbc.co.uk/bitesize/guides/z9f4srd/revision/5>, accessed 15 March 2023.

18 *Dix & Co. Directory* (1858).

19 Fairn, *History of Moseley*, p. 60.

20 *Birmingham Daily Post*, 7 May 1864.

William R. Bickley, a local historian and Moseley resident, it was 'elevated, the scenery well wooded and picturesque'.[21] Well-to-do people were prominent and visible. Seventeen gentry were listed in the 1850 *Kelly's Directory*, including Isaac Anderton, John Arnold, William Cotton, Thomas Lane of the Elms, Rev William Morrell Lawson, George Frederick Lyndon of the Henburys, James Taylor of Moseley Hall, Miss Taylor of Moor Green and Frederick Welch of the Firs. James Taylor died in 1852, having inherited Moseley Hall from his father and lived there from 1814, and in the mid-nineteenth century the era of the owner–squire was all but over. The hall was subsequently rented out to such as William Henry Dawes Esq, who was viewed in 1867 as 'a fine old English gentleman'.[22] Isaac Anderton's sisters, Sarah, Rebecca and Anne, who lived with him from 1841, inherited from him when he died in 1852 and Rebecca became noted for her benevolence. In 1854 thirty-three householders owned substantial properties, almost a doubling of the entries in four years. William J. Spurrier, writing in 1862, claimed that 'except for a few groups of cottages, there were only the large residences and a few mansions'.[23] The 1867 *Kelly's Directory* listed sixty-three private residents, nearly doubling the number of entries of 1854.[24] Moseley was establishing itself as a location for the well-to-do.

In this early phase of suburbanisation, then, development was slow and controlled. Omnibuses and horse trams underpinned development and the new station brought added impetus to expansion. Village life began to change, with new behaviours necessary on public transport, new facilities and services on offer and some disruption to the middle-class profile, but the rural environment was largely untouched.

1871–81: suburbanisation taking off

Between 1871 and 1881 the population of Moseley increased from 2,400 to 4,200, an increase of 1,800 – twice as great as in the previous phase. More land came onto the market, mostly small areas initially. For example, part of Kingswood House estate, Lady Pool Lane, came up for auction in 1871 following the death of the owner, Benjamin Cook – a development of thirty-six plots including three new roads.[25] In 1875 Kingswood House itself came up for auction. It was a large house and grounds, leased at the time to William Spurrier. The 1871 Birmingham Freehold Land Society development on

21 LBA, 392143, W.B. Bickley, p. 155.

22 A. Bold, *An architectural history of St Mary's church 1405–2005* (Moseley, 2004), p. 30.

23 SMCA, *Canon Colmore's log book*, Spurrier, *Moseley of today*, p. 447.

24 *W. Kelly & Co.'s Directory of Birmingham with its suburbs* (London, 1867).

25 LBA, Bham/Sc 1368 and 1364.

Greenhill Road was more significant, comprising eighty-seven plots and creating Prospect and Clarence Roads and Grove Avenue.[26]

A key change for Moseley came when, in 1877, the large 596-acre Anderton Park and Woodfield estate, Wake Green Road, was put on the market following the death of Rebecca Anderton.[27] A large portion of the estate had been in the Anderton family for some forty years. This development included several new roads, 100 plots varying from a quarter of an acre to two acres and the large houses Woodfield, occupied by William B. Mapplebeck Esq., and Rebecca Anderton's home Mansion House, 'a commodious family residence and pleasure gardens' having 'noble chestnut trees' (Fig. 1.7).[28] The sales catalogues detailed the short distance from Birmingham, the charming situation on the southern side of Birmingham, the 'proverbially salubrious neighbourhood', the elevated position and the gravelly subsoil with a natural fall for drainage. It noted that the estate was 'contiguous with several of the most picturesque roads in rural parts' and that the plots were 'suitable for the erection of first-class dwelling houses'. The sale posters claimed that 'a better site for rural retreats has not been submitted to public competition in this area for some years' and 'the whole will form the finest freehold building estate in the suburbs of Birmingham'. Villas only were to be erected and costs were defined to secure a middle-class development. Such a large estate coming onto the market must have created a sensation in Moseley, but no first-hand descriptions of people's reactions survive.

Plots on the Anderton Park estate did not sell rapidly, though, owing to the economic depression that had begun in 1873 (a depression that continued to 1896 and became known as the 'Great Depression'). The depression also influenced the development of the suburbs of cities other than Birmingham, such as Liverpool and Manchester, and was a defining feature of suburbanisation, rather than an interruption of it. Twenty-seven lots were readvertised in 1878.[29] They were clustered around the centre of the estate and described as 'highly valuable building land with ample frontages varying from 1,800 to 4,200 square yards'.[30] These were smaller than before, indicating that some adjustments had been made to meet the economic situation, but they were still sizeable and their status was emphasised in the description of them as 'contiguous to other building sites on which have been erected Gentlemen's residences of a superior character and the building restrictions

26 J. McKenna, *Birmingham: the building of a city* (Stroud, 2005), p. 70.

27 LBA, Bham/Sc 919, 123 and 1260.

28 *Ibid.*

29 LBA, Bham/Sc 191.

30 LBA, Bham/Sc 191.

are such as will without undue stringency preserve the character of the neighbourhood'. Moseley developers were attempting to secure better-off middle-class residents with only minor adjustments even in more demanding economic circumstances.

In fact, road and house development in Moseley generally speaks of optimism rather than lack of demand or economic constraints. Of the thirty-six roads listed by Everson, eighteen were formed in this phase, significantly more than in any other phase (Fig. 1.5). These roads encircled the village green and the railway station, highlighting the importance of transport and showing how Moseley initially developed outwards from the village green. The roads, though, were away from the busy Alcester Road and the railway line itself and skirted the southern edge of the Moseley Hall estate, suggesting that a rural ambience remained at the heart of development and was still considered crucial to attracting middle-class tenants. In total, 180 new houses were built in fifteen roads between 1871 and 1881, indicating a slight slowing down on the previous phase. Seven of these roads had more than ten new houses and Trafalgar and Kingswood Roads made significant strides. A sales catalogue's claim that villas were 'now springing up in Moseley in every direction' suggests a degree of randomness that, in turn, might reflect the greater number of locations where houses were being built.[31]

Horse omnibus services improved between 1871 and 1881, supporting Moseley's expansion, but times were inconvenient for workers and costs were still too high even for skilled workers, whose wage at the time was 20s or less per week. This helped secure the suburb for the middle classes. In 1871 horse omnibuses going to Birmingham from the Fighting Cocks ran 'very frequently throughout the day'.[32] Horse-drawn trams were popular too. The *Birmingham Daily Post* in 1873 praised their motion, ventilation, speed and cheapness.[33] Carriages were 'light, commodious, comfortable and convenient', inside seats were 'covered and backed with Utrecht velvet' and windows were 'ornamental stained glass'. The middle classes supposedly appropriated the horse tram, using them by the 1880s as a cheaper alternative to cabs – the growlers that were available for hire. The public horse buses and trams were opening up Moseley to a wider social group.

Rail services improved further during this period, stimulating Moseley's development. Local people, including John Avins of Highfield House, Church Road, successfully pressed for increases to the service, showing residents' support

31 LBA, Bham/Sc 1260. Twenty-nine auctioneer and sales catalogues (fifty-six dwellings, ten building estates and eight pieces of land) were analysed.

32 *Kelly's Directory of Birmingham and its suburbs* (1871).

33 *Birmingham Daily Post*, 8 September 1873.

Figure 2.4. Private transport, Windermere, 110 Wake Green Road, *c.*1880. MSHGC, Clive Gilbert Photographs (MC/D1/F12/10).

for the railway.[34] By about 1877 thirty trains per day went to Birmingham New Street Station from Moseley, suggesting that it was a popular form of transport that carried significant commuter traffic. The Midland Railway Company (the Birmingham and Gloucester Railway joined the Midland Railway in 1846) introduced more convenient services and, in 1872, third-class carriages. They abolished second class in 1875, giving third-class passengers the level of comfort previously available to second-class passengers. This brought more lower-middle-class individuals to Moseley, which was reflected in the building of some smaller houses and terraced rows with less garden space, such as those built subsequently in Queenswood Road.

Having a private carriage remained important to successful businessmen and their families as a status symbol and a more acceptable alternative to public transport, especially for women. Figure 2.4 shows the carriage-owning Mason family dressed in their best, outside their substantial house Windermere, 110 Wake Green Road. Samuel Mason was a Dale End manufacturer of pub fittings. The staff – a groom, coachman-cum-butler and two domestics – are

34 LBLH, B.COL 08.2;96586, *Birmingham Faces and Places*, 1/8 (1 December 1889), p. 23.

Figure 2.5. Carriage hire, Moseley village, later nineteenth century. PCRC.

dressed according to their station alongside a family clearly proud of the wealth and status their carriage, staff and house represent.

Private transport could also be hired locally. Growlers were for hire by the village green and there was a carriage-hire firm nearby. Figure 2.5 is a staged photograph that advertised the smartness of the Charles Miles Cab and Car Company's carriages for hire, its well-to-do middle-class clientele, its smartly dressed frontline staff, in their top hats, bowler hats and smart clothes, and extensive backroom staff, and presents pride, status, quality, efficiency and a service suitable for the middle classes of Moseley. Agnes Blackwell used this firm for four short journeys to Moseley and Balsall Heath Institute and Oxford and Wake Green Roads in 1896 at a total cost of 12s 6d.[35] Private carriages continued to be important, however, not only as a status symbol, but also to avoid close proximity with people from lower social groups on public transport.

This period saw the settling by the 1872 Licensing Act of the definition of the 'bona-fide traveller', a category of person mentioned in the previous section as the cause of some confusion in Moseley. It was decreed that a legitimate traveller was someone travelling further than three miles. This ruling impacted on Moseley, given that it was just over three miles from Birmingham. An image from 1873 satirises this (Fig. 2.6). It shows rough-looking, drunken men with fierce dogs outside the Fighting Cocks, suggesting that such men travelled out from Birmingham to Moseley to take advantage of the rules to drink at any time of the day. A woman and child are selling apples to the drinkers, but the woman holds a bottle. She too was taking advantage of the new legislation to

35 MSHGC, Reading-Blackwell Archive: Bills and Receipts.

Figure 2.6. '"Bona-Fide Travellers" Requiring "Refreshment"', Moseley, 1873. LBLH, WPS/WK/M6/99, by permission of the Library of Birmingham.

drink, but also to sell her wares, much to the irritation of an angry-looking innkeeper. Well-to-do pedestrians look askance at the scene. Such experiences were not what was expected in a middle-class suburb such as Moseley.

The 1872 Act did not end out-of-hours drinking by locals in Moseley or attempts by police constables to protect them and proprietors. In June 1874 PC Stevens found forty men drinking in the tap room and kitchen of the Trafalgar Hotel and reported that all except one were bona-fide drinkers.[36] The landlord, James Froggat, claimed that he had taken every precaution, even employing a servant expressly to enquire whether customers were travellers before supplying them with refreshments. Their accounts were not accepted, and James Froggat was charged by magistrates with selling liquor during prohibited hours and fined £2 and costs. Such after-hours drinking by local residents draws attention to a significant working-class contingent in Moseley.

The expansion of Moseley prompted improvements to St Mary's church. Gas and lighting were installed (1866), footpaths fenced (1869), a parapet and

36 *Birmingham Daily Post*, 14 June 1874.

pinnacles added to the tower and a new clerestory with stained-glass windows built (1870), as was a first chancel and an organ chamber (1872) and a new access roadway alongside the Bull's Head (1878).[37] The graveyard was extended (1878) and the organ chamber redecorated and improved (1879). In 1851 St Mary's had 500 seats – not enough for a growing congregation in the longer term. The solution was to build a church to the north-west of the village centre – St Anne's church, Park Hill – and also to the east of School Road – St Agnes'. St Anne's, which was consecrated in 1874 and became another District Chapelry in 1875, added about 400 seats. A temporary wooden church was built on the corner of School and Oxford Roads in 1879 to accommodate the congregation while St Agnes' was under construction. The foundation stone was laid in 1883 in Colmore Circus and the first part of the church consecrated in 1884. Those worshipping in other denominations and dissenters, such as Joseph Chamberlain, a Unitarian, and Althans Blackwell, a Baptist, had to look elsewhere for places to worship.

Shops and services were also increasing to serve the expanding suburb. Trade directories in 1875 and 1876 list seventeen different shops, mostly in Woodbridge Road and Alcester Road.[38] Four shopkeepers from the previous phase, including Thomas Hadley, were still operating and the new shops extended the goods available, providing confectionery, greengrocery, fruit, poultry, meat and fish, boots, shoes, hosiery, millinery and newspapers and magazines. In the 1870s William Dyke Wilkinson wanted to buy Moseley House opposite St Mary's church and build a terrace of shops there. He wrote, 'I saw clearly this would become the marketplace of what would be the most popular suburb of Birmingham'.[39] Abraham Lee, an architect and builder, and owner of Moseley House from the 1840s, held onto the property, no doubt also seeing the potential of the land for shops and houses. In 1878 his sons demolished the house and erected a three-storey terrace of shops and, in 1880, six rows of small workers' houses, Fern, Lawn and Moseley Terraces, Stanley Place and Church Avenue (which was amalgamated with Rodborough Place and St Mary's Terrace) to the side and behind.

Postal services improved too. Arrivals from Moseley Post Office increased from the two daily of 1871 to three in 1875 and dispatches from the one to two in 1868 and three in 1879.[40] By 1875 Moseley post office was a telegraph office.

---

37 LBA, L14.51, *Moseley Parish Magazine*, 1893, p. 6; LBA, EP/77/5/2/1 (Acc. 92/92) DRO 77/39, St Mary's Church, Moseley, Vestry Minutes Book, 1853–1940.

38 *Francis White & Co.'s Commercial and trades directory of Birmingham*, Vol. 11 (Sheffield, 1875), pp. 1418–771 and 1869–70; *Kelly's Directory of Worcestershire*, 1876, p. 1017.

39 LBA, MS/579/6/71aE, newspaper cuttings.

40 *Directory of Birmingham with its suburbs* (London: Kelly & Co., 1868); *Directory of Worcestershire* (London: Kelly & Co., 1876, 1878 and 1879); *Francis White & Co.'s Directory of Birmingham.*

Telegrams cost 1s. for twenty words, including delivery within a mile of any post office, and the telegraph boy would have been a familiar sight in Moseley. This reflected the national uptake of postal services: 862 million letters were posted in 1870 and in 1871, only a year after they had been introduced, some 75 million postcards were sent.[41] Thomas Hadley continued as postmaster until 1878 and was followed by George Johns.

In 1876, 183 private residents were listed in the *Post Office Directory*, a significant increase of 120 on 1867.[42] They included many elite members of the middle class who played an important role in the development of Moseley such as John Arnold (Moor Green), John Avins (Highfield House, Church Road), Edward Bach (The Hollies, Alcester Road), Arthur Chamberlain (Moor Green Hall), William Henry Dawes (The Red House), Frederick Elkington, JP (Moseley Hall), George Pratt Gomm (Moseley House), John Guest (The Warren, Alcester Road), Thomas Clement Sneyd-Kynnersley, JP (Moor Green House), Lister Lea (Greenhill House), George Frederick Lyndon (the Henburys), William Spurrier (Pinewood, Woodstock Road) and John Zair (Merle Lodge, Wake Green Road). In 1878 Joseph Chamberlain built Highbury at Moor Green and, though he was little involved in village affairs, his presence brought prestige.

However, concerns about the impact of development on the environment were beginning to emerge. Moseley was described in 1875 as 'a pleasantly situated village', but William Spurrier bemoaned the cutting of Park Road as 'not only the first encroachment into Moseley Park, but of the open Moseley fields'.[43] Sale particulars, though, still highlighted proto-suburbanisation features, including closeness to Birmingham ('only 2½ miles'), elevation ('stands on elevated position'), views ('extensive views of the adjacent diversified countryside'), health ('purity of atmosphere'), rural aspect ('magnificent forest trees'), drainage ('natural fall for drainage') and geology ('gravelly sub-soil').[44]

This second phase saw more roads formed than at any other stage, but also the first large estate reaching the market. An economic depression slowed house building to some extent, but horse omnibuses improved, horse trams were introduced and rail services increased. There were more shops, improved postal facilities and two new churches, and well-to-do middle-class residents predominated. The village retained its rural image, but some concerns about damage to the environment were being voiced.

41 *Bath Postal Museum guidebook.*

42 *Kelly's Directory of Worcestershire*, 1876, pp. 1016–17.

43 *Francis White & Co.'s Directory of Birmingham*; LBA, Bham/Sc 1260; SMCA, *Canon Colmore's log book*, Spurrier, *Moseley of today*, p. 447.

44 LBA, Bham/Sc 1260.

1881–91: suburbanisation intensifying

The population of Moseley increased from approximately 4,200 in 1881 to around 7,200 by 1891, an increase of 3,000, a rate of increase slightly below that of the previous decade. More land came onto the market. Some offerings were small, such as three areas opposite Moseley Park and Pool along the Alcester Road, stretching eastwards to Trafalgar Road. There were also larger areas, including Grange Farm estate, Greenhill Lane, a 125-acre freehold building estate described as an 'excellent site for residence in the country'.[45] In 1882 Woodbridge House, a freehold family residence with grounds and building sites on the corner of Woodbridge and Church Roads, came up for auction.[46]

Birmingham was in recession and capital scarce, which slowed land coming onto the market and plot sales. The sale of plots on the Anderton Park estate had not picked up significantly: only thirty-nine plots had been sold since they were put on the market in 1877 and 1878.[47] Indeed, the last lots were not sold until the 1920s. The sale of other land along Wake Green Road was sluggish too. Wintersloe, 17 Wake Green Road, was built in 1881, but its neighbour did not go up until the mid-1890s and Purbeck House (opposite Anderton Park) was part of a group built in 1926.[48]

However, while some adjustments had to be made, there still appears to have been optimism about the Moseley housing market. A considerable amount of land around the Grove Estate was auctioned in 1885 as building plots, but some failed to sell and were modified and remarketed in 1886.[49] They were accompanied by new plots and were described as 'Conveniently arranged for the erection of one or a pair of Suburban Villa Residences so much in demand in this high, dry and salubrious locality'. A Grove Avenue house deed shows that land was changing hands, which suggests the value of land was rising, so there were profits to be made.[50] These problems were not necessarily due only to recession: Moseley now had rivals, including Edgbaston, Harborne and Erdington, but also new suburbs such as Solihull and Sutton Coldfield.

Moves were afoot to develop considerable areas of the Moseley Hall grounds. In 1886 William Francis Taylor sold plots fronting Alcester Road that cut across the kitchen gardens of Moseley Hall and by the late 1880s he had planned a grid of other roads across the greater portion of the estate.[51] In

45 LBA, MS/183.

46 LBA, Bham/Sc 890.

47 LBA, Bham/Sc 1377 and 856.

48 Gilbert, *The Moseley trail*, p. 14.

49 LBA, Bham/Sc 1669, 1377, 856 and 1883.

50 PCFA.

51 LBA, MS/355198, Moseley Hall.

1890 he gained permission to make Chantry Road, running along the top of the estate.[52] Plans for draining the pool were in place, but the building estate did not go ahead as originally envisaged. Richard Cadbury's rental lease was soon to expire and, on hearing that the Taylors were planning to sell the estate or cut it up for building purposes, he persuaded them to sell the hall and twenty-two acres of land to him to save it and some green space from developers, but also with the intention of gifting the hall and land to the city as a Children's Convalescent Home, which he did in 1892.[53] This was a major act of charity that safeguarded Moseley Hall and parkland for the suburb. Richard Cadbury wanted to live in more rural surroundings and built a new home, Uffculme, in 1891 in the less built-up area of Moor Green, bordering Joseph Chamberlain's Highbury. *The Central Library Magazine* welcomed Richard Cadbury's generosity, which, for £30,000, secured some portion of Moseley Hall parkland from 'the speculative builder's hand and secures it for a wise and beneficent purpose'. It regretted, though, that Moseley Park had not been joined to Cannon Hill Park nearby, which was donated to the city in 1873 by Louise Anne Ryland to make 'a recreation ground of such beauty and magnificence' that might 'become the heritage of the toiling masses'. The magazine bemoaned the loss of such space in other suburbs and the inevitability of encroaching villadom brought by suburbanisation, the antithesis of what attracted residents in the first place:

> It is impossible to regard the disappearance of this charming park without regret. With the exception of *Edgbaston Hall*, it is the oldest residential estate in the immediate neighbourhood of the town which has escaped the hands of the spoiler. But it is useless to lament. The park not having been captured either by private generosity or public spirit to remain for ever a magnificent breathing space for the enormous population almost surrounding it, the inevitable is happening, and soon its wealth of wood and water will disappear to make way for the development of the estate into 'desirable' building sites.[54]

Other Moseley landowners saved green space too: the 560-acre Pitmaston estate at Moor Green, a freehold residence with a garden and grounds and a building estate of fifty acres, for many years the residence of John Arnold Esq.,

52 LBA, BPKNU, BCK/MC/7/3/1, Building Register for King's Norton, Plan 1260.

53 LBA, HC/BCH/1/2/4, Minutes of the Birmingham and Midland Free Hospital for Sick Children, 10 November 1890; Perrie, Maureen, '"Almost in the country": Richard Cadbury, Joseph Chamberlain and the landscaping of south Birmingham', in Dick, Malcolm and Mitchell, Elaine (eds), *Gardens and green spaces in the West Midlands since 1700* (Hatfield, 2018), p. 143.

54 LBLH, L50.7, *The Central Library Magazine.*

came up for auction in 1884 after his death.[55] Sir John Charles Holder bought the estate and lived there for many years without selling the building plots.

Recession impacted on road formation and house building, though. Only seven of the thirty-six roads listed by Everson were formed in this phase (Fig. 1.5). They lay mostly towards the south-east of the village centre, showing Moseley spreading out into its rural surroundings. Some planned roads were never built, such as a new road to Cotton Lane proposed as part of the development of the Grove Estate. Grove Avenue was new, however, and Oxford Road was extended to Billesley Lane.

The rate of house building slowed: only 194 new houses were built between 1881 and 1891 in the seventeen roads analysed. Church Road had fifty-two new houses and Blayney Road forty-one, while the rest averaged seven each. Some roads developed quickly: Mayfield Road, formed in 1889, had twenty-two houses by 1891. However, the 1885 and 1886 Grove Estate plans show few houses had been erected and villas there were advertised for sale in the *Birmingham Post* twice in 1890 and again in 1891, four to five years after the plots went up for sale. On the other hand, the 1888 Ordnance Survey map shows eighteen houses in Ascot Road rather than the nine planned, which, along with frontage changes on the corner with Oxford Road, illustrates the difference between plans and outcomes. Moseley was suffering some slowing of development, but by 1888 it was, for the first time, described as a suburb of Birmingham.[56]

The introduction of steam trams was crucial, setting Moseley on the path to intense development. They came to Moseley in 1884 and ran through the village regularly from 1887. Steam trams, though, disrupted and damaged the environment, much to the consternation of some residents. *The Dart* complained on 6 December 1884 about the widening of the main road and how the Tramway Company was spending money on Moseley by 'taking up the rails again'. 'An Old Inhabitant' complained to the *Birmingham Daily Post* of 15 November 1884 about the 'wholesale' cutting down of trees in Moseley Park to widen the road. He claimed he would rather do without trams than the beautiful trees and rookery and asked someone to step in and, at least, arrange to leave a line of trees and the 'busy rookery at the edge of the new footpath'. Tram development went ahead and the rookery was lost. By 1885 Balsall Heath House 'and its drive and orchards' opposite the village green had been demolished to make way for a new terminus.[57] Moseley's environment was damaged by steam trams in other ways too. Tram locomotives turned round

55 LBA, Bham/Sc 1377 and 856.

56 Hewston, *History of Moseley village*, p. 29.

57 MSHGC, C2/D1/F4/21, David Isgrove, 'A Snapshot of Moseley'.

Figure 2.7. A steam tram, Moseley village green, 1902. LBLH, WPS/WK/M6/6, by permission of the Library of Birmingham.

the limited space of the village green and hooked up at the other end of the trailer, which created smoke, sparks, noise and chaos.

Figure 2.7 shows their huge size. The upper deck was an area supposedly 'owned' by men, where smoking, a largely male habit, was allowed. The women in the image climbing to the top deck appear to be flouting etiquette, but 'decency panels' were fixed below the windows to protect women's modesty, suggesting that they were expected to ride there.[58] Much mention was made about women's long skirts preventing them from ascending the stairs, but the women here do not seem deterred. Indeed, women choosing the top deck were demonstrating greater female independence. Trams, then, were 'symbols of emancipation' and helped 'shape a new female presence in the public environment', giving Moseley women freedom they had not previously enjoyed.[59] The sides of the tram in the image are emblazoned with adverts for cigarettes, ales and 'Zebra Polish', testament to the commercial world.

This 'Ode to the Moseley Tram' in *The Owl* of 8 January 1886 reveals how crowded, uncomfortable, rough and unpleasant tram journeys could be. The language is coarse and the picture that emerges reflects another aspect of Moseley life, one that perhaps does not accord with perceptions of Moseley as middle-class.

---

58 K. Turner, *The lost railways of Birmingham* (Studley, 1991), p. 51.

59 Schmucki, 'The machine in the city', pp. 1065 and 1067.

'Ode to the Moseley Tram'
Ram 'em in,
Jam 'em in,
Push 'em in, pack.
Hustle 'em,
Jostle 'em,
Poke 'em in the back.
Tramp on 'em,
Stamp on 'em,
Make their bones crack.
Fat woman,
Slat woman,
Tom, Dick and Jack.
Hang on and
Cling on,
By tooth or by hair.
Hey there!
Now stay there,
And pass up your fare.

Trams could also cause fatalities. The *Birmingham Daily Post* of Wednesday 22 September 1886 reported that a very young child had been killed by a Moseley tram. Nellie Edmunds, aged one year and nine months, whose parents lived at the Coffee House, Moseley Green, ran into the path of a steam tram and was killed. The child was believed to be in the charge of a young girl of about ten years who had left her on the footpath while she took another child home. The coroner said in summing up that the parents had been negligent in entrusting her to a young girl also minding another baby. The verdict was accidental death, and the driver was exonerated from any blame.

The ruling that allowed bona-fide travellers to drink from 11.00am to 10.00pm if they were beyond three miles from town was still causing problems for Moseley. On Sunday afternoons large crowds came to Moseley by tram and then transferred by omnibuses to the Billesley Arms and the inn at Alcester Lanes End.[60] At Moseley there were 'scenes of greatest animation', with conductors of opposing omnibuses 'vehement in their solicitation of passengers', and vehicles were driven about among trams, making crossing the road dangerous. Later, between 8.00 and 9.00pm, a crowd of 400–500, mostly young men and girls, returned to Moseley and local publicans did a roaring trade. Roads and footpaths were almost impassable and there was some jostling,

60 *Birmingham Daily Post*, 5 October 1886.

which annoyed residents and those going to church. There was some singing, music-making and the ringing of tram alarm-bells. Fences were damaged by blackberry gatherers and those stealing apples and turnips, resulting in several youths being locked up. An article in *Birmingham Faces and Places* in 1889, on the other hand, presents visitors to Moseley in a more positive light:

> The time to observe the present popularity of Moseley is on a fine Sunday afternoon when tramcar and bus vie with each other in depositing their loads of people here, either to attend afternoon service at the church or to make excursions after fresh air in the country lanes and the fields.[61]

Such was the local antipathy to steam trams that Reverend William Harrison Colmore, vicar of St Mary's church, set up an 'Anti-Steam Tram Nuisance Society'. The association sent a request for an enquiry to the Board of Trade, which dealt with transport, among other responsibilities, but little encouragement was received. A conference for King's Heath and Moseley members was held at Moseley National School to discuss the renewal of the licence to use steam on tramways, due to expire on 9 June 1888.[62] The meeting was not well attended – there were 'about a dozen gentleman' there – which suggests that feelings against steam trams did not run high. George Frederick Lyndon presided and the vice-president was John Charles Holder. They were candidates for seats on Worcestershire County Council for Moseley and one of the Balsall Heath districts respectively. The association was concerned about the impact on rates, property values and rents and the difficulties of renting out houses because people's sleep was disturbed until midnight. They made several suggestions relating to the emission of steam, the type of coke burned, maximum speeds, noise and bell ringing, the size of tramcars and having inspectors. However, little change appears to have resulted from their efforts.

Between 1881 and 1891 omnibuses and horse trams were losing ground. In 1887 *The Dart* claimed that entrepreneurs had 'been too speculative' and 'could not make horse trams pay'. More passengers and a wider social group were brought in by the introduction of penny stages to the steam tram service from 1885 and a new route in 1886 via Park Road.

About thirty trains continued to run every day, as in 1877. Rail transport also allowed Moseley's middle classes to travel on holiday. Agnes and Althans Blackwell, a well-to-do couple living at the time at Brackley Dene, 30 Chantry Road, toured Scotland by train in June and July 1883. They stayed for two days at the St Enoch Station Hotel, Glasgow, at a cost of £1 4s 9d, and two

61 MSHGC, *Birmingham Faces and Places*, Vol. 1, 1889.

62 *Birmingham Daily Post*, 20 June 1888.

days at the Highland Railway Company's Station Hotel, Inverness, at a cost of 13s 6d. Bills itemise different payments, giving insights into the holiday lifestyle of a well-to-do family. In Edinburgh meals, apartments, attendance, tea, coffee and drinks cost £2 10s 8d and two days in the Foyer Hotel, Loch Ness, cost £4 2s 0d for apartments, attendances, beer, wines, claret, breakfasts, dinner and teas. They paid the Ardcheanacrochan Hotel in the Trossachs £1 12s 4d for apartments, attendances, luncheon, dinner, claret, beer and breakfast for a two-day stay and the Inversnaid Hotel 1 19s 3d for three days that included whiskey, apartments, attendance, breakfasts, biscuits, dinner and claret.

In this period St Mary's church forged ahead with the building of St Agnes' church. An architectural competition was organised between seven Birmingham architects to design the new church in 1882. Such a competition broadcast developments in Moseley and reflected its increasing status. The design by William Davis of Colmore Row was accepted in 1882, the foundation stone laid in 1883 and the church consecrated in 1884. In 1885 the north side of St Mary's was expanded to create a north aisle and an arcade of six columns and in 1891 the parish vestry was created at the west end of the church.[63] In 1888 Moseley Baptist Church, Oxford Road, was built using a design entered for the competition for St Agnes' church. Althans Blackwell was a founding member. Prior to this he worshipped at King's Heath Baptist chapel.

The number and nature of shops increased. In 1880 there were twenty-four shops, seven more than in the previous phase. Again, many were in Woodbridge Road, including four boot and shoemakers, three drapers, three butchers, two greengrocers, a chemist, a baker and confectioner, a grocer (Hadley), a stationer, a china and glass dealer, a hosier, a fishmonger and three labelled only as 'shopkeepers'. There were still twenty-four shops in 1883, but there was some change. New businesses included two tailors, two ironmongers and a tobacconist. Lloyds Bank opened a branch in 1883 and Moseley Coffee Shop was in existence by 1886. The 1890 list shows two coffee rooms and two hairdressers, testament to changing needs.

The growth of the suburb brought further services to Moseley Post Office. A cheap parcels service was introduced in 1883 and an Annuity and Insurance Office by 1890.[64] Parcels cost 3d for the first 1lb weight, with a limit of 7lb at 1s. There were three post arrivals and three dispatches in the 1880s, increasing to four from 1886. Pillar and wall boxes were introduced to Moseley by 1886. Five roads had pillar boxes in 1886. Church Road, Park Hill and Moor Green and Stoney Lanes each had four collections daily and Wake Green Road five. In 1886 wall boxes were in place in Oxford Road

63 *St Mary's Moseley*, p. 25.

64 *Bath Postal Museum guidebook.*

(three collections daily) and Greenhill and Trafalgar Roads and Moseley station (four collections daily). Such facilities helped people keep in touch. Frank, of the Stevens-Matthews family, wrote from Moseley to his sister congratulating her on the recent birth of her daughter.[65] Dr Richard Hill Norris sent his controversial book on blood to people locally, nationally and globally.[66] G. Dean of Springfield College, Moseley, like many others, replied thanking him in 1883, while R. Levett of Avonmore, Moseley, assured him in his 1882 reply of the support of the *Birmingham Philosophical Society*.[67] George Johns continued as the Moseley postmaster.

Moseley's reputation as a respectable and crime-free suburb was undermined in 1889, when the case of Henry Beresford Moore of The Firs, Trafalgar Road, attracted the attention of newspapers across the country.[68] He was a commercial traveller aged around forty-five, earning £1 per week plus commission from Messrs Thomas Woolley & Co., electro-plate manufacturers, 18 Caroline Street, Birmingham. He had only been able to get orders to the value of £10 in three months and was asked to return the firm's two cases of samples. He returned one but claimed the other had been lost on the Midland Railway. In fact, he had pawned the goods to the value of £32 3s 6d. In a second fraud, he styled himself as 'the Moseley Baronet', claiming to be the rightful heir of the Coote baronetcy and estates, Ballyfin, Ireland. Trading on these great expectations he got jewellery by false pretences from Messrs Edward Collet & Co., of Birmingham. He pawned the proceeds, went to Dublin, stayed in the fashionable Gresham Hotel and spent lavishly. The Coote family denied any foundation to his claims. The two Birmingham tradespeople involved applied for a warrant against him and he was arrested in Dublin. He was sentenced to eighteen months' imprisonment with hard labour for fraud. His case caused a sensation and was widely reported on.

Moseley still had considerable green space, and adverts in the *Birmingham Daily Post* – for example, on 1 March 1881 and 22 February 1890 – described it as 'very pleasant', 'charming' and 'delightful', though *The Dart* of 6 December 1884 complained, 'daylight has been let into Moseley village by the felling of trees in the park for a new road' and 'the old wall is being pulled down, and a rail being put up'. Moseley Hall's grounds were extensive and largely

65 CRL, MS/220/E/1/3, Letter 5, 25 May 1888, Miscellaneous Papers, Stevens and Matthews Family.

66 CRL, US/41/7/24, Correspondence of Dr R. Norris. Dr Norris (1831–1916) was Professor of Physiology, Queen's College, Birmingham from 1862 to 1891 and the letters were concerned with blood and spiritualism.

67 CRL, US/41/7/24, Correspondence of Dr R. Norris: G. Dean, Springfield College, Letter 19, Dr D.W. Simon, Letter 59.

68 *Birmingham Daily Post*, 20 and 30 July 1889 and 2 August 1889.

untouched, other than the sections to the north that had been taken for Park Road and Park Hill. When Richard Cadbury rented Moseley Hall in 1884 his children nicknamed their new home 'The Bunny House' because of the rabbits that were described 'scuttling across the grass' and 'venturing onto the lawns in the evening to nibble the softer grass'.[69] They were delighted by the 'spreading lawns, trees and woods, open fields and the beautiful pool with its tree-shaded island'.[70] Moseley was described thus on their arrival:

> Around the Village Green were low houses and old-fashioned shops, with a blacksmiths at the corner and up the street to the left could be seen the square tower of the village church. Close by the Green, and sloping steeply away from the road at right angles, was the entrance to Moseley Hall. Tall wooden gates, flanked by a little lodge on each side were thrown open under the shade of spreading trees, and showed a vista of the long drive winding between woods and fields, down-hill and up again with glimpses of the pool at the bottom of the valley. The old house, with its portico of stone pillars, its spacious rooms, and long stone-paved passages, was full of mystery and delight to the young folks.[71]

Moseley Hall was indeed a good specimen of an English gentleman's country house that many were seeking to emulate and its grounds were important to the image of rural Moseley. Views from the windows were 'very beautiful', with no houses in sight, and from the dining room, drawing room and library there was a vista to the pool and then up 'a green hillside to the thick belt of trees fringing the top of the hill', which hid Park Hill houses and where St Anne's church spire 'soared' above it all.[72] Similarly, the Moor Green area retained its rural ambience: Joseph Chamberlain's parents were delighted by the 'beautiful country which surrounded us' when they left London in 1886 and leased Moor Green Hall.[73]

In this third phase recession impacted on road formation and housebuilding. The introduction of steam trams was a major change and was fiercely opposed by some because of damage to the environment, the devaluing of property and problems around visitors the trams brought to the village. St Agnes' church

69 Helen Cadbury, *Richard Cadbury of Birmingham* (London, 1906), Chapter XIV, p. 213. The children were Barrow, William, Richard, Jessie, Edith and Helen. Margaret was born after the move to Moseley.

70 *Ibid.*, pp. 213–16.

71 *Ibid.*, p. 214.

72 *Ibid.*, p. 216.

73 M. Perrie, 'Hobby farming among the Birmingham bourgeoisie: the Cadburys and the Chamberlains on their suburban estates, c.1880–1914', *Agricultural History Review*, 61 (2013), pp. 111–34.

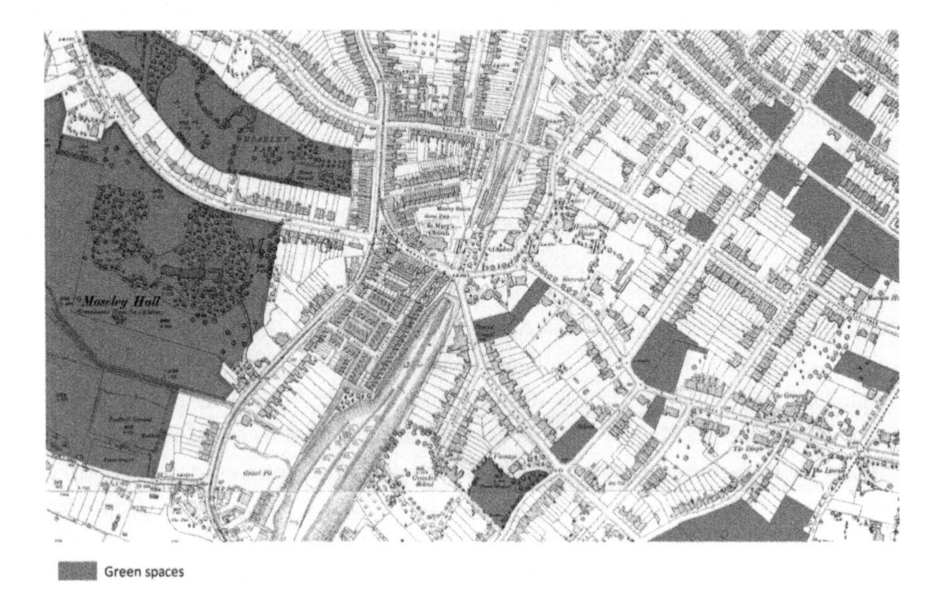

Figure 2.8. Green space in Moseley, 1900. Map constructed by Janet Berry (https://digimap.edina.ac.uk, 'Digimap', 'Historic', 'Historic Roam'. Accessed 2015). Redrawn by Sarah Elvins.

was begun and consecrated in 1884, a Baptist church was built in 1888 and the number of shops and postal services increased. The green environment was still largely secure.

1891–1901: Moseley becomes a mature suburb

The population of Moseley reached 11,100 in 1901, an increase of 3,900 on 1891, the largest increase of any decade in the second half of the nineteenth century. A newspaper drew attention to the changes, noting that 'Moseley village is rapidly undergoing great changes' and that 'Moseley as a suburb is growing larger and more important every day', echoing with pride in its development.[74] An article in the *Birmingham Post* of 14 November 1901 reported on the rapid 'process of transformation' of Moseley, its remarkable development during the last quarter of the century and especially 'within the last decade', but noted that 'little, if anything, of a century ago remains to save', which suggests nostalgia for a lost era. During this phase, land for development was at a premium and parts of gardens were offered for sale, such as the frontage of 11 Park Hill and a tennis lawn at 272 Anderton Park

---

74 *The Birmingham Pictorial and Dart*, 19 January 1900; *The Dart*, 21 August 1891. *The Dart* was a Birmingham publication and was also named *The Birmingham Pictorial* and *The Birmingham Pictorial and Dart*.

Road that would 'suit a good villa'.[75] Twelve Anderton Park estate plots came up for auction again in Woodstock, Anderton Park and Sandford Roads, but these were much smaller than those advertised in 1876 and 1877, suggesting they were aimed more at the lower middle class.[76] By the 1900s open green space for development was limited, as Figure 2.8 shows.

Eight roads out of the thirty-six listed by Everson were formed in this phase, the same number as in the previous phase (Fig. 1.5). They were located to the north-west of the village green, abutting the more rural Moseley Hall estate, and capitalised on the remaining green environment. This final developmental phase saw intense house building that included infilling in both established roads and the new roads. On 21 August 1891 *The Dart* wrote that 'New houses are being built in nearly every road [in Moseley], and the sound of hammering fills the air from six o'clock in the morning to six at night', and on 1 January 1900 that 'Moseley Hall grounds are being surrounded with large villa residences'. In total, 313 new houses were built in twenty-one roads, an average of fifteen per road, a return to the high average of 1861–71. Some roads had more than twenty-five new houses between 1891 and 1901, including Queenswood Road (twenty-nine), Grove Avenue (thirty-one), Kingswood Road (thirty-two), Sandford Road (thirty-nine) and Anderton Park Road (forty). Houses were built rapidly in two new roads, Chantry Road (fifty-nine) and Salisbury Road (thirty-five). Oxford Road was extended first to Cotton Lane and then to Billesley Lane and its houses increased from twenty to forty-two. Some areas, then, changed significantly.

This flurry of building was bolstered by the growth of Birmingham, the expansion of the professions and public services and the creation of more senior posts in clerical and executive occupations. The increased scale of industrialisation and overseas trade and the expansion of the empire fuelled commerce and finance, including banks, insurance companies, shipping and railways. Local government expanded. These all needed clerks, managers and other salaried professionals.

Moseley was still receiving plaudits. In 1893, William Spurrier described Moseley as 'one of the most beautiful residential districts in the Kingdom' with 'natural advantages which, in combination with the numerous handsome residences, make Moseley the beautiful place it is'.[77] He hailed 'the most charming views and prospects … found by Moseley Park, Anderton Park Road, and off Moor Green, Billesley and Stoney Lanes'. Spurrier was a local

75 LBA, Bham/Sc 180, D. Barr & Son, House & Estate Agents, Auctioneers & Valuers, *Property Register Booklet*, 1894.

76 LBA, Bham/Sc 970.

77 SMCA, *Canon Colmore's log book*, Spurrier, *Moseley of today*, p. 448.

worthy, so may have been expressing civic pride with a degree of hyperbole, but Austen Chamberlain expressed similar sentiments when he said that he felt like a 'country gentleman' on his farm in Moor Green.[78] Developments confirmed the advantages of Moseley: in the 1890s Moseley's reputation for the purity of its waters was demonstrated by the Pine Dell Hydropathic Establishment, an early health farm on Wake Green Road and the Moseley Mineral Water Co., which flourished for many years.[79]

In 1893 Chantry Road was cut and declared a public highway.[80] This intensified the fear of local people that the remaining northern part of Moseley Hall parkland might fall victim to residential development, with the loss of the open space and the remaining pool. A small consortium of local businessmen, residents of Chantry and Salisbury Roads, formed Moseley Park & Pool Estate Company and leased about fourteen acres around the Great Pool for forty years. A new park was laid out and opened by Austen Chamberlain in 1899. Members of the syndicate had houses in Chantry Road and Salisbury Road backing onto the park with easy access via their rear gardens and splendid views. One of these was Althans Blackwell, who built Brackley Dene, Chantry Road, in 1892. This development helped retain Moseley's rural ambience.

Other elite residents were concerned about how built up Moseley was becoming. George Frederick Lyndon moved out of Moseley and his home, the Henburys, because of building development on the adjacent Grange Estate. Richard Cadbury bought the Henburys from him in 1892 to prevent the land from falling into the hands of developers, at the same time adding about sixty-five acres to his home, Uffculme. In 1894 the Chamberlains leased some of the Henbury estate from Richard Cadbury to help retain a sense of a country estate, which was becoming difficult. Joe's third wife, Mary, wanted to keep the existing hedges 'to preserve the countrified look': she was 'afraid the iron railings and planting will make it look suburban and like all the houses in Edgbaston which have a few fields'.[81] In 1895, when a building society began to construct small houses on the Grange Estate on the far side of the railway line that marked Highbury's new border, the Chamberlains were quick to express indignation at the intrusion. Towards the end of the century Richard Cadbury's daughter, Helen, wrote that 'the town was fast pushing its long arms into the direction of Moseley and King's Heath', and their home, Uffculme, was only 'almost in the country'.[82]

---

78 Perrie, 'Hobby farming among the Birmingham bourgeoisie', p. 114.

79 Gilbert, *The Moseley trail*, p. 3.

80 LBA, H.J. Everson.

81 Perrie, 'Hobby farming among the Birmingham bourgeoisie', pp. 113–14.

82 Cadbury, *Richard Cadbury of Birmingham*, pp. 245 and 254.

Other observers showed an awareness of the changes that had befallen the village and a sense that the essence of the village was being lost. In 1894 Edward Holmes, who had lived in Moseley for sixty-two years, bemoaned the loss of the rural environment, remembering the 'Good old days … when Moseley was noted more for its green pastures than its villas'.[83] An article in the *Birmingham Mail* on 15 October 1903 remembered a time when a pleasant country walk from Digbeth to the village green could be enjoyed, lamented the loss of fields and footpaths and drew attention to the cutting up of important estates and the cutting of new roads, but also noted the handsome residences that had been built, the exclusivity of the suburb and its 'chiefly large villa-mansions' – a mixture of nostalgia and pride in progress.

Some forms of transport continued to develop and impact significantly on development, while others declined. The omnibus struggled and horse trams attracted fewer passengers. *The Dart* blamed the railway and the steam tram in an article of 31 July 1891:

> The Moseley people do not seem to take kindly to buses. One has been seen struggling desperately for the last month from Church Road to town and back again, but it has received so many rebuffs that it has at last given up the struggle. No doubt the excellent train services and the proximity of the steam tram have a great deal to do with this failure. Businessmen have to consider speed and convenience before pleasure.[84]

Steam trams contributed significantly to Moseley's growth in the final decade of the century: they were very frequent, running every ten minutes and, from 1898, every nine minutes.[85] Not only that, but journeys were rapid, taking only ten minutes to reach central Birmingham. The only drawback was the fixed route. Steam trams survived well into the age of electricity. However, they brought other unwanted visitors to Moseley. *The Dart* of 17 July 1891 described the nuisance of 'match boys', 'lavender-seller boys, and those other little torments so frequently met with in town but who seem out of place in quiet suburban districts' and expressed amazement that 'even aristocratic, sedate Moseley is not free from those little pests'.

The anti-steam lobby was still in evidence, but did not persuade everyone: 'The Trolley System', an article in *The Owl* of 10 March 1899, refers to 'grumblers against the trolley'. The *Birmingham Mail* of 13 October 1903 referenced the 'long prejudice against the steam tram' and remarked: 'This gentleman [Rev Colmore] on the appearance of the first tram registered a

83 MSHGC, C3/D2/F1/36, *Moseley Society Journal*, 1/10 (November 1894).

84 *The Dart*, 31 July 1891.

85 CRL, C1/10/11, *Moseley and King's Heath Journal*, 10 (March 1893), p. 9.

vow never to ride in one, a resolution which, we are told, he has unfalteringly maintained till the present day.' The electrification of Moseley trams in the new century brought a new lease of life to tram travel and reduced pollution.

The railway continued to attract residents, but there were concerns and conflicts. A letter from a Moseley newsagent, signing himself 'A Daily Reader', in the *Birmingham Daily Post* on 12 October 1891 suggested that the GWR should reduce the cost of its season tickets as the Midland had. He added, 'if it were not for that curve and tunnel there would be no murmur from Moseley against the Midland Service', which hints at local discomfort with the tunnel and the track. Poor punctuality was also an issue. *The Dart* of 14 August 1891 tells the story of a man who supposedly taught his dog to see him off on the early train from Moseley, then to 'trot off down the road to Mr Higgins' newspaper shop, purchase a *Post* and deliver it to his master at Camp Hill when the train reached the station'. The dog 'caught a severe cold through having so frequently to wait the arrival of his master's train at Camp Hill – and he died!' The story was told to the writer 'on the Moseley train (as it was taking a rest on the curve)'. At the same time the newspaper referred to the train delays to season-ticket holders caused by excursions, saying that 'at the best of times' there was 'always a degree of uncertainty as to what time you will reach New Street, but for the past ten days the unpunctuality of trains down to town has been beyond a joke'.

Population growth and the enhanced status of the suburb prompted King's Norton Board of Surveyors to request a new wider railway bridge, according to the *Birmingham Daily Post* of 14 August 1894. The company would not cover the additional cost of £2,500 or alter their plans unless the extra cost was raised by ratepayers. A public meeting was called to petition the county council for this extra cost and to start a public subscription list; the new bridge was completed in 1908.

Newspaper adverts related to houses for sale or rent suggest that, for some, transport and transport preferences were important. Of 318 house adverts in the *Birmingham Mail* from 1850 to 1900, 23 per cent mentioned transport, 64 per cent mentioned trains and 27 per cent trams, but few (only 8 per cent) mentioned omnibuses. Advertisers increasingly saw transport as important in the decision to move to Moseley – mentions of transport increased from 2 per cent in the 1850s to 28 per cent in the 1890s. Omnibuses featured little, trams were important in the 1880s and trains in the 1870s and 1880s, suggesting that house owners were more likely to be attracted by accessibility to train services.

Train travel increased in popularity and enabled adventures locally and further afield. On 28 April 1893 Agnes and Althans Blackwell, still living at Brackley Dene, purchased from Thomas Cook & Son, Tourist and Excursion Offices, Stephenson Place, Birmingham, six sets of tickets at £11 16s 3d (£70

17s 6d), 120 days of Hotel Coupons at 8s 9d (£52 10s 0d) and Circular notes (£100), making a total of £223 7s 6d. Hotel coupons were launched in 1868 to pay for accommodation and meals bills instead of money, and circular notes, first issued in 1874, were the forerunner of traveller's cheques.[86] The Blackwells continued to visit places in England, including Ilkley Wells Hydropathic Company Ltd, Ilkley, Yorkshire, from 20 to 27 September 1894, where board, lodging and attendance, drinks and amusements cost £8 17s 9d. They also holidayed in Scotland again, staying twice at the Craig-Ard Hotel, Oban, in 1893 for three days each time. The first visit involved bus and baggage, tea, apartment, attendances, breakfasts, biscuits and dinner at a cost of £3 6s 3d. *The Dart* noted in 1891 that 'Moseley is very quiet at present, nearly everyone of note [is] at the seaside. Mr Heath, of "Armadale", Wake Green Road, and family, have been recruiting their health at Llandudno for some time', the vicar of St Anne's went for 'a long rest and holiday on the continent' and 'Mr and Mrs Johnston are travelling on the continent and have reached Vienna'.[87]

No records exist that imply an increase in crime during such holiday absences, which suggests an effective police presence and that Moseley's reputation as a crime-free suburb was well founded. *The Dart* of 17 July 1891 reported that a new police station and court house was 'about to be erected', 'probably' on a site in Woodbridge Road, and this was in operation in 1896, according to *Kelly's Directory of Worcestershire*. Moseley was not a crime-free suburb, though. For example, on 22 April 1892 the *Birmingham Daily Post* reported a 'Daring Burglary' in which thieves ransacked The Mount, a large detached villa in School Road, the home of a Mr Hookham, and stole a £5 note, silverwork and a sovereign and half-sovereign in gold, which the newspaper described as 'Impudent Thefts'. The burglary was attended by Sergeant Hill and Constable Wainwright of the Moseley police.

Despite the improvements in public transport and the options available, private transport thrived. Building plans accessed show there was an increase in the building of stables and coach houses in the 1890s.[88] Newspaper adverts for houses for sale or rent paint a more nuanced picture: coach houses and stables were less frequent in 1891 adverts compared to those in 1881. Coach houses and stables remained important signs of wealth and status and perhaps more so as the social character of the village changed and the now more crowded public alternatives brought passengers into close contact with lower social groups.

---

86 https://www.theguardian.com/travel/2018/nov/22/thomas-cook-the-father-of-modern-tourism-archive-1958. Hotel Coupons and Circular Notes. Accessed 2022.

87 *The Dart*, 7 and 14 August and 4 September 1891.

88 A total of 111 building plans (407 dwellings) was analysed covering sixteen central Moseley roads that reflected different middle-class social levels. Of these, 82% were from the 1890s.

Figure 2.9. Luker, the Woodbridge Road baker and confectioner, *c.*1909. The man in the foreground is Henry Samman. The men are preparing home deliveries, a service that reflects middle-class consumer behaviours. MSHGC (C3/D1/F5/4).

Facilities developed further. At St Mary's the chancel was enlarged and the lady chapel added in 1897, funded by church members. Another religious denomination was satisfied when the modest Moseley Presbyterian church on the corner of Alcester and Chantry Roads was begun in 1898. The number of shops increased: in 1896 Everson listed twenty shops, including a chemist; Thomas Luker, baker and confectioner (Fig. 2.9); and Matthias Watts, an art dealer and framer.[89] There were two bakers, butchers, grocers and bootmakers, a poulterer, a fruiterer, a booksellers, a newsagent, a tailor, a milliner, a dressmaker, a hairdresser, a watchmaker, a dealer in furniture and ironmongery and the village coffee shop. The Victoria Parade of shops was built in 1901 along the former boundary of the Moseley Hall estate, which involved the demolition of the original entrance gates and gatehouse. An entrance to the hall and estate was provided through the ornate archway in the centre of the parade and access to the hall was then along a drive that crossed Salisbury Road. The building of Victoria Parade caused an outcry because of the destruction of a bluebell copse and elm rookery which a public fund failed to save.[90]

---

89 Fairn, *History of Moseley*, p. 55.

90 *Ibid.*, p. 54.

By 1894 new sites for pillar boxes were added at Springfield Road (three collections) and College, Park, Mayfield, Woodbridge and Woodstock Roads (four collections). Pillar and wall box collections increased and in 1894 Clarence Road was given a wall box. They were cleared once on Sundays throughout the nineteenth century. There were no arrivals at the post office on Sundays and only one dispatch. Weekday postal arrivals and dispatches increased to four after 1890 and six after 1897, with one dispatch on Sunday.

For a short time, Moseley had its own fire brigade, formed in 1897 and sited in premises erected 'near Mr Bullock's house', according to the *Moseley Society Journal*. The Fire Station had 'a fire escape, hose cart, a Toziers patent hand engine and several hundred feet of hose'.

The final phase of the second half of the nineteenth century saw the largest increase in population, intense house building and the loss of much public rural green space. Some areas were saved by the philanthropy of Richard Cadbury and other residents. Steam trams and the railway dominated and more convenient and cheaper transport brought the lower middle classes and artisans to Moseley, changing its social and physical character. Facilities such as shops and postal services continued to expand and residents enjoyed holidays using public transport, some venturing abroad. Some residents looked back with nostalgia, but others took pride in the progress made.

Three Moseley roads: Park Hill, Chantry Road and Queenswood Road

A comparison of three roads serves to exemplify how development varied across the suburb in the second half of the nineteenth century (Figs 2.10–2.12). Park Hill and Chantry Road are both north of Moseley Hall Park and west of the busy Alcester Road, and Queenswood Road lies to the east of the railway line. All three had easy access to public transport along Alcester Road and via the railway station. The roads were formed at different times. The Taylor family cut Park Hill through their Moseley Hall estate in 1865 and the first building leases were tendered immediately. The development was advertised in *Aris's Birmingham Gazette* on 9 December 1865: 'a portion of beautiful park attached to Moseley Hall has recently been laid out for the erection on building leases of villa residences exclusively, for which it is admirably adapted'. Queenswood Road was formed in 1875 by John Avins. William Francis Taylor lodged a planning application for Chantry Road on 25 March 1890 and it was formed and built up by the end of the century.

The pace and timing of house building differed. Plots in Park Hill were sold off piecemeal over time and houses were built over the second half of the nineteenth century. *Aris's Birmingham Gazette* of 9 December 1865 advertised them as 'first-class villas'. They were mostly well spaced to secure views of Moseley Hall's park. Two houses were built in the 1860s,

Figure 2.10. The development of Park Hill, Moseley, 1860–1900. Map constructed by Janet Berry (https://digimap.edina.ac.uk, 'Digimap', 'Historic', 'Historic Roam'. Accessed 2015. Research by Paul and Pam Rutter, Roy Cockel and Janet Berry). Redrawn by Sarah Elvins.

The Shrubbery at the top of the road, the home of George Padmore, a manufacturer of ivory goods, and Park Hill House, nearer the bottom of the road, a substantial house with large grounds, the home of John Pickering, a tallow chandler.[91] The census shows twelve houses in 1871 in Park Hill, at least seven houses on the north side and a small group beyond, all substantial detached residences. In 1881 there were eighteen houses there, in 1891 thirty-five and in 1901 fifty-one. Most building took place towards the end of the century in the 1880s and 1890s. The first two houses were built in Queenswood Road by 1881 and between 1881 and 1890 a run of small semi-detached houses was completed. Between 1890 and 1901 short blocks of terraced houses continued the run and small semi-detached houses were begun on the opposite side of the road. The census shows nine houses in 1891 and thirty-eight in 1901, a significant increase. These houses, though smaller than those in more prestigious roads in Moseley, were far from the tunnel-back terraces of other less salubrious areas. The plan for the first

91 Research by Paul and Pam Rutter, Roy Cockel and Janet Berry.

Figure 2.11. The development of Queenswood Road, 1881–1910. Map constructed by Janet Berry (https://digimap.edina.ac.uk, 'Digimap', 'Historic', 'Historic Roam'. Accessed 2015). Redrawn by Sarah Elvins.

house in Chantry Road was entered in 1891 and all plans were in by 1900 except for 'No 5'. The census shows that Chantry Road had fifty-nine houses in 1901, the road having been subjected to intensive building work. Thirty-nine houses were built between 1891 and 1895, seventeen between 1896 and 1900 and three in 1901. Residents on the north side of the road were annoyed by the houses built on the south side, because they obscured their views of the Moseley Hall parkland.

Chantry Road, then, was quickly built up. It had major advantages, running as it did along the top of Moseley Hall parkland and close to other status residences as well as to public transport. The quality of its development shows that the well-to-do middle class still wanted to move to Moseley even though it had become a mature suburb. The differing patterns of development of these three roads illustrate the variables in Moseley's progress to suburbanisation.

Moseley changed beyond recognition from a tiny rural village near Birmingham to a bustling, built-up, middle-class suburb over the half-century 1850 to 1900. Pre-development features and local influences

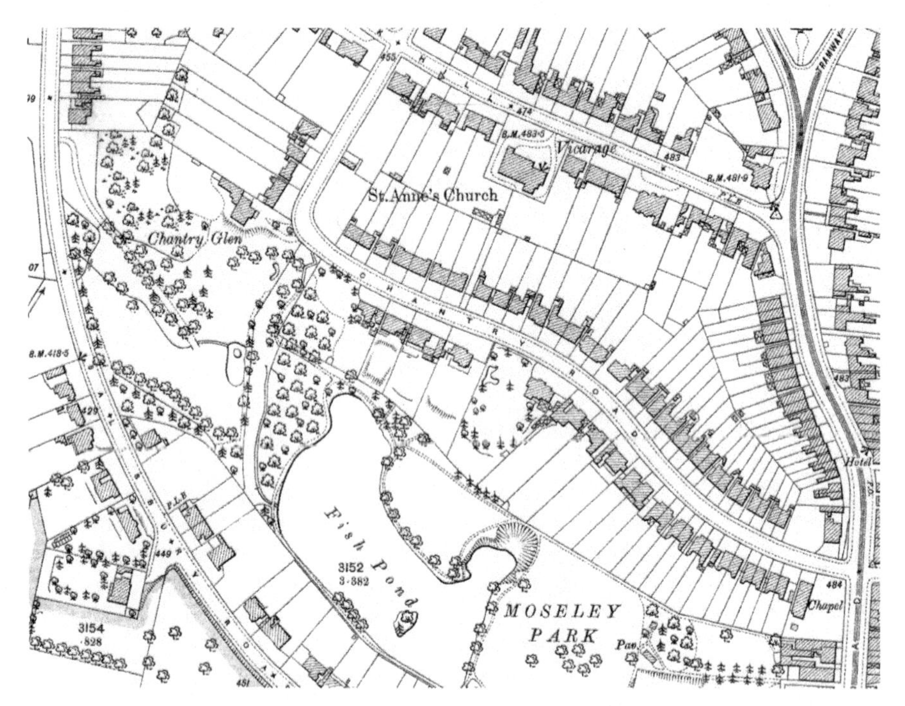

Figure 2.12. Chantry Road, Moseley, 1900s. Map constructed by Janet Berry (https://digimap.edina.ac.uk, 'Digimap', 'Historic', 'Historic Roam'. Accessed 2015).

continued to be influential, however. The role of transport and particularly that of the station and steam trams is clear. Development, though, required the intervention of people. The next chapter explores who built Moseley and what they built.

3

Shaping the landscape: builders and buildings

The development of Moseley as a suburb involved many middle-class men and women with various levels of engagement and included a large local contingent. What they built was led by the desire to attract the middle classes and when problems or concerns arose these residents came together in pressure groups.

The developers and builders of Moseley

Landowners and the building-lease system

Landowners were the prime movers, who generally took the first 'overt' step in development. They had various options when developing their land. They could sell land directly to interested parties, realising the capital value of assets, especially in a favourable market, or use the building-lease system, described below. The Blayney family drew £300 19s 5d per annum from their estate, according to the 1840 tithe apportionment, but chose to sell their land on from 1843 through to 1886, when they sold their remaining land, a large tract opposite Moseley Park.[1] The building-lease system was used extensively in Moseley. The consortium of local businessmen who leased fourteen acres of Moseley Hall grounds for forty years on the Taylor estate in the last decade of the nineteenth century to form Moseley Park also acquired building plots for themselves on improved ground rents. One consortium member was Althans Blackwell, who built Brackley Dene, Chantry Road, in 1892. William Shorthouse released small parcels of his Moseley land over time using the building-lease system, such as Lots 1–15 on Ladypool Lane (later Church Road) in 1853 and Lot 1, 'A very desirable freehold estate' between Cotton Lane and Bully Lane (later Billesley Lane), in 1868.[2] The Birmingham and District Land Company took on the role of developers for the 595-acre Anderton Park estate following the death of the owner, Rebecca Anderton, in 1877, including the formation of new roads and drainage systems.

Under the building-lease system, land was leased from the landowner by a developer (an individual or individuals, a firm or a building association) for a ground rent. Developers generally organised road building, installed drainage,

1 Gilbert, *The Moseley trail*, p. 11.

2 LBA MS/383200, Shorthouse's Greenhill Estate Plans, 1853 and 1858.

sewerage and a water supply and marked out plots. The plots were then let by the developer on another building agreement at an 'improved ground rent', usually on a 99-year lease. These improved ground rents were intended to recoup site development costs and provide developers with a profit over the ground rent payable to the freehold landowner. The ground rent paid by the developer to the landowner was based on an estimate of the likely profit from the 'improved ground rents', with about one-third of this profit going to the developer and two-thirds to the landowner. During the first one or two years a peppercorn rental was often offered by the landlord to help developers' cash flow while infrastructure development was carried out. The landowner–developer building lease also stated what was to be built together with covenants relating to maintenance, insurance and other obligations, and these were passed on in the plot lease.

Ground rents and improved ground rents varied according to plot size, location and current market forces. William Francis Taylor of Kingscote Park, Wooton Under Edge, Gloucestershire, who had an official position with the Taylor estates, granted leases on land in the northern part of the Moseley Hall estate (Park Road, Park Hill and Chantry Road) over the second half of the nineteenth century. The ground rent on Piercefield, 11 Park Road, on a 99-year lease granted in 1863 to John Abbott, a coal and iron merchant, cost £13 10s 0d per year. The ground rent on the 2,880 acres in Chantry Road that William H. Langley leased from William Francis Taylor in 1891 for 99 years cost £30 pa. The annual ground rent paid by Henry Pickering, a soap and candle maker, on a 99-year building lease on land for 30 (later 78) Park Hill in March 1896 was £7, payable quarterly.[3] Between 1892 and 1897 Althans Blackwell paid two quarters ground rent twice a year at about £21 to William Francis Taylor Esq. through Willmot, Fowler & Willmot, Land Agents & Surveyors, 6 Waterloo St, Birmingham. Sales catalogues noted annual ground rents costing from £7 2s 6d to £85 15s 7d.

Ground rents and improved ground rents had capital value and were bought and sold like any commodity. The ground rents of all the houses in Trafalgar Road came up for auction in 1895 in sixty lots that included twenty pairs of semi-detached houses, twenty-four double-fronted houses and thirty-six 'residences'.[4] These ground rents varied in price from £9 3s 8d to £23 4s 7d for pairs of semis, £8 17s 6d to £20 2s 0d for double-fronted houses and £6 0s 8d to £14 for residences. The variation reflected the length of leases (from fifty-five years to eighty years, with most in the seventies), type of house, stabling (six pairs of houses and twenty-eight detached properties had stabling)

3 PCRC, Deed, 30 March 1896.

4 LBA, Bham Sc 1364.

and location in the road (some houses backed onto the railway and some were close to Balsall Heath, a less salubrious area).

The covenants attached to building leases helped secure Moseley for the middle classes by designating house types, sizes and costs that excluded less well-to-do people and by imposing high levels of maintenance, controls and rules about the use of the land and the property. The building lease for 78 Park Hill (formerly number 30), the plot that Henry Pickering bought, stipulated that only a private residence was allowed and that the house built should cost £800.[5] All gutters, drains, sewers, privies, chimney stacks, greenhouses, vineries, walls and fences had to be kept in good repair and the outside and inside of the house painted every three years. The reversioner (the person entitled to an estate in reversion, or their agent) was legally entitled to view the property and any repairs found to be necessary had to be completed within three months. Houses could not be used for manufacture, carrying on any trade or business, the employment of a schoolmaster or school mistress, the instruction of youth (other than by governesses) or as a hospital or charitable institution. No other house or building was to be built on the site. The lessee had to insure against loss by fire in 'the Lancashire or some other respectable office of Insurance' for a sum equal to two-thirds of the value of the property and produce the policy of insurance and receipts for premiums from time to time to the reversioner. Insurance money received in the event of buildings being destroyed or damaged by fire was to be spent on rebuilding and repairing the property.

The building-lease system was popular because it enabled landowners to make money from ground rents with no outlay, watch the land grow more valuable and take advantage of increased rent at the end of the lease when they re-entered into full possession of the land with all its improvements and in good condition and repair. Future generations benefited from the eventual property reversion because land that was of negligible worth at the start of such leases was often of immense value at the end. The system was very flexible: plots could be put up for sale when the market was ripe, sold over time and reorganised and put back on the market if left unsold, as in the case of the Anderton Park estate in 1877, 1878 and 1892. Financial risks were spread over several building contractors, while the involvement of more than one established developer expanded marketing effort. There was a need to invest wealth and the property market was structured to appeal to the private investor wanting to capitalise on inherited income, money earned in trade or a profession, or profits from selling land and other assets. Ground rents offered security and a fixed return to investors.

---

5 PCRC.

The building-lease system was not necessarily problem-free, though: population growth was unpredictable, which impacted on demand; investors could be distracted by other opportunities, particularly transport developments; and financial sources were dependent on saving by the middle classes, which might fluctuate. Additionally, lessees might not fulfil their original contract. William H. Langley contracted to build 'one or two at the most' houses when he leased the land in Chantry Road in 1891. In 1893, though, no houses had been built and he sought to change the contract, wanting to build two or three houses to be completed by 29 September 1894 with 99-year leases at £30 rent and spending at least £800. Ultimately, he built two houses (21 and 23 Chantry Road) and in 1896 sub-leased 960 square yards to a Mr Thomas who built 25 Chantry Road.

Investors and entrepreneurs

Like many others in Moseley, John Avins involved himself in housing development and made a significant mark on the village. Before retiring to Moseley in 1858 he had done well for himself in the family firm of japanners, wood turners, sawyers by power and timber merchants living and working in Birmingham in and around Worcester Wharf, a key Birmingham canal junction. He bought up parcels of land around his Moseley home, Highfield House, and employed building contractors to manage development. He was named as owner on four of the seven building plans accessed for the 1880s, which involved forty-two of the forty-six houses planned in that decade in Church or Queenswood Roads. Sanitary Rates Assessments reveal he had nineteen houses and five pieces of land in Church, Coppice and Woodstock Roads in 1876, twenty-one houses and five pieces of land in Church, Coppice, Queenswood, Anderton Park and Oakfield Roads in 1886 and, in 1891, thirty-seven houses and five pieces of land in Church, Coppice, Queenswood, Anderton Park, Woodhurst and Forest Roads.[6] He was taking advantage of lucrative investment opportunities on his doorstep, but he was also controlling his immediate environment by building good-sized houses with large gardens and imposing strong covenants with 99-year leases, which meant middle-class residents and high maintenance standards.

According to Everson's Directory, Avins formed seven roads, Oakland Road (1870), Coppice, Forest and Woodstock Roads (1871), Queenswood Road (1875), Sandford Road (1877) and Woodhurst Road (1883).[7] Not all his plans reached fruition. He submitted a building plan in 1887 to build the Highfield estate, twenty-two houses on the meadow adjoining his home, Highfield

6 LBA, BCKJ/MB/6/13/ 4, 9 and 11.

7 LBA, H.J. Everson.

House, Church Road, that stretched up to Wake Green Road. The estate was never built, probably because Avins suffered a long illness before dying in July 1891. The land was not built on until the 1920s, after the death of his wife, Eliza, in 1919. After Avins' death his housing portfolio was managed and developed by a trust. Both trusts and executors of wills were important players in the housing market. In 1896 the John Avins Trust was managing thirty-four houses and three parcels of land in Church, Woodstock, Queenswood and Forest Roads.[8]

The extent of speculation and entrepreneurship in Moseley varied. Many investors were small-scale. Some owned only one house. Of the twenty-five investors named on the 1877 Anderton Park estate plan, fourteen chose one plot and seven wanted two plots, but only four took three or four plots. Of owners identified on building plans, 36 per cent submitted plans for only one house;[9] 45 per cent of owners of Moseley houses identified by Phillida Ballard owned only one house each and the rest three to fifteen houses.[10] Sanitary assessments also show that between 1881 and 1896 few owned properties other than the house they occupied. Some people, though, had large portfolios: in 1881 Thomas Wilkinson had twenty-nine houses.[11] By 1891 there were more men with larger holdings and Thomas Wilkinson had forty houses.[12]

A wide range of the Moseley middle classes invested in property development, including private individuals, individual investors, executors of wills, trusts, building societies, architects, architect firms, building companies and jobbing builders. Many Moseley residents were involved in developing the suburb: 48 per cent of owners whose addresses were given on building plans were Moseley residents, 15 per cent were from surrounding suburbs and 36 per cent from inner-city Birmingham, the latter mostly architect firms with Birmingham offices. The purchasers named on the 1877 Anderton Park Estate Plans were almost all well-known local middle-class residents.[13] Other Moseley residents built and bought houses near where they lived: in the 1870s Isaac Ford of Hildathorpe also owned numbers 5, 6 and 7 Park Hill (now 34, 36 and 40). William Willcox from 54 Park Hill purchased the plot next door and built Eversleigh in the 1880s. Many outsiders, though, were also attracted by the potential of the Moseley housing market: few of the fifty-five different owners

8 LBA, BCKJ/MB/6/13/23.

9 LBA, BPKNU, BCK/MC/7/3/1.

10 P. Ballard (ed.), *Birmingham's Victorian and Edwardian architects* (Wetherby, 2009). Analysis of data in lists of Architectural Works at the end of chapters and information within the text.

11 LBA, BCKJ/MB/6/13/15.

12 LBA, BCKJ/MB/6/13/11.

13 LBA, Bham/Sc 919.

of 118 Moseley houses identified by Phillida Ballard were from Moseley.[14] Building was encouraged as a capitalist activity. Moseley building sites were 'certain to be let at remunerative rents. Affords an unequalled opportunity … to a Capitalist in search of a small ripe and attractive Building Estate possessing all the elements for successful enterprise' and had the 'prospect of good tenants'.[15]

Freehold land societies

Freehold land societies were significant in the development of Moseley. My building plan sample revealed four examples of building societies. In 1894 Birmingham House Building, L & P Co. Ltd built a detached house on the corner of Church and Coppice Roads and Birmingham District & Land Co. built two semi-detached houses in Sandford Road.[16] In 1895 Birmingham Building & Investment Co. built two semi-detached houses in Chantry Road and in 1896 Birmingham House Building Land and Investment Co. Ltd built two semi-detached houses in Chantry Road.[17] Sanitary assessments reveal many entries for the Birmingham Freehold Land Society, particularly in the 1880s, when it had upwards of thirty-five plots on the Anderton Park estate and many in Woodbridge Road.[18] This society developed land on the other side of Greenhill Road too, providing eighty-seven plots and creating three new roads – Prospect, Avenue and Clarence Roads – in the 1870s as well as land near the village centre and the railway, which envisaged the future Oxford and Ascot Roads. Freehold Land Societies were an important means of enfranchisement and had a significant impact on suburbanisation.

Architects

Architects played an important part in the development of Moseley, sometimes as private individuals and sometimes representing a firm. As well as carrying out their function as architects, they could also be purchasers of plots, builders and owners. Essex, Nicol and Goodman were associated as architects with eighty houses in and around Moseley between 1884 and 1900, thirty of which were in Chantry Road.[19] In 1886 they designed the Highfield estate for John Avins that was never built. Oliver Essex bought land and built two houses in 1886 (11 and 13 Park Hill), two in 1887 (128 and 130 Anderton

14 Ballard, *Birmingham's Victorian and Edwardian architects*.

15 LBA, Bham/Sc 890 and 1260.

16 LBA, BCK/MC/7/3/1, 1916 and 1894.

17 *Ibid.*, 1996 and 2534.

18 LBA, BCKJ/MB/6/13/6, 9, 11, 15, 23, 24 and 26.

19 Ballard, *Birmingham's Victorian and Edwardian architects*, pp. 216–18.

Park Road), two in 1889 (32 and 34 Wake Green Road) and four in 1892 in Chantry Road.[20] John Goodman bought land and built houses in Salisbury Road in 1896.[21] These included Beverley, 52 Salisbury Road (which he built for himself and which was one of the first houses built in this new road cut through Moseley Hall grounds in 1896), numbers 48 and 50 there in 1897 and two others in 1899. Jethro A. Cossins of Cossins, Peacock and Bewlay bought land and built 45 and 47 Mayfield Road in 1883, two villas in Forest Road in 1884 and 1890, a house in Anderton Park Road in 1894 and one in Mayfield Road in 1896.[22] Ernest Chawner Bewlay was from Moseley. He designed and built The Cottage, 39 Park Hill, for himself and lived there from 1898 to 1914. He designed 35 Park Hill for George F. Piggott in 1898, 37, the Red House, for John R. French in 1899, and 39, 43 and 45 in 1899 for W.E. Adland. Thomas F. Newton of Newton and Cheatle built Greengate, 42 [98] and Arden Bank 44 [102] Park Hill in 1898 in his own name and, according to *The Building News*, had 'done several houses on the estate'.[23]

Builders

Owners, architects and builders formed relationships to develop land in Moseley. Oliver Essex joined forces with John Parker, a builder, on ten houses, while John Coulson Nicol and the builders John Parker and E.J. Charles collaborated on six. Some builders worked for particular owners: George Bayliss of Newport Road, Balsall Heath and his son worked closely with John Avins and his trust in the 1890s.[24] Builders often became architects, designing houses aided by building journals and plan books such as *The builder*, S.H. Brooks' *Rudimentary treatise on the erection of dwelling-houses* (1860) and C.J. Richardson's *Picturesque designs for mansions, villas, lodges*. Builders kept up to date, understood their clients' taste, had an architect in the background to ensure standards and used a standard house plan for single family occupation with slight variations.

Family partnerships among builders were also a feature of the building trade. George Bayliss and his son operated as owners, architects and builders. George Bayliss senior was involved in twenty-three building plans accessed (sixty-eight houses) as the owner and builder. Of these, he was also the architect in thirteen plans (twenty houses) and the owner, architect and builder in another thirteen (thirty-six houses). George Bayliss junior was involved in twelve planning

20 *Ibid.*

21 *Ibid.*, pp. 200 and 216–18.

22 *Ibid.*, pp. 244–6.

23 *Ibid.*, pp. 479 and 495–7.

24 LBA, BCKJ/MB/6/13/1, 6, 9, 11, 15, 23, 24 and 26.

projects (fifty-six houses) as the architect and was the builder on three of them (twenty-four houses). Father and son collaborated on ten building-plan projects (thirty-two houses) with George Bayliss junior as the architect on all the plans, while his father was the owner and builder. Such combinations of roles and family partnerships promoted the speedier erection of houses and was an economic use of time and money. Overall the building plan sample shows that the Bayliss pair concentrated on terraced houses (fifty-four) along with twenty-five semi-detached houses and fourteen detached houses in the area north of Wake Green Road. Sanitary assessments show that George Bayliss Senior's involvement increased significantly from two houses in the 1880s to twenty in 1891 and sixty-eight in 1896, the period of the great expansion of Moseley. No other builders were on the same scale in Moseley.

George Bayliss lived in Balsall Heath. Eleven other builders in the sample building plans where addresses were given were from nearby suburbs, such as King's Heath and King's Norton, and eleven were from Birmingham. However, the local builders were responsible for more houses (forty-one: three detached houses, twenty-six semi-detached and twelve terraced), while the Birmingham builders were responsible for twenty-seven houses (two detached and twenty-five semi-detached). Taken together with the building plans of Bayliss father and son detailed above, this makes a large contribution by local builders to the domestic built environment of Moseley. Building plans accessed did not reveal any Moseley-based builders.

The extent of the involvement of builders in Moseley developments varied. Sales catalogues identified eight builders in thirty-three entries who were responsible for eighty-six houses, an average of almost eleven houses each, suggesting some intensive activity. Of the builders on building plans accessed 74 per cent appeared only once but together were responsible for seventy houses, an average of about three houses each. Five builders or firms, a Mr Dowse, Thomas Wilkinson, Mills & Sons, Harry Hyde and Richard Folland, appeared only twice and planned thirty-eight houses, an average of nearly eight houses each. John Parker appeared five times and Fred Charley six times, as proposed builders of twenty-four and nineteen houses respectively. Builders worked mostly in the same or adjacent roads. John Parker built the twenty-four houses referred to above in Chantry Road in the 1890s, Thomas Small fourteen houses in Church Road in 1885, Mr Middleton ten in Trafalgar Road in 1892 and Richard Folland eighteen in Kingswood Road in 1898.

As the suburb developed, new shops became an important part of the built environment. In 1867 George Bayliss planned two shops as the owner and builder on the corner of Church Road and Newport Roads.[25] The shops had domestic quarters consisting of a hall, parlour, kitchen, scullery, a dressing room, two bedrooms, one closet and two cellars, one of which was a wine cellar. In the yard there were spaces for coal and ashes and a WC. An 1891 building plan was entered for three shops in a terrace in Woodbridge Road owned by George Underhill.[26] The domestic area had a kitchen, three bedrooms, an attic and cellar, and there was a yard with a WC and storage for coals and ashes. Josiah Fitter of Trafalgar Road planned a shop in Woodbridge Road in 1899 opposite the Trafalgar Hotel.[27] The domestic quarters comprised a parlour, three bedrooms, a bathroom and in the yard storage for coals and ashes and a WC. While these domestic areas were lower status, they were still comprehensive.

Plots were marketed at builders. In 1892 the sale particulars for twelve Anderton Park estate plots were directed at 'builders and investors' and the plots described as 'sound building sites'.[28] The capacity of the building industry to cope with development demand was crucial. The building industry underwent major changes with the emergence of the building contractor. Small building firms transformed into capitalist building firms employing members of different building trades as waged workers, including labourers and skilled craftsmen such as bricklayers, carpenters, plumbers, glaziers and sanitary engineers. They are the 'invisible' builders of Moseley whose record in history is meagre. They can be glimpsed in trade directories: the Johns family, for example, were a well-known Moseley family of carpenters, joiners and builders and the Bullock family were plumbers, glaziers and painters. Both were working from the 1850s well into the 1890s. Another important unremarked-on group of workers were the suppliers of materials. Some materials were locally sourced: there were quarries in Moseley and the Moseley area, including one on John Avins' land, and many houses in Moseley were built of King's Norton bricks, but the railway allowed builders to use new materials from further away, such as Welsh slate.

Levels of failure and bankruptcy were high among builders, particularly smaller outfits. They lacked management skills and had low levels of capital, and their investment in land was short-term and small. George Bayliss had financial problems and was supported by the John Avins Trust, which advanced him money on two occasions – in 1892 when he was 'in difficulties' and in 1894 when they gave him £2,500 at 5 per cent interest. They were

25 LBA, BPKNU, BCK/MC/7/3/1, 861.

26 *Ibid.*, 437.

27 *Ibid.*, 126.

28 LBA, BhamSc 970.

keeping Bayliss 'on his legs' in 1896 and he was in 'crisis' in 1898.[29] The Trust may have supported George Bayliss and his son in this way because of John Avins' close relationship with them and the financial and moral commitment the Trust had as developers and owners of the ground rent. It was also in their interest that projects were completed rather than see Highfield House, the Avins' home, and other properties they were managing and marketing surrounded by abandoned building sites. The Bayliss father and son worked on lower-status housing where, perhaps, margins were tighter.

Connecting houses to the main drainage system was a problematic issue for builders. On 26 November 1879 the *Birmingham Daily Post* reported that Joseph Breeden of Sycamore House, Park Road, had formally charged Alfred Palmer, a builder and contractor, with overcharging him for connection to the main sewer. The charge for the work was £49 17s 1d, including £36 0s 2d for excavations. Breeden also objected to paying 1s each for six-inch pipes, claiming they could be acquired for much less. Moseley property holders met at the Trafalgar Hotel on 8 December 1879 and a District Property-Owners' Protection Association was formed, which suggests that problems such as this were frequent.[30] A committee was established that conferred with Mr Till, the borough surveyor, as to a proper charge to be paid. 'The one case was chosen and it will in all probability be regarded as a test case by other property owners'.[31] Ultimately the contractor admitted an error and proffered an amended bill of £46 16s 8d, to laughter from the audience.

The peace and serenity of middle-class Moseley must have been disturbed, particularly in the final decade of the century, by the many building sites, the invasion of workers, the noise of hammering and sawing, the mixing of mortar and the many carts bringing materials. According to Jane Ellen Panton, an interior designer, novelist, poet and journalist famous as a spokeswoman for suburbia, the 'demon builder' was 'the cause of so very many of our domestic woes and worries'.[32] Covenants guarded against some negative aspects of building work: the Anderton Park estate sales catalogue stipulated that nothing constituting a nuisance could be carried out on site, such as brick or tile making, the burning of clay or lime or the excavating of gravel.[33]

29 LBA, MS/1672 (Add l) (Acc 1991/137), Minute Book 1, John Avins Trust, Meetings 34–35, 43, 51 and 63 (18 August 1892, 28 January 1895, 10 January 1896 and 18 July 1898) and Special Meeting 67 (22 March 1894).

30 *Birmingham Daily Post*, 9 December 1879.

31 *Birmingham Daily Post*, 26 November 1879.

32 J. E. Panton, *From kitchen to garret: hints for young householders* (London, 1890), 7th edn, Project Gutenberg, eBook, 2016, p. 160.

33 LBA, Bham/Sc 919.

Women and middle-class housing development

No Moseley women were identified as architects or builders, but there were roles for women in the housing market: in renting and owning their own homes, owning a property or properties other than the one they lived in and developing housing portfolios. Only three women were named as owners on the building plans accessed – a Miss Ellis, Mrs K. Parker and Mrs A. Bradley – which suggests that it was unusual for women to plan houses. 'Miss Ellis' was Amelia Ellis, who put in a building plan in 1877 for two semi-detached houses in Trafalgar Road.[34] The 1881 census shows her as the household head in Trafalgar Road, aged forty-nine and living with her younger sisters, Ann and Ellen, both forty-three. Sanitary assessments for the 1880s show her as owning two houses in Trafalgar Road, one of which she occupied. Assessments for the 1890s show Ann Ellis as the owner–occupier of one house and the owner of another in Trafalgar Road.[35] Mrs Parker planned a detached house in Oxford Road in 1895 and Mrs Bradley two semi-detached houses on the corner of Queenswood and Church Roads in 1899.[36] In planning more than one house Miss Ellis and Mrs Bradley were acting as small-scale entrepreneurs.

Sanitary assessments reveal Moseley women owning and renting out houses. In 1881 sixteen women owned houses in five roads in central Moseley and eight of these were living in houses they owned, leaving women owning eight houses they rented out.[37] In 1891 twenty-four women owned houses in the same roads, a significant increase.[38] Six of these women were living in the house they owned and eighteen were renting out houses they owned. Renting was very acceptable: buying was not considered socially necessary. In the October 1896 sanitary assessment Eliza Howes owned a house in Park Road that she did not live in. Her husband, Walter, had died in 1896, so she may have inherited not only her home but also the other house. Walter was a surveyor of land and houses, as was their son, Walter junior, making the family experienced in the world of house speculation.

Some women owned more than one house other than the one they lived in. Ann Williams owned 86 and 88 Trafalgar Road in 1886 and 1891. In 1891 she was a widow and household head aged seventy-five, living at 20 Trafalgar Road with three sons, all clerks and aged between forty and fifty-five years of age, and three daughters aged from thirty-eight to forty-four. She was still living there in 1899. Mary Johns had three houses in Woodbridge Road in the 1880s, but she

34 LBA, BPKNU, BCK/MC/7/3/1, 117.

35 LBA, BCKJ/MB/6/13/ 6, 11, 15, 23, 24 and 26.

36 LBA, BPKNU, BCK/MC/7/3/1, 583 and 2002.

37 LBA, BCKJ/MB/6/13/15.

38 LBA, BCKJ/MB/6/13/11.

was a widow living on the Alcester Road in 1881, aged sixty-five, with two sons in their twenties and a daughter aged forty-two. Jane Yardley owned eighteen houses in Woodbridge Road in the 1890s. Her husband, Matthias Yardley, was a house speculator and in 1891 they were living alone at 10 Laburnum Grove. Matthias died in June 1895 aged seventy-three and as a widow aged fifty-eight Jane was still living in the same house in 1901.

Most of the women owners lived in the roads where they owned other houses and the majority had houses in one road only, suggesting that it was easier for them to take advantage of nearby opportunities. Eliza Evans, for example, lived at Beaufort, 96 Trafalgar Road, and owned one other house in the road. In 1881 she was a widow aged sixty-seven and she was still there in 1891. A few women owned houses in roads where they did not live. Elizabeth Austin lived in Brighton Road, but owned houses in Chestnut Road. She was a forty-five-year-old widow, a grocer and provisions dealer in 1891 with three sons aged between twelve and twenty and three daughters aged from fourteen to sixteen.

Matilda Beynon (1834–87) owned two houses in Trafalgar Road in the 1880s sanitary assessments.[39] In the 1881 census she was living at Woodvale, 37 Woodstock Road, with her sister Fanny Beynon (1836–81). They were single and joint household heads and co-principals of a 'Ladies College' there. They had twelve pupils and three servants. The youngest two pupils were sisters aged nine and thirteen and the other ten ranged from fifteen to twenty-one years, an older age group more typical of a college than a school. The 1891 census shows that Annie Benyon (b. 1846), the younger sister of Matilda and Fanny, was the principal of the school following the death of her sisters. She was still there in an 1896 sanitary assessment and in trade directories including 1900.[40]

Many of the women living independently and owning houses other than the ones they lived in were widows: 50 per cent of women owners were widows in the 1881 sanitary assessment sample, 52 per cent in 1891 and 88 per cent in 1901. Only two in 1881, Matilda Beynon and Ann Ellis, and two in 1891, Annie Beynon and Ann Ellis, were spinsters. In 1891 Catherine Alabaster was married but was the owner of the house she and her husband lived in, 20 Park Hill. Prior to 1870 married women who held property were required to give up all rights to it to their husbands on marriage. A long-running campaign led in 1870 to the Married Women's Property Act, which allowed any money a woman earned to be her own property. This was extended in 1882 to allow married women to have complete personal control over all their property.

39 LBA, BCKJ/MB/6/1/13/15 and 24.

40 LBA, BCKJ/MB/6/1/13/23.

Some widows acted independently by buying a house for their family. Emma Hadley's husband died in 1878 when they were living at 15 Islington Row, Birmingham. In 1881, aged sixty-six, she was household head at Southfield in Ascot Road, giving a home to her two sons, John, a printer compositor aged thirty-four, and William, a thirty-two-year-old dentist, and her thirty-five-year-old married daughter, Ellen Umbers, her grandson, John Umbers, five months, and one servant. Trade directories show Emma was still there between 1882 and 1886, but an Emma Hadley of King's Norton died in 1883 aged sixty-nine, according to the death index. The house was advertised for a rent of £44 in 1889 by Messrs Hadley, Dentists, 45 Bull Street, Birmingham – presumably her son William's business. The family were keeping the house on to generate income.

Sanitary assessments show that some women had extended property portfolios. Selena Fowler lived in one of the three properties she owned in Trafalgar Road (No. 88), according to the 1886 sanitary assessment. In April 1896 she also had two houses in Oxford Road and four in Church Road. In October 1896 she also had four in Oxford Road and four in Kingswood Road, a significant holding. By April 1896 Margaret White had three houses in Kingswood Road, compared with one in 1886. Emma Gray owned two houses in Woodbridge Road in the 1880s and 1890s other than her home. She was a widow aged sixty-one in 1881 and was described as having 'income from property'. She moved upmarket in 1891 to Yew Tree Cottage, Taylor Road, and in 1896 to Laburnum Cottage, Taylor Road. Sarah Green owned a property in Woodstock Road in the 1880s and two houses there in 1891, one of which she occupied in 1896. The 1881 census described her income as coming from mortgages. She was forty at the time. In 1891 she lived at 43 Woodstock Road.

These women were mostly widows. They were often women with family at home to support, but they were not just widows and unmarried women making a safe investment while also providing a home; they were taking the opportunity to generate income and invest speculatively. Women were clearly a significant force in the Moseley property market.

Peripheral professionals

Solicitors, surveyors, auctioneers and estate agents were vital cogs in the housing market. Solicitors had control over the legal knowledge involved in land and house purchasing, securing the title to a property and facilitating financing or marketing; they also had a monopoly over conveyancing law. John Arnold of Moor Green was a well-known Moseley solicitor, Edward Holmes of School Road an architect and the chairman of King's Norton Board of Surveyors, and John Avins was the surveyor for King's Norton.[41] Francis

41 *Worcestershire Chronicle*, 6 April 1870; *Birmingham Daily Post* 3 April 1868 and 8 April 1872.

Willmot, who had a large house, Wake Green House, on the corner of Wake Green Road and Billesley Lane, was a surveyor.

Auctioneers and estate agents managed the sales process – preparing plans, drafting particulars and conditions of sale, planning, printing and issuing catalogues, advertising sales and auctions through posters and newspaper advertisements and running auctions. By 1901 there were more than 100 auctioneers in Birmingham. Three firms were extensively involved: Thomas and Bettridge, whose involvements included an eighteen-acre building estate in 1875; James Lister Lea and Son, who were responsible for the sale of the Grove estate in 1885 and 1886; and Grimley and Son, responsible for selling Anderton Park estate in 1877 and 1878. Edward Bettridge of Thornhurst, Wake Green Road, and James Lister Lea at Greenhill House, School Road, were Moseley residents, active in the community. They both attended St Mary's church vestry meetings and Edward Bettridge was a member of the John Avins Trust.

Professions related to housing development ran in families. Edward Holmes' son-in-law, the husband of his fourth daughter, Alice, was a house agent in 1881 and an auctioneer and agent employing staff in 1901. His second daughter, Gertrude Fanny Holmes, was married in 1882 to George Birch, a house agent, and his son, George Henry Holmes, was a clerk to an estate agent. Francis Willmot's son, Philip H. Willmot, was a solicitor's clerk in 1881 aged nineteen and his other son, George, seventeen, was a surveyor's clerk at the time. His father, George Willmot of Wake Green Road, was a road surveyor.

The reputation of housing market professionals was enhanced by the establishment of the Institute of Surveyors in 1868 and its acquisition of a Royal Charter in 1881 and the founding of the Estate and House Agents Institute in 1872, the Auctioneers' Institute in 1886 and the Land Agents' Institute, all of which guided and regulated the identity and practices of their members.[42]

What they built

The middle classes sought single-family houses to distance themselves from the world, to show off to their neighbours and to support a suburban life of individual domesticity alongside others of similar status. John Claudius Loudon (1783–1843), botanist, garden designer and writer on suburban architecture, wrote in 1846: 'Every man who has been successful in his pursuits, and has, by them, obtained pecuniary independence, may possess a villa.'[43]

---

42 https://www.rics.org/about-rics.

43 J.C. Loudon, *An encyclopaedia of cottage, farm, and villa architecture and furniture* (London, 1833), p. 763.

House types

The middle class encompassed a wide range of economic states and the different types of house built in Moseley – detached, semi-detached and terraced – was a response to this. Size varied within each house type to accommodate the subtle layers of the social hierarchy. Highbury, Joseph Chamberlain's home, and Uffculme, the home of Richard Cadbury, topped the social pyramid of new builds in Moseley. Below them came the large detached houses of the elite, such as Highfield House, John Avins' home, and, on Wake Green Road, Sorrento, lived in by the Ellis family and later the Adams family. Below them were smaller detached houses, some sizeable and others less so. Semi-detached houses, the ultimate reduction of the country house, came next in the status stakes, followed by terraced rows. Centrally placed front doors in semi-detached pairs unified the façade to give a larger villa-like appearance and terraced rows were built in short blocks, suggesting semi-detached houses, to raise their status. The hierarchy was complex – the size of semi-detached and terraced houses varied and detached houses could be smaller than semi-detached ones.

House prices on building estates illustrate this variety and overlap. The covenant attached to the 1877 Anderton Park estate development designated that detached houses would sell at no less than £1,000, £750, £500 and £350 and pairs of semi-detached houses at no less than £1,750, £1,400, £900 and £600 (£875, £700, £450 and £300 per house). Some semi-detached houses here were more expensive than some detached houses. The difference of £50 between some of these detached and semi-detached houses appears small, but this was equivalent to approximately £3,309 in 2017.[44] Houses on the Grove estate were to retail at £1,500, £800 and £500 for a single house and £900 for a pair (£450 each), more expensive than those on the Anderton Park estate. In 1893 the two lower-middle-class villas George Bayliss planned in Church Road were intended to be sold for at least £250.[45] Owners and tenants were very aware of where they stood in this hierarchy and of the many subtle differences that complicated the layers further.

Semi-detached villas were characteristic of Moseley in the second half of the nineteenth century. Of the houses in building plans and sales catalogues accessed, 64 per cent were semi-detached properties, 22 per cent were detached and 14 per cent terraced (494 houses in total). Terraced and smaller semi-detached houses were built for the lower middle class who were moving to Moseley encouraged by higher wages and more convenient and cheaper transport. The changing social profile impacted even on higher-status roads:

44 See https://www.nationalarchives.gov.uk/currency-converter.

45 LBA, MS/718/9, Abstract of the title of George Bayliss.

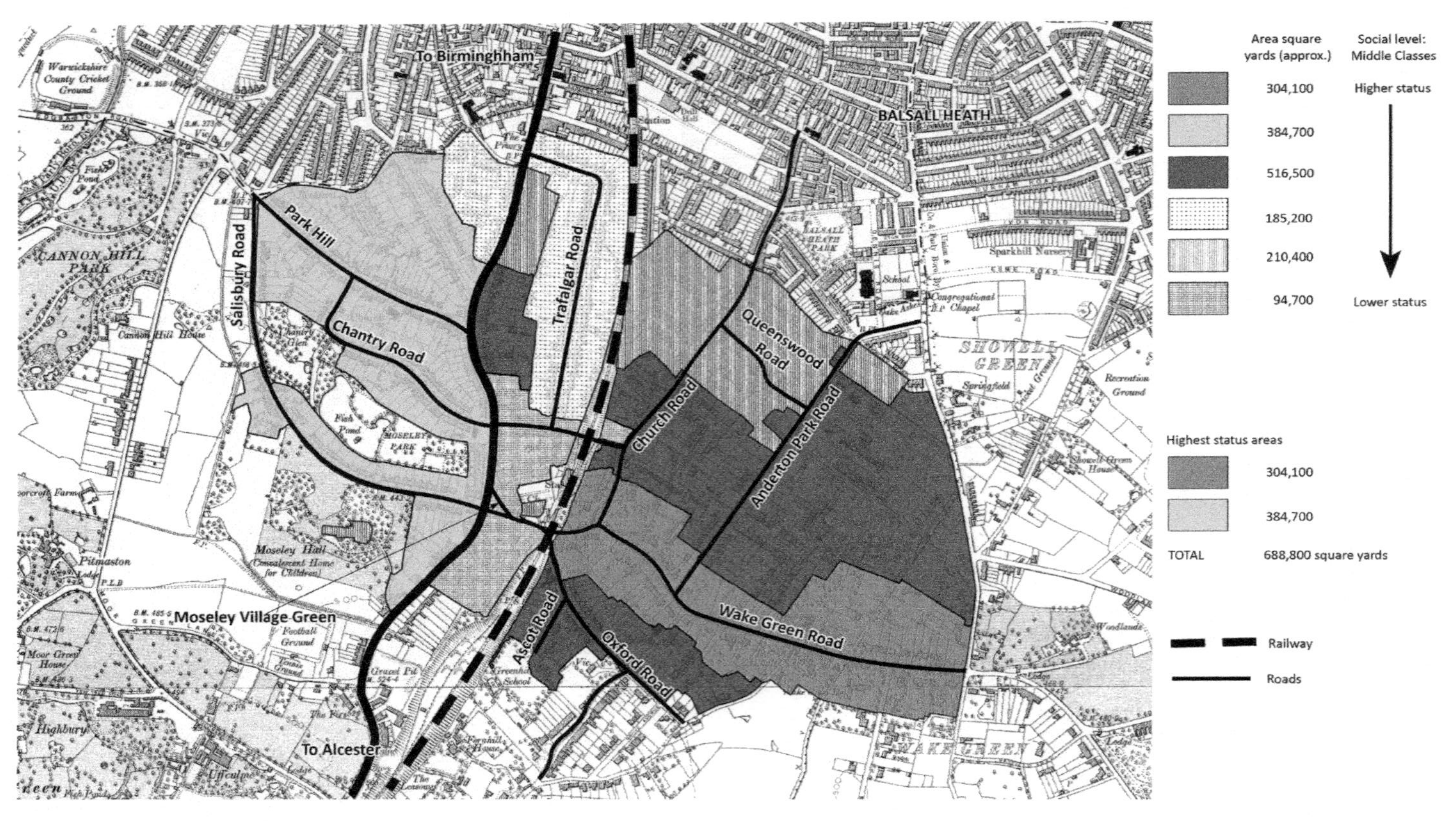

Figure 3.1. Social zoning in Moseley. Map constructed by Janet Berry (https://digimap.edina.ac.uk, 'Digimap', 'Historic', 'Historic Roam'. Accessed 2016). Redrawn by Sarah Elvins.

initially, the houses in Chantry Road were large and detached, but then groups of semi-detached villas were built. Seventeen of the nineteen houses built in Park Hill in the 1870s and 1880s were detached, but the fourteen built there in the 1890s were mostly semi-detached. Smaller semi-detached houses were built in Queenswood Road in the 1880s, but terraced houses went up in the 1890s.

The proportion of the different types of house varied in roads, defining their status. Wake Green Road comprised detached houses, signalling the road as superior, while Queenswood Road's lack of detached houses and its small semi-detached and terraced houses indicated a lower status. Differing proportions were subtle status markers noted by residents, because the 'niceties' of social status were important. Park Hill had slightly more detached houses (56 per cent) than semi-detached and Church and Chantry Roads significantly more semi-detached houses than detached villas (69 per cent and 68 per cent respectively). Ascot Road was almost exclusively semi-detached houses (80 per cent). There were advantages from proximity to people of a higher status: association with more elevated people could enhance personal status and the mix of different types of housing brought a social diversification that might have contributed to social cohesion. House types, sizes and location contributed to social zoning in Moseley – marking out areas of similar social status.

Location

The 'right address' was crucial to suburban respectability, with the 'possession of it a source of indefinable satisfaction', and location was an important factor in social zoning (Fig. 3.1).[46] The 'right' address in Moseley meant higher status and rural areas such as those around Moseley Hall and Moseley Park and Pool, Moor Green to the south-west and the ancient route, Wake Green Road. The importance of the 'right' address is reflected in the frequent use in the 1881 and 1891 *Birmingham Daily Mail* adverts and in sales catalogues of phrases such as 'in the best parts', 'best class', 'very best part of Moseley' – one talked about 'land contiguous on other Building Estates on which have been erected Gentlemen's residences of superior quality'.[47]

A lower-middle-class area developed to the north of Wake Green Road because of its proximity to Balsall Heath, a less salubrious area nearer to the city. This meant two properties at the Balsall Heath end of Trafalgar Road had to be advertised fifty times each and eight other properties in roads close by between eighteen and forty-eight times in the 1881 newspaper advertisements. The 1881 and 1891 adverts show that properties in roads near to Balsall Heath, such as Church, Trafalgar, Kingswood and Woodstock Roads, changed

46 Dyos, *Victorian suburb*, p. 23.

47 LBA, Bham/Sc 869, 919 and 1259.

hands frequently, suggesting a more transient population. The middle classes required the working classes to service their needs, but working-class housing and lower-class terraced housing was built on less attractive plots near the railway line, behind the St Mary's Row shops and close to the busy Alcester Road. An 1895 building plan shows owner George P. Underhill hoping to build fifty-one houses on the Bank House estate land along Alcester Road (a private school in the 1880s run by Hannah Sansome); they were built to a basic ground-floor pattern of a front room, a room behind, a kitchen and a yard.[48] These were much smaller houses and were built over a larger area than Moseley had previously experienced. They were not welcomed by the editor of the 1899 *Moseley and King's Heath Journal*, who denounced them as 'Villadom' and claimed: 'such projects mean the rurality of Moseley is fast passing away'.[49]

Moseley displayed its social and cultural pretensions in road and house names. The more refined 'Road' was used exclusively rather than 'Street', which was symbolic of working-class areas. Many of the names of Moseley's roads referenced old country estates, such as Anderton Park Road and Park Hill. Others were named after trees, such as Forest and Coppice Roads, reflecting the dream of a rural idyll that had brought many to Moseley. Many house names reflected plots, surroundings or the rural idyll, such as Chantry Glen and The Vale, and many also referenced trees, including the Beeches and Oakfield House, underlining the importance of conveying a rural ambience. Others demonstrated owners' aspirations: Ivanhoe referenced Sir Walter Scott's novel of 1814 and the house owner's literary status; The Grange suggested a substantial property and the gentry, while Highbury associated the house and owner with Joseph Chamberlain and his home of the same name. Many house names referred to holiday places such as Windermere and Sorrento, highlighting the owner's travel adventures.

Architecture

Domestic architecture was crucial to social status and added to the elements that helped define where a home sat in the social hierarchy. It provided opportunities for middle-class suburbanites to display wealth, taste, fashion and individuality and to express and reflect status and identity.

Styles that emerged in the first half of the nineteenth century influenced architecture post-1850. These included the Georgian style, which featured the Classical and particularly the Palladian, with its symmetry and restrained elegance; the Regency style, which drew on the 'Picturesque'; and the Gothic

48 LBA, BPKNU, BCK/MC/7/3/1, 2152/3/4.

49 Gilbert, *The Moseley trail*, p. 21.

style, which harked back to the early Tudor period with its pointed arched openings and windows filled with delicate arched glazing bars and leaded lights. The Italianate style, inspired by Renaissance palaces, with its tall first-floor windows, square towers and overhanging eaves supported by scrolled brackets, was popular from the 1830s. In 1833 John Claudius Loudon's highly influential *Encyclopaedia of cottage, farm and villa architecture and furniture* contained over 2,000 designs for houses in a variety of 'romantic' styles and was edited and published in a new edition in 1846 by his wife, Jane. Augustus Welby Northmore Pugin (1812–52) published *True principles of Gothic architecture* in 1841, ushering in a serious and analytical approach to the use of Gothic architecture.

A Gothic Revival was part of the mid-century picturesque and romantic movement inspired by medieval design. It was fostered by John Ruskin (1819–1900), an art critic and influential commentator on architecture who was himself influenced by Pugin. Ruskin's three-volume treatise *The stones of Venice* brought an eclecticism never seen before, along with increased ostentation, ornamentation and decoration.[50] Gothic Revival was seen as a quintessentially English style and its elements included pointed arched window surrounds, painted brickwork, ornamental ridge tiles and finials, carved capitals and stonework, semi-turrets, stained glass, rustic porches and Tudor-style decoration and chimneys.

In the 1870s the Queen Anne Revival style, a 'kind of architectural cocktail', developed, taking hold fully in the 1890s.[51] It comprised 'a little genuine Queen Anne, a little Dutch, … Flemish … Robert Adam … Wren and … Francois I'.[52] Houses in this style were built predominantly from red brick, often with details in a lighter stone that were sometimes richly carved. It included dominant tiled roofs, massive chimneys, Dutch gables, dormer windows, decorative brickwork, terracotta panels, panels of strapwork (ribbon-like patterns), smaller panes of glass, curving bay windows, white sash windows and other paintwork, wooden balconies, porches and verandas, and stained glass. The Queen Anne Revival rendered suburban building 'sympathetic, harmonious, English, at once modern and connected to the past'.[53]

At the very end of the century Arts and Crafts, a simpler architectural style, emerged as a reaction to both the ornate styles previously popular and to machine-made building parts and fittings. Houses in this style resembled

50 Ruskin, John, *The stones of Venice* (London, 1851–3).

51 M. Girouard, *Sweetness and light: the Queen Anne movement 1860–1890* (New Haven, CT and London, 1977), p. 1.

52 *Ibid.*

53 Sarah Bilston, *The promise of the suburbs: a Victorian history in literature and culture* (New Haven, CT and London, 2019), p. 103.

Figure 3.2a. Architectural styles: Park Hill, 1870s. Ian Berry.

Figure 3.2b. Architectural styles: Park Hill, 1880s. Ian Berry.

Figure 3.2c. Architectural styles: Park Hill, 1890s. Ian Berry.

simple cottages, with low roofs, wide eaves, horizontal windows, white, rough-cast exterior walls and exposed beams and brickwork.

An eclectic mix of these historic architectural styles flourished in Moseley as a result of the suburb's fifty-year development (Figs 3.2 a–c). They satisfied middle-class aspirations, offering opportunities for individualism and display that were important to status, but at the same time were deeply rooted in tradition. Ironically, these historic architectural styles were used on new houses and built using new technology, new methods and mass production. Architecturally, the suburban villa itself was ideal for the middle classes because it allowed individuality and variation within a basic pattern. Catalogue descriptions, such as 'artistically built in the Queen Anne style', 'pleasant Gothic residence' and 'Gothic porch', show that advertisers believed that architectural house styles were important to those seeking property and also suggests that potential buyers were knowledgeable about the different architectural styles on offer.[54] Houses were frequently described as 'superior' in 1881 *Birmingham Daily Mail* advertisements, but as 'handsome', 'elegant', 'modern' and 'artistically designed' in 1891, suggesting that style became

54 LBA, Bham/Sc 811, 863, 869, 877 and 1394.

BROXTOWE

Figure 3.3. Ornamentation. Peter Leadbetter.

more important. Sales catalogues described houses as 'handsome and distinguished'.[55] Such phrases in adverts drew on the architectural pretensions of potential suburban residents or those looking for an upgrade.

Special features drew attention and raised status. Striking steps and entrances were 'an added bulwark' for privacy, but, according to Loudon, writing in the 1840s, 'The porch indicated a superior description of dwelling', colonnades, verandas and arcades were 'evidences of elegant enjoyment' and chimneys produced 'the kind of effect and beauty required in a villa'.[56] Other structural features, such as balconies, brought kudos, while the introduction of plate glass in 1857 and the reduction and then abolition of glass and window taxes made larger windows like French and bay windows possible. Façades were enhanced with new gable ends, porch roofs, pillared porches, French doors, bay windows and balconies, bringing houses up to date and signalling the importance of being in fashion. Such features made for 'a show of outward appearances noticed by neighbours'.[57]

Ornamentation was crucial in the quest for individuality, differentiation and status (Fig. 3.3). The degree of ornamentation varied with house type, size and location, but not exclusively. Mostly, but not always, decoration was greater in higher-status roads. Generally, detached houses were more decorated than semi-detached or terraced houses, but detached houses could be very ornate or simple and vary within the same road. Terraced houses in Moseley were the least decorated, on the whole, because of the costs involved. Architectural features and embellishments enabled house owners to distinguish their homes, raised the status level of lower-status house types and roads and helped give Moseley a varied character architecturally.

Building controls

High-quality housing was necessary to attract the middle classes. Architects and builders in Moseley were controlled by the Royal Sanitary Authority of the King's Norton Union. Building plans were accompanied by a comprehensive questionnaire that asked about materials, the thickness of walls, the type of closets (lavatories), receptacles for house refuse, ventilation and drains. This related to concerns about quality, fire safety, privacy – especially in relation to party walls – waste collection, coal and gas fumes and health and hygiene. Space surrounding the house was seen as a priority, to judge by the questions about the clear open space at the rear, the width of the street (streets had to be at least thirty-six feet wide), open space opposite the building, how far the house was from

55 LBA, Bham/Sc 863, 869 and 1394.

56 J. Calder, *The Victorian home* (London, 1977), p. 172; Loudon, *Encyclopaedia*, p. 763.

57 Thompson, *The rise of suburbia*, p. 8.

the road and the building line. The King's Norton Sanitary Authority checked all stages of building, requiring notices of inspection for commencement before foundations were laid, of the damp course, drains and drains being covered up and of completion. These notices went from Moseley to the Rural District Council of King's Norton or their surveyor at 23 Valentine Road, King's Heath. Building could not progress until these inspections were completed.

The inspections were rigorous. Owner, architect and builder Fred Charley of 50 Vaughton Street South, Birmingham, was given a list of works to be done before the two semi-detached villas he was building in 1896 in Woodstock Road could be occupied. Changes required included: suitable receptacles or a place for ashes to be rendered in cement; no surface water to be connected to the sewers (the overflow of the soft water cistern); vent shafts to be open at the top and covered with a cage; and the two rooms on the second floor with no fireplaces to have special means of ventilation. He had to make improvements to two semi-detached houses he was building in Chantry Road in 1896. These included thickening the cellar walls to fourteen inches up to the first floor, altering drains and adding a window two feet by one foot in the WC.[58] S. Roberts & Sons, builders and contractors, of 55 Oldfield Road, were taken to task in 1898 for encroaching on the building line when building ten terraced houses in the new Kingswood Road. Mr Roberts explained that he had been ill and the foreman had made the measurements. Builders could seek advice: William M. Masters, a builder and contractor of 49 Oldfield Road, consulted the surveyor of King's Norton District Council about building a projection of half-timber work on an upper storey on one side of two houses he was building in Anderton Park Road.[59] He added a sketch map of his proposals and asked if this would satisfy 'your Building Council'.

The notices of inspection caused some builders intense frustration. George Bayliss wrote to Mr Godfrey, surveyor at Valentine Road, about six semi-detached villas he was building in Oakland Road for which he was also the owner and architect: 'Re: Damp Course put right. Want to proceed with the work. My men are waiting'.[60] Fred Charley was clearly angry that he had had no response to a request to inspect the footings and damp course which he had left at the office in Valentine Road. His men were 'compelled to lose time' and 'it is really too bad', he stated.[61] Builder J. Woodcock of Northfield, who was building a detached house in Chantry Road for owner and architect Thomas de Lacy Aherne in 1896, also experienced hold-ups. He

58 LBA, BPKNU, BCK/MC/7/3/1, 2534.

59 *Ibid.*, 2941.

60 *Ibid.*, 2211.

61 *Ibid.*, 2290.

wrote to King's Norton to request an inspection of the damp course 'in the morning as we are at a standstill with work'.[62] Such hold-ups carried financial liabilities, delaying the possible sale or rent of the buildings and incurring more extended wage payments where workers continued to be paid. For workers not receiving continued payments this meant hardship. Such delays suggest that the engineers and surveyors at Valentine Road were under pressure from the building peak of the period.

Building leases and their covenants were important in ensuring the quality of houses built. The building lease for Hillsborough, 30 Park Hill, stipulated that the frontage space and building line had to be kept clear of any buildings, porch, veranda or other (except for a fence). The house had to be built in a good and substantial manner with chimney stacks, greenhouses, vineries and hothouses having flues for fire smoke.[63] Materials were specified: oak, red deal or good timber, well-burnt bricks, tiles or slates and good mortar. The outside walls had to be nine inches thick and proper drains and sewers made. Quality materials were crucial: *The Building News* of 31 May 1880 reported that 96 Park Hill was built of dark red bricks with red Broseley tiles, while the front fence and gate were of cleft oak.[64] High standards were required of cheaper houses too. In his 1893 Church Road villas, George Bayliss had to use the 'best front bricks, good sound timber and materials of all kinds', make the windowsills of stone and keep them in good substantial repair (painting the outside wood and stone once every three years and inside every seven years).[65] Concrete was widely used. This, too, was inspected by the King's Norton Union surveyors. Mr Roberts, the building and contractor of ten terraced houses in the new Kingswood Road in 1898 referred to above, wrote to them: 'The concrete is laid on the building site ready for your inspection'.[66] In 1894 an architect claimed the brick walls of a detached house on the corner of Anderton Park and Forest Roads were to be set in concrete and in 1896 King's Norton Union surveyors insisted that the drains be concreted in the outbuildings to a house, Hango Mount, in Trafalgar Road.[67]

Poor suburban housing was much commented on at the time and was part of the stereotyping of suburbs. Jane Ellen Panton highlighted particular problems, such as ill-fitting windows.[68] John Ruskin valued the idea of preserving the

62 *Ibid.*, 2340.

63 PCRC, House Deed, 30 March, 1896.

64 PCRC.

65 LBA, MS/718/9.

66 LBA, BPKNU, BCK/MC/7/3/1, 3348.

67 *Ibid.*, 1821 and 2439.

68 Panton, *From kitchen to garret*, p. 62.

place where one's family had lived as a way of honouring it and providing continuity from generation to generation.[69] To him the new suburban houses signalled a disruption to society in that they reflected an aspiration or desire for social and physical mobility. He denounced new houses that were poorly built, uniform and in 'gloomy rows of formalised minuteness', because they offended the eye, destroyed the countryside and were a corrupting influence on 'our national greatness'. Ruskin, however, belonged to a high-status social group and perhaps had little understanding of the limited financial resources of many suburbanites.

Moseley catalogues stressed that houses were 'substantially built', 'thoroughly well-built' and 'well built'. Newspaper adverts in 1861, 1881 and 1891 used descriptors such as 'substantially well-built', 'Superior', 'Good', 'Capital' and 'Excellent' for Moseley houses. These descriptions were part and parcel of the advertising process, but the controls available to the King's Norton Union surveyors, the tight building leases and covenants and extant buildings suggest that building standards were high in Moseley. Builders sometimes had to remind building officials to come along for an inspection, though: Thomas Mills of 35 Leopold Street, Birmingham, reminded them to come and pass the remainder of the drains on the eight semi-detached houses in Anderton Park Road he was building for owner H. Lucas of Thirlmere, Anderton Park Road, and architect E. & J.A. Harper of 57 Colmore Row.[70] Moseley houses were far from the gloomy rows of small, uniform dwellings that Ruskin depicts, but suburban housing did reflect a mobile population.

Health and hygiene

The middle classes moved to Moseley for a healthier life and the new domestic built environment post-1850 promoted this in various ways.

The new middle-class houses had 'Outdoor Offices', outside yards with various storage facilities and lavatories. All the building plans accessed had storage facilities for ashes and coal and a privy or water closet (WC) in their outside yard. Privies had no water supply and no drains. They had a fixed wooden seat with a round or oval hole over a void (the midden or cesspit).[71] Cesspools were often unlined or only partially bricked, which could allow seepage into nearby wells, contaminating drinking water.[72] Dry privies (earth-closets) developed and were manufactured from the mid-1860s. In these, the privy waste in the pit was covered with earth or ash to deodorise it and break

69 John Ruskin, *The seven lamps of architecture* (London, 1849), p. 180.

70 LBA, BPKNU, BCK/MC/7/3/1, 169/7.

71 D.J. Eveleigh, *Privies and water closets* (Oxford, 2011), pp. 7–8.

72 *Ibid.*, p. 11.

it down to create a rich manure. New ash privies had waterproof brick walls and were smaller, mitigating the contamination of wells and springs. The pail or tub closet developed: a galvanised or enamelled iron bucket, which could be removed from the rear, was located underneath the privy seat and a side hopper delivered ashes. These buckets were collected regularly and sometimes disinfected before being returned. Only three building plans had privies in the yards in the building plan sample. These plans were for five terraced and one detached house and were all in houses built in the 1870s in lower-status Trafalgar and Woodbridge Roads.

All the other properties in the building plan sample had water closets (WCs) in their yards. However, in the early days most of these lacked connection to sewers and, like privies, drained into cesspools. Given the amount of water used, a cesspool connected to a WC was more likely to overflow than one connected to a privy.[73] The wider use of WCs was stimulated by the spread of the water-carriage system in towns from mid-century and by the success of the WCs in the Crystal Palace 'retiring rooms' at the 1851 Great Exhibition installed by Josiah George Jennings (1810–82). The WCs in the first-class refreshment halls were expensive mechanical valve closets.[74] Valves opened and closed the inlet in an overhead tank and an outlet to piping in a simultaneous action using a flush handle. The WCs in the second-class refreshment halls were a new type, 'the monkey closet', a modified basin trap closet with a water-sealed trap below a basin containing a shallow pool of water. The trap was the bend at the back of the toilet that led the waste to the piping that took it away.

In 1858 Jennings patented 'the plug closet', which had a plunger or piston at the rear or side of the basin that, when pressed, discharged waste and, when raised, released flush water.[75] In 1863 John Shanks (1825–95) introduced his version with an india-rubber ball for a plug.[76] After 1870 the pace of development increased. In 1884 the 'Pedestal Vase' was introduced, a wash-out closet with the trap in the pedestal, a chain pull and a small overhead cistern containing enough water for one flush.[77] A new type of basin-and-trap water closet emerged – the wash-down, in which the trap was set higher to become a continuation of the basin and meant the water level was shared between the trap and the basin.[78] By the 1890s most makers had added a pedestal wash-

73 *Ibid.*, p. 17.

74 *Ibid.*, p. 41.

75 *Ibid.*, p. 42.

76 *Ibid.*, p. 43.

77 *Ibid.*, p. 47.

78 *Ibid.*, p. 53.

down to their range, such as Doulton's 'Simplicitas' (1820–97), Shanks' 'The Citizen' (1825–95) and Thomas Crapper's 'Marlborough' (1836–1910) and 'it was the wash-down – simple, reliable and (importantly) cheap and affordable – that went forward to become the universal toilet of the twentieth century'.[79]

Sanitary conditions in Moseley came under the spotlight in 1872 with an outbreak of typhoid fever.[80] The Rural Sanitary Committee for King's Norton Union met at Selly Oak workhouse on 14 December 1872 and Thomas Plant of Moseley claimed that almost every other house in Moseley was 'more or less affected' with fever. At a meeting of residents at the National School on 28 December 1872, the first concern was the reputation of Moseley. Many believed the reports exaggerated but about fifty residents had been diagnosed with enteric fever and six had died from typhoid in Trafalgar Road and on the Alcester Road towards Balsall Heath (Fig. 2.1). The chairman stated that the fever cases occurred in the houses of the 'better class' and were thus related to their WCs.

Tests on samples of well-water in Moseley revealed twenty grains to the gallon of organic matter and escapes of 'dark matter' – in other words, sewage – were found on the Moseley Road.[81] 'Something like a panic has set in among the residents of both suburbs [Moseley and Balsall Heath] some of whom are leaving their houses'.[82] A 'memorial' (i.e. a petition) asking for a special commissioner to investigate and report on the situation and be sanctioned to act was taken to George Dixon MP. The commissioner attributed the outbreak to the pollution of well-water by an adjoining privy and stated that the system of dumb-wells and ash-pit privies caused serious pollution of the soil and well-water and that the cementing of dumb-wells and the regular emptying of their contents on the land were not sufficient to arrest the danger.

Residents responded quickly. A committee of Moseley residents recommended the substitution of the Birmingham Waterworks Company for the existing well-water supply and that earth-closets and a more satisfactory system of sewers for the surface water and ordinary house drainage be adopted. The Birmingham Waterworks Company, founded in 1826, provided most of the water for Birmingham and its surroundings. The King's Norton Rural Sanitary Board appointed a Parochial Committee, including three local men, given that there were 'many gentlemen of experience and standing at Moseley who would be glad to serve on the committee and would render great assistance'.[83]

79 *Ibid.*, pp. 56 and 59.

80 *Birmingham Daily Post*, 21, 24 and 29–31 December 1872, 16 and 29 January, 13 February and 22 May 1873.

81 *Ibid.*

82 *Ibid.*

83 *Ibid.*

The 1875 Public Health Act consolidated previous acts of parliament relating to public health and introduced urban sanitary districts overseen by local government boards. The Act required the provision of clean water, the disposal of rubbish and sewerage and the sale of safe food. Homes had to be connected to the main sewerage system and new houses built with such connections. In the same year Birmingham Council took over the Birmingham Waterworks Company noted above and set up a Birmingham Tame and the Rea District Draining Board to provide an integrated drainage system over a wide area that included Moseley.[84] Gradually Moseley houses were joined to the Birmingham sewerage system and water was brought to Moseley houses by the Birmingham Corporation.

These measures were supported by the founding of the Sanitary Institute in 1876 which rigorously tested water closets at its annual trade shows and the many publications on sanitation that appeared, such as *The Plumber and Sanitary House* (1877) by Samuel Hellyer, the inventor of the 'Optimus' patent water closet in 1870 and campaigner for better plumbing.[85] The Sanitary Institute and the publications drew attention to the insanitary nature of some methods of sewerage.

Concern among Moseley residents about sewerage and sanitary conditions continued, exacerbated by the expansion of the suburb, and lighting and pavements also became an issue. Moseley residents met at the Trafalgar Hotel on 3 February 1877 to discuss the formation of a new local board with King's Heath and the ecclesiastical district of St Anne's, under the provisions of the 1875 Local Government Act.[86] Clearly, little had changed. The system of dumb-wells and open middens still operated, which the *Birmingham Post* considered surprising 'in a fashionable suburb where there is a large and growing population even if health is generally good'. There were broader concerns about 'the annexing disposition of Balsall Heath': 'It is feared that Balsall Heath has set a hungering eye on the rich [rates] of Moseley and is eager to fold it into its arms and the inhabitants of Moseley naturally object.'

There was opposition to street lighting on the grounds that 'it will tend to "unruralise" the neighbourhood'. William J. Spurrier, looking back to the past in the *King's Heath and Moseley Journal* in 1893, explained that 'There were no gas lamps, for the very good reason there was no gas, it was specially brought to our house for us', but by 1903 he described the roads in Moseley as 'well-lighted'.[87] Gas to Birmingham and nearby villages was generated by two

84 *Ibid.*

85 Eveleigh, *Privies and water closets*, pp. 43–4.

86 *Birmingham Daily Post*, 3 and 5 February 1877 and 22 May, 4 July, 18 and 24 August 1883.

87 SMCA, *Canon Colmore's log book*, Spurrier, *Moseley of today*; *The Dart*, Friday 27 January 1893.

private firms, the Birmingham Gas Light and Coke Co., and Birmingham and Staffordshire Gas Co. Chamberlain negotiated a municipal take-over in 1875. Althans Blackwell at Brackley Dene got his gas from the Birmingham Gas Department in the 1890s. There is no mention of the provision of gas in the building plan questionnaires.

In 1883 the issue of a separate sanitary board for Moseley and King's Heath had not been resolved and lighting was still causing concern.[88] *The Birmingham Daily Post* advised its readers that 'in almost every suburban place in England the lamps are not lighted during a particular portion of the summer, but they need to be lit when there is no moon and it is dark'.[89] Moseley residents agreed and a deputation visited the King's Norton Sanitary Authority to persuade them to relight the lamps in these circumstances. The Lighting Committee refused and 'great dissatisfaction was expressed by the ratepayers'. Representatives met at Councillor Moore's home in Forest Road, Moseley, to 'consider how the government of the district could be amended and brought more into harmony with the wishes of the inhabitants'. The group wanted the parish divided into wards and more representatives for Moseley and King's Heath, given they were being 'thickly populated and heavily rated'. The Rural Sanitary Authority relighted the districts as residents had demanded and was told by the Local Government Board, in a reproof that reveals the status of Moseley residents, that:

> it must not attempt to govern these large and important districts in a huckster-like manner. … it may be reasonably hoped that the Rural Sanitary Authority will see fit to endeavour, for the remainder of their term of office (which expires in April next), to attempt to govern the districts more in harmony with the wishes of the inhabitants and consistent with their ratal importance.[90]

A sub-committee was retained as a 'Ratepayer's Protection Association' to 'very forcibly call attention to any derelictions of duty on their part, such as putting out the lamps, or making a mess of sewerage matters, as they had done in the past' and 'to ensure the nomination at the next election, and future elections, of proper persons to represent the ratepayers of these districts on the Rural Sanitary Authority'. The Moseley middle classes were taking control of their own environment.

Health and hygiene problems rumbled on. Two years later, in 1885, a Wake Green Road resident, Henry B. Barnett of Ivythorpe, wrote to the *Birmingham*

---

88 *Birmingham Daily Post*, 22 May, 22 June and 2 July 1883.

89 *Birmingham Daily Post*, 22 May 1883.

90 *Ibid.*

Daily Post regarding sewer gas. He looked back nostalgically to a supposedly idyllic rural past:[91]

> When I took up abode here this road was a beautiful country lane and the air was worth a guinea a mouthful. Certain Goths have comparatively destroyed the beautiful country lanes by a ruthless cutting down of the trees; and certain Sanitarians have absolutely destroyed the other with sewer gas. Pedestrians nauseate, and horses actually sniff in affright as they pass.

Fears about sewer gas were widespread. Bad smells were still felt by many to cause illness, despite developments in germ theory at the time by such as Louis Pasteur. Such smells were not appropriate in a middle-class suburb. Henry Barnett's 'Sanitarians' were probably the enthusiasts in Moseley intent on improving local sanitary conditions in the suburb, but Joseph Chamberlain's urban redevelopment scheme in central Birmingham would have received considerable publicity.

The responses on building plan questionnaires suggest that the water carriage system improved in the last decade of the nineteenth century. Only one of five mentioned 'Corporation' water in the 1860s, 1870s and 1880s plans. Other water-related mentions are 'tap' (two), 'Water Works' (one), and 'Company Water' (one). The change is significant in the 1890s questionnaires: 83 per cent used terminology associated with Birmingham, such as 'Birmingham Corporation', 'Corporation', or 'Town Water', but five used 'Water Works' and one 'South Staffordshire or Birmingham Water Works' and others 'tap' (one) and 'mains' (two). Althans Blackwell's water at Brackley Dene, Chantry Road was supplied by Birmingham Corporation Water Department in the 1890s. One question asked about the outlet of drains. 'Sewer' was the most frequent descriptor (thirty-four) and others included 'sewer in road' (thirteen), 'main sewer' (six) and 'street sewer', 'sewer in yard', 'into existing sewer' and 'main culvert' (a total of four). In 1878 the main sewer was laid by the United Drainage Board on the Anderton Park Estate and the Birmingham Corporation put down water mains along all the intersecting roads there.[92]

Household water was monitored, reflecting the importance of water quality: building-plan questionnaires noted 'h & c water', 'rainwater' also termed 'soft water', 'tap water' and 'Corporation tap water'.[93] Althans Blackwell received a document in 1892, signed by John Houghton, inspector to the Rural Sanitary Authority, that certified there was 'within reasonable distance of the house an

---

91 *Birmingham Daily Post*, 7 January 1885.

92 LBA, Bham/Sc 919.

93 LBA, BPKNU, BCK/MC/7/3/1, 2304, 1535, 627, 532, 1485, 1483, 811 and 1194; LBA, Bham/Sc 1194 and 890.

available supply of wholesome water … sufficient for consumption / use for domestic purposes'.

The building plan questionnaire required information about the size, fall and position of drains. George Bayliss had to 'make all proper drains and sewers for carrying off foul wastewater and soil from the land and any buildings' at his 1893 Church Road villas and cleanse, keep in good order and repair sewers and drains.[94] Robert Kerr, writing in 1864, advised siting windows away from outside smells and taking care in the positioning of 'dust heaps' (dust and other household rubbish, but mostly fine cinders and ashes from coal fires), 'gully-holes' (an opening to a drain or sewer) and 'offensive apartments' (privies) in outbuildings.[95] Given fears of miasma, ventilation was important and was achieved through 'air bricks', 'ventilating plates', iron ventilators and 'room windows placed high up in walls'.[96]

Complaints about footpaths and the state of roads arose again in the 1890s, revealing the tension between the rural romance and urban practicality in the voices of Moseley residents. 'Mollie', in her column 'Tittle-Tattle from Moseley' in *The Dart* on 21 August 1891, wrote:

> I wonder why it is that the footpaths of a great many of the roads in Moseley are so abominably pebbly and rough? Is this their chronic condition? Church Road, Woodstock Road, Sandford Road and Woodbridge Road are all the same, indeed I don't believe there is one footpath in Moseley that you could call smooth. Not only are these footpaths most uncomfortable to walk on, but they are also ruinous to light summer shoes, as I for one, have found to my cost, and no doubt other ladies have also.

A letter to the *Birmingham Daily Post* from A.B. Bowden published on 15 November 1892 brought up the subject of lighting again:

> What has become of the Surveyor to King's Norton Rural Sanitary Authority? I hope he may not be invalided. But I am constrained to think he must be, or surely he would not have neglected the lighting of so important a thoroughfare as Chantry Road, situated as it is in the heart of Moseley. We are in the middle of the garrotting and 'burgling' season and the gentlemen who follow these avocations must look upon Chantry Road as a safe hunting ground.

Garrotting was a dramatic exaggeration, given Moseley was renowned as crime-free, though not entirely robbery-free.

94 LBA, MS/718/9.

95 R. Kerr, *The English gentleman's house or how to plan English residences* (London, 1864), p. 87.

96 LBA, BPKNU, BCK/MC/7/3/1, 1458.

On 27 January 1893 *The Dart* again criticised the state of the roads and complained about how muddy they were. By 1903, though, Spurrier described the roads in Moseley as 'good'.[97] Good roads and pavements that were well lit were important because they signalled a sophisticated and modern suburb. Improved sanitation and roads came at a cost: the 1896 lease for 78 Park Hill shows the owner had to contribute to the local authority for sewering, paving, kerbing and guttering of roads bounding the land and comply with the provisions of the Public Health Act of 1875 and additional Sanitary Acts.[98]

The management of household rubbish was an important aspect of health and hygiene. The building plan questionnaires show that there were 'dust' or 'tub' rooms for bins, sometimes referred to as 'place', 'pit' or 'house' in the yard. Receptacles for house rubbish were referred to as 'tubs', 'pails' or 'bins', some of which were 'galvanised as now required' and some 'covered' or with 'proper doors and covering'. One had an 'Adams Patent Ash Tub' but by 1897 the regulations insisted on 'galvanised pails with lids'.[99] Only one plan, a terraced house, shared a 'dust' space for household rubbish, unusual for Moseley's middle classes. Before 1875 many suburbs had no regular rubbish collection and residents arranged and paid for refuse removal themselves. From 1875 refuse was removed by the municipality as a legal obligation.

Upmarket homes had a wider range of outdoor offices. Two of the three houses planned in Wake Green Road had dairies – John Padmore's large home built in 1875 and The Grange owned by George Jackson, gentleman, built in 1895.[100] Clovelly, 22 Chantry Road, built in 1891, had a washhouse. Other larger properties had a rainwater cistern room and wood and tool stores. Bicycle sheds were labelled in five house plans from 1892 to 1898 – two detached houses in Chantry Road and Park Hill and three semi-detached houses, Overdene, 4, Chantry Road, and two in Oxford Road.[101] This reveals very progressive and well-to-do families: bicycles in general were not widely produced until the 1870s and expensive until very late on in the century.

Outbuildings associated with private transport differentiated those with rank and wealth and highlighted a male world. Coach houses were few in building plans: only 6 per cent had coach houses. Ten were in detached houses and three in semi-detached houses. In the 1870s, when public transport was more limited, 23 per cent of the houses had coach houses, in the 1880s 2 per cent and in the 1890s 9 per cent.The drop in the 1880s might reflect increased

---

97 SMCA, *Canon Colmore's log book*, Spurrier, *Moseley of today*; *The Dart*, 27 January 1893.

98 PCRC, Deed.

99 LBA, BPKNU, BCK/MC/7/3/1, 3015.

100 *Ibid.*, 18 and 2139.

101 *Ibid.*, 1460, 2340, 2686 and 3630.

public transport and a greater number of smaller houses being built; the rise in the 1890s may indicate private coaches becoming a status symbol that differentiated the elite and a preferred means of travelling, particularly for elite women, given an increasing number of lower-status people on public transport. Few stables, loose boxes and harness rooms were identified on these building plans – three in detached houses in the 1870s and five stables in the 1890s, four in detached houses and one in a semi-detached house. A semi-detached house built in 1891 in Chantry Road, Clovelly, number 22, had a corn house, and the semi-detached Hopwood, 18 Chantry Road, a hay loft as well as coach houses and stables.[102] There was, then, a small but significant 'carriage class' in Moseley.

Moseley was developed by a range of people in complex relationships. Many residents were involved in mostly small-scale investment, but there were also some larger operators. House type and size, plot size, location and strong covenants secured Moseley for the middle classes and differences created a social hierarchy that coalesced into social zones. Architecturally, Moseley was eclectic in nature and services and facilities underpinned the health and hygiene for which Moseley was noted, ably influenced by residents forming strong pressure groups.

The houses were set in gardens that were important in attracting people to Moseley and securing the green environment. The next chapter explores some middle-class gardens in Moseley in the second half of the nineteenth century and considers what influenced their design.

102 *Ibid.*, 1435 and 1498.

4

Gardens, garden design and gardening

Gardens were an important attribute of the middle-class suburban single-family house and at the root of the demand for suburban living. They fed into the dream of the rural idyll, the nostalgia felt by those brought up in the countryside and images of the life of a country gentleman. They helped provide a salubrious and healthy environment, an escape from urbanisation and industrialisation and the sanctuary, peace, privacy and safety the middle classes were seeking. Gardening was considered a Christian activity that reflected 'God's work on earth made visible'.[1] The bond between individuals and nature was believed crucial to identity and its loss responsible for personal crises, giving gardens an important role in well-being.[2] Gardens allowed each homeowner to 'create his or her own utopia within walls and hedges' and offered opportunities to display wealth and aesthetic skills and mark the individual apart from others.[3] The ideal suburban garden was one 'in front to impress the outside world with a display of neatly-tended possession of some land and one at the back for the family to enjoy'.[4] Gardens, garden design and gardening came to have a special role for the newly emerging suburban middle classes, who formed a powerful gardening lobby. This chapter introduces contemporary garden styles, shows how these were interpreted in Moseley and explores other influences on the choices Moseley residents made.

Surviving photographs of Moseley gardens from the second half of the nineteenth century are invaluable records of suburban middle-class garden design and planting schemes. They include the gardens of the super-elite middle class such as at Uffculme, Moor Green, built in 1892; of the elite middle-class, such as at Sorrento, a large house in Wake Green Road, built in the 1870s; and of the middle-middle-class, as at Brackley Dene, Chantry Road, built in 1892, or the restored garden of a smaller semi-detached house in Park Hill, built in the 1870s. No images have been located of the gardens of Moseley new builds further down the middle-class hierarchy. Photography was

---

1 H. Barrett and J. Phillips, *Suburban style: the British home, 1840–1960* (Boston, Toronto, London, 1993), p. 169.

2 A. Helmreich, *The English garden and national identity: the competing styles of garden design, 1870–1914* (Cambridge, 2002), p. 10.

3 *Ibid.*, p. 113.

4 Thompson, *The rise of suburbia*, p. 15.

an elite and expensive pursuit at the end of the century and photographing their homes and gardens shows that Moseley residents wanted to record their status in a new medium. The bills and receipts preserved by well-to-do Althans and Agnes Blackwell relate to the development of their new-build garden at Brackley Dene. They reveal the plants, equipment, fertilisers and soil improvers they bought for their garden, the outside labour they employed, the nurseries they patronised and the costs involved.

Garden styles in the second half of the nineteenth century reflected both the formal and informal, and this was played out in Moseley. Interest in the formal garden was stimulated by three developments across the second half of the nineteenth century. The 'Italian Garden', popular at mid-century, was favoured by John Claudius Loudon (1783–1843) and championed later by James Shirley Hibberd (1825–90), one of the most popular and successful gardening writers of the Victorian era.[5] The later 'Queen Anne style', 'The Old-fashioned' or 'Old World' artistic and architectural garden, was an offshoot of the picturesque that harmonised with 'Queen Anne' architecture popular in Moseley from the 1870s, and was promoted by John Dando Sedding (1838–91), an English church architect, artist, garden designer and author. Subsequently Reginald Blomfield (1856–1942), also an architect, garden designer and author, espoused the revival of 'Jacobean' features, further undermining the natural garden. He claimed that formality provided quiet and shelter from the outside world.

The terraces, balustrades, stone steps, vases, urns and bedding-out plants in the gardens of Sorrento and Uffculme (Figs 4.1–4.2) reveal the influence of these formal styles. Many of the structural features of formal gardens were constructed from new materials such as concrete, or older artificial materials such as coade stone or decorative stone not found locally but brought in by rail. Cast-iron features, industrial intrusions into the natural garden such as that shown attached to the plinth in the rear garden at Sorrento, often adorned formal gardens (Fig. 4.1). Cast iron was also used to imitate rustic features such as benches. The smaller gardens – Brackley Dene and Park Hill – do not display these formal structures to any great extent.

Shrubberies, evergreens (such as conifers and easily clipped privet and laurel) and topiary were popular formal elements and are visible in the Uffculme and Sorrento photos (Figs 4.3–4.4). Althans Blackwell bought several shrubs for the garden of his larger detached house: among others a camelia (2s 6d) in 1894 and a ceanothus (2s) and a hypericum (1s) in 1897. Specimen trees and plants were set in lawns and beds to show them to their full advantage, planted where they could be seen and admired from all angles, as at Uffculme and Park

5 J.C. Loudon, *The suburban gardener and villa companion* (London, 1838); Loudon, *Encyclopaedia*, p. 763.

Figure 4.1. The rear terrace, Sorrento, 1899. PCRC.

Hill (Figs 4.4–4.5 and 4.7). The specimen tree in the Park Hill lawn is a more formal element in a largely 'natural' garden. Herbaceous plants were also bought, including, by Althans Blackwell, specimen plants such as heuchera, poppy and campanula.

Borders of 'old fashioned flowers' were recommended later for the more formal garden – particularly lilies, roses, poppies and sunflowers – as well as box hedging, trellised walks, bowers and climbing flowering plants up walls, as at Uffculme (Fig. 4.7). Althans Blackwell bought twenty-nine roses in 1893 and 1894 costing a total of £8 13s 6d and twenty bulbs and seventeen lilies for 15s 8d in 1895. Such expenditure would have been beyond the pocket of many: in 1890 it would take a skilled tradesman approximately a month to earn £8 13s 6d and around two days to earn 15s 8d.[6]

The 'natural' or 'wild garden', a looser style with softer and more fluid lines, less rigid planting and using natural materials, was proposed by William Robinson (1838–1935), a gardener, writer and magazine editor, in his 1870 book *The Wild Garden.*[7] This approach was represented in Moseley by garden shrubs in their more natural state as in the Park Hill garden and some parts of the Sorrento and Uffculme gardens (Figs 4.5–4.7). Uffculme had rustic bridges and seating and Sorrento a rustic arch (Fig. 4.6); the Blackwells of

6 https://www.nationalarchives.gov.uk/currency-converter.

7 William Robinson, *The wild garden* (London, 1870).

Figure 4.2. The rear garden from the dining room, Uffculme. The Barrow Cadbury Trust. (BCT).

Figure 4.3. The front garden, Sorrento, 1899. PCRC.

Figure 4.4. The rear lawn, Uffculme. BCT.

Figure 4.5. The rear garden, Park Hill. Courtesy of the current owners, 2015.

Figure 4.6. The rear garden, Sorrento, 1899. PCRC.

Figure 4.7. The east garden, Uffculme. BCT.

Brackley Dene bought a rustic seat in 1895 for £1. Ponds, lakes, water rills, streams and collections of plants in special 'natural' settings, such as ferneries and rockeries, were also natural garden elements. Uffculme had a large wild garden, woodland area and lake and a rockery/fernery on a grand scale (Fig. 4.8). Park Hill's 'natural' water feature included rills, waterfalls and a pond (Figs 4.9 a–b) and Brackley Dene had a pond, rockery and fernery. Ferneries or fern-houses were highlighted in 1881 and 1890 adverts and catalogues, signalling them as attractive features to prospective buyers and tenants.[8]

The English Cottage Garden style that emerged from the natural garden favoured native herbaceous plants in borders of densely planted hardy perennials and shrubs with loosely shaped beds of shrubs and hardy plants, as well as flowering climbers. The natural garden incorporated a display of flowers and shrubs in their natural state, rather than manicured, and plant combinations such as roses with the newly introduced sub-tropical plants, including yucca and palms. Ground cover and alpine plants with lilies in borders were also popular. Althans Blackwell ordered eight creeping fig (*Ficus repens*) plants at 6d each in 1893, which would have served as ground cover.

Wide, dry gravel paths linked different parts of garden designs and provided convenient private walkways for the family and their guests, especially females. Paths were straight in more formal garden areas, as at Sorrento and Uffculme (Figs 4.1 and 4.4). In more informal gardens, as at Park Hill and Brackley Dene, and also in the natural garden areas at Uffculme and Sorrento, they were likely to be curving, following the contour of the land (Figs 4.5–4.7 and 4.10).

At the end of the century the garden designer Gertrude Jekyll (1843–1942), working with the architect Edward Lutyens (1869–1944), combined elements of the formal and natural, formulating a new balancing of the architectural and horticultural to achieve aesthetic harmony. Jekyll was a follower of Robinson and her inspiration was the profusion of the cottage garden and its essential Englishness. For her the vernacular meant topiary, water, summer houses, simple natural materials, climbers and subtle herbaceous borders. She brought back architectural features such as antique urns and vases, pergolas, brick and stone paths set in patterns, reflecting ponds and a sense of linked rooms.

The 'battle' between the formal and informal generated fiery debates: the difference was not just about individual taste, but about what the garden said about English identity. Both were promoted as essentially English, but which showed more Englishness? What garden style was chosen as the leading style mattered greatly if the garden symbolised Englishness, because 'each form inscribed a different, nearly opposing, appearance and set of meanings on

8 LBA, Bham/Sc 890 and 1260.

Figure 4.8. The rockery and fernery, Uffculme. BCT.

Figure 4.9a. Water feature, Park Hill. Courtesy of the current owners.

Figure 4.9b. Water feature, Park Hill. Courtesy of the current owners.

landscape'.[9] Julia Cartwright (1851–1924), an art critic and historian of the Italian Renaissance, claimed that gardens held the possibility of cultural unity, because the formal and informal were both part of England's history and identity.[10] She saw the formal garden as 'within the reach of humbler persons' because it required much less space, but advised gardeners to express 'an individual idea'.[11]

Lawns were a quintessential part of Victorian garden design, particularly for larger houses and villas, emerging as a strong theme in the 1860s (Figs 4.2–4.5, 4.7 and 4.10–4.11). They were mentioned frequently in advertisements for the sale or rent of houses in Moseley. In 1891 newspaper advertisements referenced the large, levelled lawn at Treaford Lodge, Anderton Park Road, and two lawns at The Vale, Wake Green Road. The 1877 sales catalogue for Mansion House described a 'beautiful lawn belted by numerous fine grown ornamental shrubs and noble chestnut trees'.[12]

Edwin Beard Budding, an engineer from Stroud, Gloucestershire, invented the lawn mower in 1830, paving the way for this later Victorian obsession with lawns. From the mid-1850s, lighter and quieter lawn mowers were introduced, as well as models in various sizes with minor modifications, all of which were dependent on human power. These developments underpinned the widespread devotion to lawns and made lawns feasible for a wider social group. Motorised mowers appeared in the 1890s as lightweight petrol engines and small steam-power units became available but, by 1900, petrol-engine mowers were market winners.[13] Neat lawn edges were important, as seen in many of the garden images reproduced here, and iron or terracotta rope- or scallop-pattern edgings became very popular. They, like ironwork, were mass produced in manufactories – another example of the contradiction between the natural and the industrial.

Robinson, the foremost champion of the 'natural garden', claimed that the heart of the garden was a bold informal sweep of lawn and defended the practice of bringing lawns and planting right up to the house, something John Dando Sedding opposed. Sedding saw the house and its architecture as an integral part of the design of a garden, with the area immediately outside the house needing to link with the architecture through, for example, a gravel or stone surround or, where there was a drop, a balustraded terrace with stone steps leading down into the garden area. The garden was another room

9 Helmreich, *The English garden and national identity*, p. 135.

10 Julia Cartwright, 'Gardens', *The Portfolio* (London, 1892), p. 144.

11 *Ibid.*

12 LBA, Bham/Sc 919.

13 <www.oldlawnmowerclub.co.uk>, accessed 2016.

Figure 4.10. The rear garden, Brackley Dene. MSHGC (C3/D2/A/F10/13).

Figure 4.11. Rear garden balcony, Sorrento, 1899. PCRC.

extending from the house, or, in the case of larger gardens such as Uffculme and Sorrento, a series of rooms divided by hedges and walls, gravel walks, herbaceous borders and orchards of fruit trees (Figs 4.6–4.7). Both approaches were taken up in Moseley in gardens of different sizes, signalling the independent attitudes of some Moseley gardeners. At Brackley Dene the lawn swept up a slope close to the house but was separated from it by a narrow path and planting (Fig. 4.10). Lawns and planting were separated from the house at Sorrento by a wide terrace, hedged borders and narrow pathways (Figs 4.1, 4.3, 4.6 and 4.11).

Garden designers recommended a graduated transition from the house to the wilderness, with the most 'frankly manipulated' features such as terraces and formal bedding located near the house and the increasingly naturalistic following on as the landscape moved outwards.[14] This was taken up by Moseley gardeners of both larger and smaller gardens. The terraces, garden walls, balustrading and walks at Uffculme and Sorrento advanced the line of the house into the garden (Figs 4.1–4.2, 4.4 and 4.7). The water features, rockery and fernery at Uffculme, Sorrento and Park Hill and the pond and vegetable garden at Brackley Dene were located at the end of their gardens (Figs 4.8–4.9a–b).

Some Moseley gardeners held onto some planting styles despite criticism and others yielded to the fashion of the day. Bedding-out, a Victorian fashion that brought huge amounts of bright and previously unknown colour to gardens, was considered 'gaudy' by natural gardeners, but Moseley gardeners continued in its use: Uffculme, Sorrento, Park Hill and Brackley Dene gardens show close planting of one variety or colour of plant or flower in beds and ribbon bedding alongside paths (Figs 4.4–4.7 and 4.10). Beds varied in shape and were often geometrically complex and symmetrical when viewed from an upstairs window. Althans Blackwell subscribed to this style, ordering fourteen tradescantias and sixteen begonias costing 4s. Bedding-out left the ground empty from autumn to early summer and the middle classes, who, unlike the aristocracy, did not decamp for the season to London, filled the gap with spring bulbs and dwarf conifers.

None of the Moseley photographs show vegetable plots. Few suburban villa gardeners grew vegetables to any great extent other than specialist types. For them, not growing one's own vegetables was an indicator of gentleman status and purchasing ability. The railway brought fresh vegetables and fruit and a wide range of good-quality produce from around the world. However, the Blackwells grew basic vegetables, some bought as plants and many from seed. In 1893 and 1894 they also grew specialist types, including two cucumbers

14 Helmreich, *The English Garden and National Identity*, p. 170.

(1s 6d), asparagus (two for 2s and one for 5s) and two dozen tomato plants (8s). Growing vines and fruit bushes was considered suitably middle-class because it was a specialist, skilled activity. In 1881 and 1891 *Birmingham Daily Mail* advertisements highlighted vineries, as did sales catalogues.[15] In 1894 Althans Blackwell bought gooseberries and currants (16s 6d) and a vine (7s 6d) from the same places as his vegetable plants. Larger Moseley gardens, such as Uffculme and Treaford Lodge, Anderton Park Road, had kitchen gardens. Mansion House was advertised as having a 'large and productive Fruit, Flower and Kitchen Garden. Vinery in full bearing. Melon House, Forcing House, Greenhouses'.[16] Woodfield nearby was noted in 1877 as having an 'extensive Fruit, Flower and Kitchen Garden well planted and very productive and is surrounded by a lofty wall covered with Fruit Trees of the best kinds'.[17]

The colourful new exotic plant species coming from around the globe promoted enthusiasm for gardening and innovative design in the second half of the nineteenth century, impacting on the character of gardens. Plants acquired by Althans Blackwell, for example, came from the Americas (tradescantias), Brazil (begonias), North America (heucheras), Japan (camelias), China (clematis) and East Asia (*Ficus repens*) – and flowers from different countries were grown together. The use of exotic plants brought status and signified affluence and gardening expertise: Joseph Chamberlain's extensive glasshouses filled with orchids at Highbury were renowned. In 1896 the Blackwells purchased orchid peat, suggesting that they were trying their hand at growing orchids in their small glasshouse (Fig. 4.10). Even the lower middle classes might procure specimens to impress visitors. Assimilating plants from around the world brought suburbanites into contact with ideas about ethnicity, race and exploration – places and people from distant regions – and was an expression and demonstration of British imperialism. At the same time, gardens were considered to represent 'Englishness', making gardens and gardening a complex arena of perceptions of 'us' and 'them' for the suburban middle classes.

The development of small 'Wardian' cases from the 1830s meant that tender plants could be brought back alive from around the globe and then nurtured, propagated and hybridised in conservatories and greenhouses, bringing cheaper plants to the middle classes. Botanical gardens stimulated the development of greenhouses. The Birmingham Botanical Gardens, designed by John Loudon, opened in Edgbaston in 1832. Edinburgh's palm house was completed in 1834 and Kew Gardens' famous palm house, the largest in

---

15 LBA, Bham/Sc 890 and 1260.

16 LBA, Bham/Sc 919.

17 LBA, Bham/Sc 123.

the world at the time, was built between 1844 and 1848. New technology in ironwork, glazing and heating was crucial, along with the repeal of tax on glass in 1845, the abolition of the brick tax in 1850, the easing of timber duty in 1851 and the construction of Crystal Palace, built for the Great Exhibition of 1851. Glasshouses were also encountered on visits to country houses such as Chatsworth and Trentham and to the gardens of the local elite.

Conservatories and greenhouses became cheaper and were produced in a range of sizes, making them accessible to more people. Thomas Clark, 55 Lionel Street, was a significant Birmingham greenhouse manufacturer. Loudon considered conservatories the 'most desirable additions to villas' and 'a mark of elegance and refined enjoyment', which marked the house 'as the abode of gentility'.[18] They raised status, being small-scale imitations of the plant houses and orangeries of country estates, and were a public space for consumption and display. They impressed with the marvels of their iron and glass construction and the richness and rareness of their contents. Conservatories linked the house and the garden. Moseley conservatories varied in size considerably, highlighting the middle-class social hierarchy: the Uffculme and Sorrento conservatories were very large and impressive, both influenced by the design of the Botanical Gardens at Edgbaston (Figs 4.1 and 4.3). The Brackley Dene conservatory was much smaller and simpler (Fig. 4.10).

Greenhouses were more workstations than sites for display, but were still status buildings. They were usually sited away from the house, as at Uffculme and Sorrento (Fig. 4.4), but were nearer the house in smaller gardens, as at Brackley Dene (Fig. 4.10). Building regulations ensured standards: George Bayliss was required to use a flue or chimney stack for heated greenhouses when building two villa residences in Church Road in 1893.[19] Garden buildings were another category of construction that spoke to status and differentiated the middle classes. In 1881 adverts identified many, including summer arbours. Uffculme had a decorative ornamented pavilion and a gothic-style summer house to match the house (Fig. 4.2).

Local botanical gardens with their large glasshouses stimulated visiting gardeners. Moseley Botanical Gardens, which opened in the 1890s in the grounds of Pine Dell Hydropathic Establishment on the corner of Wake Green and College Roads, contained extensive and varied garden areas and large and small greenhouses holding rare plants. The entrance lodge had an intricate rustic archway that alluded to the idealised rural myth of the simple cottage garden and epitomised the Arts and Crafts movement. Adverts on the boards at the entrance broadcast the leisure activities available to visitors. The Moseley Botanical

18 Loudon, *Encyclopaedia*, pp. 975–6 and 849.

19 LBA, MS/718/9.

Gardens emulated the Birmingham Botanical Gardens in nearby Edgbaston, which were strongly supported by Joseph and Neville Chamberlain. Various features and buildings were added at the Birmingham Botanical Gardens, including the fountain (1850), the lily house (1852), the palm house (1871), the bandstand and the terrace (1884) and the rock garden (1896), developments that would have attracted visitors from Moseley.[20] The development of these botanical gardens reflects a commitment to the ideal of the garden that went beyond the limits imposed by the financial means of individual householders.

Vistas of the rear garden and beyond from inside the house and views of the house from the garden were important aspects of garden design. A 'prospect' was increasingly sought after for its aesthetic quality. The essential advantage of the new suburbs was that they were on the edge of the countryside with open views beyond, but, as suburbs became built up, such views disappeared for many. Uffculme had views to the Lickey Hills and Rednal, while other homes, such as Brackley Dene, had fabulous views of the parkland and lakes of Moseley Hall grounds and Moseley Park (Figs 4.2 and 4.4). Smaller houses and those closely surrounded by others had more restricted views. The images show views of the house from the garden at Uffculme and Sorrento and views over the garden from the house at Park Hill (Figs 4.3, 4.5 and 4.7). In Figure 4.11 a lady at Sorrento views the garden from her balcony. The 1877 sales catalogue for Mansion House notes the pleasures of the view from the house: 'the lawn of rich old turf is belted by flowering shrubs of luxuriant growth and grand old chestnut and other splendid trees and presents from the house a picturesque and attractive scene'.[21] The ground floor of Brackley Dene was raised, allowing views from all three reception rooms, and there were lovely views of the house from the garden (Fig. 4.10).

Some garden features were thought particularly attractive to prospective middle-class purchasers or renters. Gardens and 'own grounds' were mentioned in nearly half of the 1881 *Birmingham Daily Mail* adverts and a third of 1891 ones relating to Moseley properties for rent or sale. They were described as 'good' in 19 per cent of the 1881 adverts and in 11 per cent of 1891 adverts. In sales catalogues gardens were 'well-stocked', 'exceedingly well-stocked', 'well planted' and 'tastefully laid out and arranged', with 'lawns tastefully laid out', or they were described as 'pleasure gardens', suggesting that good design and mature gardens were a particular draw.[22] The term 'pleasure gardens' conjures visions of large spaces for leisure and entertainment. Plants in the form of 'shrubs' and 'flower beds' were noted, highlighting fashionable

20 <https://www.birminghambotanicalgardens.org.uk/the-gardens-history>, accessed 15 March 2023.

21 LBA, Bham/Sc 919.

22 LBA, Bham/Sc 890, 1260, 877, 1890 and 869.

planting schemes.[23] 'Large' was the most frequent descriptor, appearing in 17 per cent of adverts in 1881 and 14 per cent in 1891, and there were frequent references to 'large garden' in sales catalogues too.[24] These adverts helped market Moseley as a garden suburb.

Garden size – overall, front, side and rear – was a significant element that differentiated the suburban middle classes and marked a family's wealth and place on the social ladder. The images reproduced here capture this hierarchy, showing Uffculme at the top, followed by Sorrento, Brackley Dene and Park Hill. Most detached houses had larger gardens than semi-detached houses and semi-detached houses larger gardens than terraced houses, but this was not necessarily always the case: the garden of a semi-detached house in Park Hill, at 1,396 square yards, was larger than that of detached Brackley Dene. The largest lot on the Anderton Park estate in 1877 was approximately 11,400 square yards and the smallest 1,700 square yards.[25] Garden size also contributed to the status of roads and social zoning in the suburb: on average, gardens in Trafalgar Road were much smaller than those in higher-status Park Hill and the plots of the semi-detached and terraced houses in Queenswood Road were significantly smaller. Loudon did not appear to attach much consideration to status and garden size, writing that 'a very small portion of land … will contain all that is essential to happiness'.[26]

The most highly sought after type of property was a villa set back from the road, such as Sorrento (Fig. 4.3). A large front garden not only signalled wealth and established the residents as socially significant, but also hid the house from the prying eyes of passers-by and allowed a more impressive drive. Sweeping drives gave a good aspect of the house and evoked images of the carriage class and country houses. Frontages were a very visible indicator of social difference separating the elite from others and their size in Moseley varied considerably. On the Anderton Park estate 62 per cent of frontages were up to fifty yards in depth, 33 per cent exceeded that and a few (5 per cent) were over 100 yards.[27] Some substantial detached houses, such as Brackley Dene, though, had small front gardens, challenging the status accorded to frontage size. Trafalgar and Woodbridge Roads, less highly ranked areas, had larger average frontages than Chantry Road, a higher-status road.

---

23 LBA, Bham/Sc 179 and 811.

24 LBA, Bham/Sc 1260 and 1790.

25 LBA, Bham/Sc 919.

26 J.C. Loudon, *The villa gardener* (London, 1850). This was edited by Jane Loudon. It was aimed at those owning plots from one perch (30¼ square yards, 25.29 square metres or 0.00625 acres) to fifty acres.

27 LBA, Bham/Sc 919.

Loudon considered side space essential in a 'perfect villa', not only to preserve privacy from neighbours but also to avoid contact between the family and members of the lower social orders, such as delivery staff and workmen.[28] Detached houses were mostly set in their own grounds with plenty of side space, but not always: a detached house in Trafalgar Road was very close to its neighbours.[29] Semi-detached houses offered less side privacy, given the shared party wall. Uffculme had a signposted tradesman's entrance and separate rear access, but even smaller houses had tradesmen's entrances labelled on building plans. Terraced housing had no side space and not much privacy, though some had 'entries', shared passageways between the houses that gave access to the rear of the properties.[30]

Rear gardens were important to status and privacy and significant in preserving a sense of a rural environment, especially as the suburb became built up. Of advertisements placed in the *Birmingham Daily Mail* in 1881 and 1891, 43 per cent and 34 per cent respectively mentioned rear gardens.[31] Rear gardens were usually significantly larger than front gardens, but varied considerably in size, and there was a wide variety within house types and between roads. The average size of the rear gardens of detached houses in building plans accessed was about 387 square yards, those of semi-detached houses about 290 square yards and those of terraced houses about 145 square yards. The average width, though, varied from seven to 218 yards for detached properties, five to twenty-nine yards for semi-detached properties and eight to ten yards for terraced properties. This shows that rear gardens of detached properties were not always larger than those of semi-detached houses and those of semi-detached houses were not always larger than terraced rear gardens, as might be expected, complicating the hierarchy of houses further.

Garden size influenced what design style residents adopted and the features they could incorporate, which in turn impacted on status. Smaller properties such as Brackley Dene and Park Hill could accommodate only small rockeries, ferneries and ponds and modestly sized flower beds and lawns compared with those at Uffculme and Sorrento. Many Moseley gardens were smaller still. Larger gardens had the space to respond to both formal and informal styles on a grander scale as they became fashionable, whereas smaller gardens, as at Brackley Dene and Park Hill, were predominantly informal in style, shown by their curving paths and informal planting (Figs 4.5 and 4.10). Sorrento and Uffculme were at the top end of middle-class accommodation and not

28 Loudon, *Encyclopaedia*, p. 768; LBA, BPKNU, BCK/MC/7/3/1, 866 and 2340.

29 LBA, BPKNU, BCK/MC/7/3/1, 28 and 26.

30 LBA, BPKNU, BCK/MC/7/3/1, 1458.

31 LBA, Bham/Sc 1260, 869, 456, R2 and 1658.

typical of the majority of Moseley gardens. The grounds of Uffculme, built by Richard Cadbury in 1891, 'developed somewhat haphazardly with little regard for current fashion in garden design', and its formal but individualistic style was much derided by Joseph Chamberlain, Cadbury's neighbour.[32] Chamberlain favoured the natural parkland style in his extensive grounds, but, when developing new garden areas between 1899 and 1904, he used the now fashionable geometrical features and straight lines that he had disliked at Uffculme.[33]

Larger gardens and grounds such as those at Uffculme could easily and more closely imitate country houses with meadows and hay fields. Even smaller establishments could incorporate a small meadow, like that at Highfield House, where a meadow extended from the house to Wake Green Road. Other larger houses had space for a variety of features that would have set them apart and raised their status: the 1881 *Birmingham Daily Post* adverts detail orchards and fruit trees, while sales catalogues mention fowl runs, pig pens, an aviary and dog houses.[34] A property in Church Road had a cow house for five cows and piggeries attached, while in 1877 Woodfield had a large lawn, extensive formal geometric gardens, many trees, three large fishponds and substantial greenhouses.

Privacy was a key component of the 'trappings' of the middle-class suburban 'way of life' and crucial to garden design, irrespective of garden size.[35] Loudon noted: 'The great object, whether in small villas or extensive ones, has been to shut out everything belonging to the neighbourhood, which could indicate that there was any other proprietor or resident in the vicinity.'[36] Privacy was maximised by walls, trees, shrubs, hedges and gates, important also in protecting and marking all the boundaries of the property. Trees, hedges and shrubs provided privacy in sectioning off garden 'rooms' at Uffculme (Fig. 4.7). The side boundaries of the Park Hill garden and a path in the rear garden at Sorrento were screened by trees and shrubs, which also gave shade to the walkways (Figs 4.5–4.6). The 1877 sales catalogue describes approaching Mansion House on the Anderton Park estate along a 'pretty shaded walk through the shrubbery'.[37] Shrubs and trees supposedly shielded dry gravel paths and other family-walk areas from the eyes of servants and also spared

---

32 Perrie, '"Almost in the country"', p. 150.

33 *Ibid.*, pp. 155–6.

34 LBA, Bham/Sc 1890, 1260, 869, 456, R2 and 1658.

35 Simon Gunn, 'Translating Bourdieu: cultural capital and the English middle class in historical perspective', *The British Journal of Sociology*, 56/1 (2005), p. 53.

36 Loudon, *Encyclopaedia*, p. 766.

37 LBA, Bham/Sc 919.

the family from having to observe outdoor servants at work. The Blackwells moved into Brackley Dene in August 1892 and by the end of the year they had bought many trees and shrubs, plus hedging, suggesting that they were planting for privacy, given that Chantry Road was a newly developing road and their house overlooked Moseley Park. A local commentator wrote later: 'Tall trees, a vegetable patch, flowering borders and thick hedges made the house completely private, restricting visibility from the park.'[38]

Covenants required boundaries to be marked. George Bayliss, the Moseley builder, was required by the covenant attached to his building lease on two villas in Church Road in 1893 to 'fence and partition off the premises' with 'substantial brick walls 9" thick and properly coped'.[39] The abolition of the brick tax in 1850 helped the less well-to-do afford such walls. Walls also protected produce from the elements and the working areas of the garden from the family and visitors. As much as signalling a desire for quiet and privacy, however, recently constructed walls and new hedges, shrubs and trees marked out a new community and planting would take time to grow to maturity. This underpins the significance of the many mentions of established trees in sales catalogues: houses were 'surrounded by mature trees', 'beautifully timbered', 'shaded by fine grown trees' and 'trees in full growth'.[40] Adverts from the 1891 *Birmingham Daily Mail* described The Vale as being 'nicely timbered'. Mature trees offered privacy, but also created a sense of the long-established country estate rather than a 'new build'.

Costs involved in developing gardens also dictated what could be achieved by residents and tied them to the social hierarchy that differentiated the middle classes. In 1875 the cost of establishing and maintaining a garden was estimated to require an annual income of between £400 and £500.[41] The Blackwell bills show that the family spent nearly £300 on their garden between 1892 and 1897, though this may not represent all their garden spending. It does not include the amount spent on planning the garden and implementing the plan at the outset in 1891/92, before they moved into their new build. Those renting or moving into more established properties would not necessarily be burdened by such an initial outlay and smaller gardens required fewer items. The bills suggest that seed was affordable, even by the less well-to-do: a wide array of vegetable seeds (eleven ounces of seed, fourteen packets and 1lb of shallots) cost the Blackwells 14s in February 1893, and they paid 1s for a packet of polyanthus seeds and 3d for nigella in 1896. The average cost of 456 plants

38 MSHGC, C3/D2/A/F10/16, Contemporary comment on Chantry Road.

39 LBA, MS/718/9.

40 LBA, Bham/Sc 919, 1861, 890, 811 and 1260.

41 James Anderson, *The new practical gardener and modern horticulturist* (London, 1875), p. 2.

bought by the Blackwells in 1890s was 11d per plant, a feasible outlay for many middle-class Moseley residents. Structural features involved greater expense: in 1893 the Blackwells invested in a modest greenhouse, fernery and rockery, which cost them just over £70 for materials, plants and labour. Few lower-middle-class households could afford these features except on a very small scale and not everyone had the necessary time or skills to devote to building such features.

A large gardening industry developed, stimulated by the new enthusiasm for gardening. Althans Blackwell mostly used Birmingham nurseries, but also a few from the West Midlands and some from further away, including in Matlock, Chester, London and the Lake District. Some orders were significant: in October 1892 James Smith & Sons, Darley Dale Nurseries, Nr. Matlock delivered plants, including nearly eighty shrubs and twenty trees, to Camp Hill station, just over two miles away from his home. In 1894 Richard Smith & Co., nurserymen and seed merchants of Worcestershire, sent seventy-eight plants and a bundle of straw by Midland Railways. Rapid railway transport of plants and horticultural items meant nurseries and market gardens were increasingly freed from restrictions of locality. The Blackwells used some firms frequently, especially Thompson & Co., nurserymen, seedsmen and florists of 20 High St, Birmingham (1892–7), but also the Royal Seed Establishment, Reading (1894–7), Richard Smith & Co., nurserymen and seed merchants of Worcester (1894–6) and Robert Sydenham, 'Importer of really good bulbs/seeds', of Tenby St, Birmingham (1895–7). The introduction of the penny post enabled seed companies to offer free delivery, making seeds by post even more viable for the less-well-to-do.

For purchases of soil, potting loam, leaf mould, manure and gravel the Blackwells used local suppliers such as T. Hadley & Son, Moseley House, Moseley, and William Parker, general haulier, of Gravel Pits, Billesley Lane, Moseley. They also bought tools and equipment locally, from, for example, James Williams General Furnishing Ironmonger, St Mary's Row, Moseley. The gardening bills were all made out to 'Mr' or 'Althans' Blackwell, but this may have been the convention of the day and did not necessarily mean that Mrs Blackwell was not involved in selecting what to buy. Gardening linked the middle classes to the public world of commerce through their purchases, undermining the perspective of the home as a retreat from the public world.

Trade directories list several gardeners and landscape gardeners locally, including Joseph Walker, active in the 1870s and 1880s, who lived in Moseley Terrace, off Alcester Road, near the village centre. Joseph Chamberlain employed a landscape gardener, Edward Milner, to design the gardens of Highbury, but Richard Cadbury designed the gardens at Uffculme himself. Cadbury employed many gardeners to manage his Uffculme estate. John Avins employed a live-in groom-cum-gardener in 1871 and his widow Eliza Avins a live-in gardener in 1901. Gardeners given accommodation thereby became part of the Moseley community, but were working class. Althans Blackwell at Brackley Dene employed a gardener, G. Seeley. Bills show he worked 35½ hours in 1893 at an average of 4s 6d per hour. He dealt with and charged for deliveries of soil, manure and leaf mould, rolled and mowed the lawn, dug borders, fixed the vine, weeded the pond, clipped verges and wheeled rubbish from the yard – the more manual tasks. He may well have worked many more hours than those billed to keep the gardens at Brackley Dene in order: it is unlikely that the Blackwell family did the remaining garden chores.

On the other hand, many publications reflect a 'do-it-yourself' approach, suggesting that most middle-class gardeners worked in their gardens themselves – but this would not be 'back-breaking' work, just lighter tasks such as design, planting and maintenance.[42] Gardening was considered an acceptable form of recreation because it involved 'physical effort and some intelligence' and was not 'associated with idleness, a corrupting vice'.[43] The 99-year leases on Moseley new-builds included strict rules about the upkeep of gardens, which prompted residents to maintain their gardens and helped keep Moseley looking neat, enhancing it as a status suburb. The middle classes had more leisure time and gardens offered them physical, intellectual and leisure opportunities. Health became an increasing concern, leading to an appreciation of fresh air and exercise. Families could enjoy walking round, resting, socialising and reading, and could undertake hobbies, play garden games or take tea in the garden. Figures 4.2, 4.4 and 4.10 show seats and Figure 4.13 that tea in the garden for the family living at Sorrento meant a table complete with white linen tablecloth. Croquet was a popular Victorian garden game and larger gardens, such as Sorrento and Highfield House, just around the corner in Church Road, had tennis courts. Gardens offered a relaxing contrast to work and pleasure in achievement.

Suburban gardens were a locus of 'modernity', integrating technology, science and the intellectual as well as the aesthetic in a new context that was neither city nor country. Lawnmowers and glasshouses testify to new technology, mass production and scientific ideas. The market was flooded with new tools, equipment and gadgets. Scientific understanding of the physiology of plants, the composition of soils and the process of photosynthesis increased and effective fertilisers and insecticides were developed, resulting in improved

42 Stephen Constantine, 'Amateur gardening and popular recreation in the 19th and 20th centuries', *Journal of Social History*, 14/3 (1981), pp. 388–9; Helmreich, *The English garden and national identity*, p. 118.

43 Constantine, 'Amateur gardening', p. 96.

Figure 4.12. Tea in the garden, Sorrento, 1899. PCRC.

methods of cultivation. There were new practical skills to learn, such as pruning. The Blackwells understood the need to improve the soil: in February 1893 they bought ten loads of soil, four loads of leaf mould and two loads of manure and in October eight more loads of manure and leaf mould for 12s from Hadley & Son, Moseley House. In 1895 and 1896 they bought eight bags of potting turf, five loads of soil, two loads of potting loam and two loads of manure, along with fertiliser and insecticide. By integrating science and technology and the products of the British empire, gardens encompassed two opposing visions of England – 'the workshop of the world' and 'a green and pleasant land'.

Local horticultural societies were a source of inspiration and support to Moseley gardeners and their garden produce shows brought access to local elite gardens. Many middle-class Moseley residents belonged to the Moseley and King's Heath Horticultural Society, where gardeners honed their gardening skills, demonstrated their horticultural expertise and mixed with the upper middle classes, Joseph Chamberlain being a keen member. The horticultural society shows hosted by Moseley's elite were an important part of the gardening and social calendar and widely reported on in the press. The first Moseley and King's Heath Horticultural Show was held at Moseley Hall in 1880 and the eighth Moseley, King's Heath and Balsall Heath Horticultural

Society Annual Exhibition in 1887 took place at the Henburys, when the owner, George Frederick Lyndon, opened his conservatory, greenhouses and fernery to visitors.[44] At a horticultural show in 1883 Joseph Chamberlain 'threw open' his greenhouses and conservatories and 5,000 attended. At the Moseley, King's Heath and Balsall Heath Horticultural Society's Fourteenth Annual Exhibition in 1893 he again opened his orchid houses and conservatories and 3,790 attended.[45] Attractions in 1893 included a bee tent and the exhibits were pronounced 'very good'.[46] In 1891 at the Moseley, King's Heath and Balsall Heath Horticultural Society there were athletic sports and fireworks, but 'unfortunately a rick on an adjoining field was found to be set on fire in the evening'.[47]

As well as providing opportunities to view elite gardens, glasshouses and produce on display, these shows enabled local gardeners to enter flower and produce competitions and receive recognition for their achievements. There were divisions for specific plants, such as roses, and a wide range of fruit and vegetables, as well as divisions for professionals, gentlemen's gardeners and 'amateurs or gentlemen who do not regularly employ a gardener', highlighting another social hierarchy associated with gardens. This suggests that they were men-only, but a 'Mrs Horton' frequently appeared in the winners' lists. Other well-known local people appeared as winners of different sections, including James Lister Lea, John Padmore, Francis Willmot, John Charles Holder, Richard Cadbury and Joseph Chamberlain. Some shows were fundraisers: *The Dart* of 5 July 1891 reported on the annual flower show at St Mary's church, which raised money for the Children's Hospital that year. The shows brought together people from different walks of life and from Birmingham and other local suburbs, reinforcing gardens and gardening as a signifier of social status. They also brought kudos to Moseley, highlighting it as a status suburb.

The gardens and grounds of the Moseley elite also had social and political roles. Queen Victoria's golden and diamond jubilees were celebrated in the grounds of Moseley Hall in 1887 and 1897. Many children and adults were entertained with tea, balloons, fireworks, prizes and presents. These were opportunities for residents of Moseley to come together, supporting cohesion between different social and religious groups. Joseph Chamberlain used his garden at Highbury for political purposes. He designed the long straight terrace in front of Highbury to serve as an elevated platform from which he could address assemblies of his supporters at the garden parties and rallies

44 *Birmingham Daily Post*, 31 August 1880 and 2 August 1887.

45 *Birmingham Daily Post*, 9 August 1893.

46 *Ibid.*

47 SMCA, *Canon Colmore's log book*, p. 395.

held in the garden, which enabled him to reach substantial audiences for support or to celebrate achievements.[48] In 1881 the gardens were opened for a rally by the Junior Liberal Association of Birmingham to strengthen its forces. Over 1,000 attended and entertainment was provided. A rally was held in 1887 during difficult political times for Chamberlain, who was fighting for control of the Birmingham Liberal Association. He consolidated local support, bringing together local branches of the National Radical Union. After Joseph Chamberlain married Mary Endicott in 1888, he began the annual practice of inviting his constituents in West Birmingham to a garden party in August when parliament ended, addressing them on the current political situation from the terrace.[49] Such political events put Moseley on the map and linked it to Birmingham, other local suburbs and beyond.

Getting garden design 'right' for those who could not afford a garden designer was a cause of anxiety for some. Many were new to the locality, away from family and making and maintaining a garden for the first time. Books, magazines and articles were published to educate and aid the amateur gardener, stimulated by the growing enthusiasm for gardening. Garden literature was crucial to the development of suburban gardens and had a major impact on how suburban gardens looked and were managed. Practical advice was dispensed, the latest horticultural knowledge disseminated and new plant introductions promoted. Writing on gardens and gardening was a platform for debate on horticultural techniques and, later, on style and taste. James Shirley Hibberd started the magazine *Amateur Gardening* in 1884 (still published today) as well as many books, including *The rose book* (1864). William Robinson published the magazines *The Garden* (launched in 1871) and *Gardening Illustrated* (1879), which, along with *Amateur Gardening*, appeared as cheap penny weeklies but continued to attract the middle classes. He wrote many books, including *The wild garden* (1870). John Dando Sedding edited three magazines, including the *Amateur Gardener* (launched in 1884 and still published today), and wrote *The town garden* in 1855, *The amateur's flower garden* in 1878 and *Garden-craft old and new* in 1892.[50] Reginald Blomfield's response to Robinson came in his 1892 book *The formal garden*.[51] Newspapers also carried gardening articles, such as 'The Villa Garden' in the *Birmingham Daily Post* of April 1874, which explained how to train plants up walls and fences and which plants to use.[52]

48 Peter Marsh and Justine Pick, *The house where the weather was made: a biography of Chamberlain's Highbury* (Alcester, 2019), pp. 7–8 and 15–16.

49 *Ibid.*, p. 22.

50 John Dando Sedding, *Garden-craft old and new* (London, 1892).

51 Reginald Blomfield, *The formal garden* (London, 1892).

52 *Birmingham Daily Post*, 8 April 1874.

Books were published specifically with women in mind; many were written by women. Jane Loudon (1807–58), the daughter of a wealthy Edgbaston manufacturer, worked closely with her husband John Claudius Loudon over many years and edited and published earlier editions of his works, including *The villa gardener* in 1850, after his death in 1843.[53] She also published her own works, including *Gardening for ladies* and *The ladies companion to the flower garden*, first published in 1841 with a seventh edition in 1858. Her works from the 1840s until the early 1880s focused on pragmatic advice, while her writings from the mid-1880s to the 1900s were more aesthetic in emphasis.[54] Isabella Beeton published *The book of garden management* in 1862, and Gertrude Jekyll published *Wood and garden* in 1899 and *Home and garden* in 1900. These publications encouraged women into the garden.

Gardens, garden design and gardening constituted a gendered arena. There was some concern about the 'delicacy' of women, but Jane Loudon, while writing that 'digging appears at first sight a very laborious employment, and peculiarly unfitted to small and delicately formed hands and feet', assured her readers that all gardening was possible for 'ladies' and proceeded to unravel its mysteries.[55] J.B. Whiting, in his 1849 *Manual of flower gardening for ladies*, asserted that, even if ladies were not doing all the work themselves, they needed to know about every aspect. In an interview for the *Birmingham Daily Post* published on 4 August 1890, Mrs Grace Harrison stated that 'a woman can easily do every part of it except winter digging, the mulching and the pruning'. Isabella Beeton claimed that a 'knowledge of garden management is as essential to every possessor of a garden as a knowledge of domestic management to every mistress of a house'.[56] Victorian garden writers asserted women's instinctive love of gardens and their affinity with the plants they nurtured and depicted women as light gardeners, matronly garden supervisors or ornaments or decorative spectacle, thereby sanctioning and furthering high conservative ideals of women's limited social role.[57] Figures 4.10 and 4.11 suggest these different attitudes: in one a woman admires the view of the garden from her balcony and in the other a woman is in the garden seemingly poised for action. Smaller gardens were considered ideal for women: they did not require too much work but were large enough to give satisfaction and exercise.

---

53 Loudon, *The villa gardener*.

54 Bilston, *The promise of the suburbs*, p. 115.

55 Jane Loudon, *Gardening for ladies and companion to the flower garden*, ed. A.J. Downing (New York, 1840), p. 1.

56 Mrs Beeton, *The book of garden management* (London, 1862).

57 Michael Waters, *The garden in Victorian literature* (Aldershot, 1988), pp. 241–5.

The garden was an extension of the private sphere outdoors, and advice texts aimed at women gardeners furthered this vision of the suburban garden as not-home. For women with time, the garden had potential as a venue for personal fulfilment and freedom, an outlet for physical, intellectual and technical energies and a vehicle for creativity, artistic and imaginative experimentation, consumerism and connection to the modern world. Gardens took women beyond the home and garden too. Buying or ordering plants and other items for the garden involved journeys to market gardens and stores, the use of catalogues and visits to the post office. As noted above, women attended horticultural societies and participated in shows, which provided social encounters that expanded their horizons and provided opportunities for networking. Such contacts, and the gardening and garden design expertise derived from work with their own gardens, their visits to various gardens and their access to gardening literature, presented the possibility of moving towards the professional role of garden designer.

The middle classes influenced the growth of interest in the value of gardening for the working classes. Their horticultural shows were models and literature on gardening, both visual and literary, occurred because of the 'practical demands of middle-class villadom'.[58] In the 1860s and 1870s the middle classes established municipal parks in most provincial towns and cities, motivated by philanthropy and civic ambition and no doubt often with the intention of shaping working-class behaviour. Louisa Ryland (1814–89) donated Cannon Hill Park, Moseley, which opened in 1873, to the citizens of Birmingham as a place of healthy recreation. It was intended for the working classes of the immediate area, but postcards show middle-class people in the park, which brought an air of respectability to the enterprise. Private landowners were responsible for much of the provision of allotments: by 1902/3 there were forty-one sites in Birmingham covering 192 acres, all mostly in private hands.[59] Moseley's gardens and green spaces must have impacted on the city's reputation, providing a counterbalance to images of the city as heavily industrialised and polluted.

The success of suburbs such as Moseley may have helped inspire the building of similar environments for the working classes. Richard and George Cadbury moved their factory out of Birmingham in 1879 with ideas about building some kind of model village for workers. Richard Cadbury moved to Moseley in 1884 to be nearer the factory and what he saw there may well

58 M. Gaskell, 'Gardens for the working class: Victorian practical pleasure', *Victorian Studies*, 23/4 (1980), p. 486.

59 MSHGC, C1/D3/BB1/2, Thorpe, Harry, Galloway, Elizabeth, B., and Evans, Lynda, A., 'The Rationalisation of Urban Allotments Systems – A Case Study of Birmingham', p. 4.

have influenced ideas behind the development of Bourneville. However, only a few semi-detached houses for senior foremen and, in the 1880s and in 1892, some cottages were built at Bournville in the early years.[60] In 1895, some sixteen years after the factory move, George Cadbury set up the Bournville building estate and houses were finally released by the estate between 1896 and 1900. These houses were not part of a model village for workers or 'a great social experiment', though, because their cost (substantially more than the £150 planned) restricted them to the middle classes.[61] However, the level of horticultural activity was exceptionally high, which demonstrated the value of planning gardens in direct relationship to housing development and community life. Ebenezer Howard proposed a 'Garden City Movement', involving settlements around cities that embraced the best of town and country, in his 1898 book *To-morrow: a peaceful path to real reform* and formed the Garden City Association in 1899.[62] George Cadbury joined the Garden City Association and the first 'Garden City Association Conference' was held in Bournville in 1901.[63] Thereafter, garden cities developed and a growing encouragement of the new idea of town planning emerged.

Moseley gardens, then, were sites of display and status that fed into the social hierarchy. Their gardens brought opposites together: 'Englishness' and the wider world; technology and mass production versus the rural idyll; private and public. Moseley's middle-class residents asserted their individuality, were actively engaged and sought inspiration from texts, garden visits and horticultural societies and shows. Moseley gardens and gardening offered opportunities to women, served as models for the value of gardening for everyone and were important to the reputation of Birmingham.

Having described the homes and gardens of the Moseley middle classes, the next chapter considers the residents who moved to Moseley, to understand what households were like, where responsibilities lay and how people managed the stages of their life-cycles.

---

60 A.R. Bailey, 'Constructing a model community: institutions, paternalism and social entities in Bournville 1879–1939', PhD thesis (University of Birmingham, School of Geography, Earth and Environmental Sciences, 2002), p. 2; M. Harrison, *Bournville: model village to garden suburb* (Chichester, 1999), p. 26.

61 J.R. Bryson and P.A. Lowe, 'Story-telling and history construction: rereading George Cadbury's Bournville Model Village', *Journal of Historical Geography*, 28/1 (2002), pp. 29–30; A. Mah, 'Demolition for development: a critical analysis of official urban imaginaries in past and present UK cities', *Journal of Historical Sociology*, 25/1 (2012), p. 162.

62 E. Howard, *Garden cities of tomorrow*, 2nd edn (Rhosgoch, 1985), pp. 8–12.

63 *Ibid.*; D. Hardy, *Utopian England: community experiments 1900–1945* (London, 2000), p. 66; P. Hall and C. Ward, *Sociable cities: the legacy of Ebenezer Howard* (Chichester, 2000), p. 29; W.L. Creese, *The search for environment, the garden city: before and after*, 1st edn (Hartford, CT, 1966), p. 498.

5

Families and households

Understanding who lived in Moseley in the second half of the nineteenth century and the variety of their experiences is important in appreciating the character of the suburb. Moseley's middle-class households and their roles, responsibilities and relationships varied greatly. They also changed across time and with life-cycle stages: these included moving to the suburbs and establishing a suburban home, marriage, having and raising children, growing old and death.

Two surveys undertaken as part of this study offer opportunities to consider the breadth of the households of Moseley. The first is a detailed analysis of the decennial censuses of four roads – Church, Ascot, Queenswood and Chantry Roads – from 1851 to 1901. Church Road, of mixed middle-class status, was an ancient highway; Ascot Road, housing those from the middle ranks of the middle classes, was formed in about 1873 and developed quickly; Queenswood Road, a lower-status road, was created in 1875 but was slow to expand; and Chantry Road, with its first house built in 1892, was built-up by the end of the century and was higher status. The survey analysed 426 households and 2,279 household members in a longitudinal study that not only reveals households in specific roads but also suggests a picture of the suburb as a whole. It takes an overall perspective of the half-century and highlights continuity and change.

The second survey explores the lives of nine families from different social levels within the middle classes from the roads surveyed and nearby. These include John and Eliza Avins, living from 1858 at Highfield House, a substantial detached early Victorian mansion on Church Road (Fig. 5.1); Thomas and Marion Ellis at Sorrento, a well-to-do detached establishment built in the late 1870s in Wake Green Road, a high-status ancient highway, and William and Martha Adams, living there from 1891 (Fig. 4.3); Althans and Agnes Blackwell, living at Brackley Dene, a detached house built on Chantry Road in 1892 (Fig. 5.2); three households who succeeded each other at Maycroft, a modest 1870s semi-detached house in Ascot Road: William and Rosalie Genge in 1881, Charles Tanner in 1891 and William and Fanny Crompton in 1901 (Fig. 5.3); James and Rhoda Barston, living in 1881 at a small semi-detached house listed as 8 Queenswood Road, and Ann Cook resident there in 1891 (Fig. 5.4); and, in 1901, Sarah Powell at Elleslie, listed as 24 Queenswood Road, a terraced house (Fig. 5.5).

Figure 5.1. Highfield House, Church Road, *c.*1900. Courtesy of Mike Rhodes.

Moving to the suburbs

Much is made of suburbs representing a flight from the city, but Moseley residents included not only many who were born in Birmingham but also many who were born in a range of places in Britain and abroad. Only just over a third of Moseley residents (excluding servants) in the census sample were born in Birmingham. Of all Moseley residents, 12 per cent were born in Moseley and 7 per cent in other Birmingham suburbs; a large number, 31 per cent, were born in Worcestershire, Warwickshire and Staffordshire; 13 per cent were born elsewhere in Great Britain, including twelve in Scotland, six in Ireland and one in South Wales; and sixteen were born outside the country: one each in France, Germany, the colony of Demerara, Spain, Lisbon, the West Indies, Australia, India and South America, three in the USA and four in Canada. Many Moseley residents, then, had moved out of Birmingham to take advantage of a more rural environment, but more people moving to the area chose to live in Moseley rather than in Birmingham. A majority of these came from the surrounding counties, while the small proportion from outside of Great Britain brought global and imperial connections and some cultural diversity to Moseley.

This pattern was reflected in the case-study families. Those born in Birmingham were John Avins and his son Charles by his first wife, Hannah, as well as Althans and Agnes Blackwell, Thomas Ellis, the three Genge children – two daughters and a son – Ann Cook and her two sons and two daughters and Sarah Powell and her two sisters. Eliza Parthenia Avins (John Avins' daughter by his second wife, Eliza) and the youngest child in the Ellis

Figure 5.2. Brackley Dene, Chantry Road, 1891. MSHGC (C3/D2/A/F10/9).

Figure 5.3. Maycroft, 11 Ascot Road. Author's own collection.

Figure 5.4. Semi-detached houses, Queenswood Road. Ian Berry.

Figure 5.5. Terraced houses, Queenswood Road. Ian Berry.

and Adams families were born in Moseley. Eliza Avins was born in King's Heath and Charles Tanner and his brother and sister in Lichfield. William and Martha Adams and three of their four daughters were born in Sheffield, William Genge in Somerset and his wife, Rosalie, in Surrey. Marion Ellis was born in Ireland, Ernestine, Charles Tanner's niece, in France and the other Ellis children in New Zealand.[1] Some families moved around the country, revealing a highly mobile population: William Crompton was born in London, his wife, Fanny, in Newport and their sons in Monmouthshire and Liverpool; James Barston was born in Yorkshire, his wife, Rhoda, in Hereford, their older sons in Yorkshire and the youngest one in Surrey. Frequent moves, including to suburbia, provided opportunities for the middle classes to reinvent themselves.

For some, moving to and within Moseley reflected climbing the social ladder. John Avins made his money in Birmingham. He retired to Highfield House in Moseley in 1858 and to life as a suburban gentleman, an influential member of St Mary's church, a Moseley resident active in improving the village and involved in local civic endeavour and a significant philanthropist. Thomas Ellis emigrated to New Zealand sometime after 1850 and succeeded in business there as the first proprietor of the Golden Fleece Hotel, Christchurch and also as lessee of the Ashley Gorge Station, some forty miles from Christchurch.[2] He returned in 1878 to educate his family and built Sorrento. Althans and Agnes Blackwell moved up in the world by degrees when they moved from 341 Moseley Road, Balsall Heath (1876–88), to Monterey, 11 Park Hill (1888–92) and then to the house they built in Chantry Road – Brackley Dene. Two Park Hill families moved further down the road as it developed – John Pickering of Park Hill House to Glen Lyn in 1890 and Thomas Arter of Helvellyn to Mariemont in 1896. In 1901 George Thomas Piggott of Clydesdale moved over the road to No. 35, Newlands. People moved frequently, as houses in the case studies show: Maycroft in Ascot Road and the houses in Queenswood Road had different occupants at each census and Maycroft was being advertised again in 1892.[3] Frequent house moves highlight suburbs as socially shifting spaces. Moving house cost money. In 1892 Althans Blackwell paid John Hudson & Son £3 16s 9d for removing furniture from Park Hill to Chantry Road. This involved three men for fourteen and a half hours at a cost of 4s per hour and a small van with three men for seven and a half hours costing 2s 6d per hour.

Setting up an independent home on marriage was important for a middle-class man. Most people rented their homes – buying was not considered

1 A. Griffiths, *The history of the Ellis family: the Sorrento connection* (Studley, 2013), p. 5.

2 *Ibid.*

3 *Birmingham Daily Post*, 1 March and 2 February 1892.

socially necessary – but the adverts for houses for sale or rent in Moseley in the *Birmingham Daily Mail* suggest that buying became more popular. Of the 1881 adverts accessed, 13 per cent gave information on sale prices, but in 1891 this had risen to 37 per cent.[4] This was at the end of the recession, though, so property owners may have been keen to shift houses. A substantial income – in the region of £300–£600 – was needed to buy a house in Moseley. An income in the upper-middle-class bracket has been rated at over £1,000 per annum, one in the middle-middle-class bracket at £200–£1,000 and one in the lower-middle-class bracket at £150–£200.[5] An engineer might earn £110 per annum in the mid-1860s and in the 1880s a civil service clerk started at £80, rising to £200. A post office clerk earned £90 rising to £260, a school board teacher £75-plus and a female telegraph head-clerk £110–£150.

Rents and house prices varied according to house size and location, which fed into social zoning. Rents averaged £55 for thirty-six properties in the sales catalogues accessed. In adverts from 1881 rents varied from £25 to £90 and averaged £42, and in 1891 they varied between £18 and £90, averaging £41.[6] There were more rents of £50 and over in 1891 (30 per cent) compared with 1881 (23 per cent), which suggests a continued desire of the well-to-do to move to Moseley. Prices for houses for sale were given in eighteen entries in the 1881 adverts: costs varied between £225 and £3,300 and averaged £797. This highlights wide differentiation within the Moseley middle classes and the economic resources needed to move to the suburb. In 1891 prices for sixty-six houses were identified. These varied between £200 and £1,270 and averaged £643 – lower costs that suggest recession and smaller houses built to meet the needs of the lower middle classes, who were increasingly moving to Moseley. Both rents and house prices varied within and between roads, highlighting the variety of accommodation in Moseley. In 1891 the rents for four houses in Trafalgar Road were £40, £45, £60 and £65. A George Bayliss house in Church Road was costed at £250 in 1893, but 30 (later 78) Park Hill cost £800 at the end of the century.

The costs involved in living in Moseley were high too. Rates on property and land were a form of local taxation based on a rateable value (RV), the rent at which properties might reasonably be let from year to year with deductions for repairs, insurance and other expenses. Moseley RVs accessed for the 1880s

4 Adverts accessed in 1881 included 125 different properties or developments: 142 houses and in 1891 172 different properties or developments: 217 houses.

5 F. Musgrove, 'Middle-class education and employment in the nineteenth century', *The Economic History Review*, NS, 12/1 (1959).

6 Forty-four adverts for houses out of 142 in the 1881 adverts and seventy-six of 217 houses in 1891 in the *Birmingham Daily Post* gave information on rents.

and 1890s varied from £25 10s 0d to £153, reflecting the status of the house and location. Amounts paid annually varied from 9s 7d to £2 11s 0d. In 1879, when Althans Blackwell was living on the Moseley Road, Balsall Heath, Balsall Heath Local Board of Health charged him a district rate of £4 16s 0d and in the same year he paid £5 0s 10d for income tax and house duty. His expenses increased as the suburb developed and with the move to a larger home, Brackley Dene. From 1893 to 1896 he made four payments of just under £10 per annum for income tax, house duty and land tax, and just under £10 twice a year towards the King's Norton poor rate. Between 1893 and 1897 he paid about £5 twice a year for King's Norton special expenses rates and about £2 2s 6d per year for King's Norton United Drainage rates.

Other costs involved in running a home in Moseley included payment for a water supply – up to 3s per week, often for an intermittent supply. In 1893 Althans Blackwell paid £6 8s 0d per annum for water and a 'bath supply' at 10s per annum and, on average, about £3 7s 0d twice a year between 1893 and 1897 to Birmingham Corporation Water Department. He paid about £3 13s 0d three times per year between 1882 and 1897 to the Birmingham Gas Department.

Some found maintaining a middle-class home difficult. On Saturday 13 February 1892 the *Birmingham Daily Post* reported that George William Herbert from Moseley, aged fifty-two and a toy manufacturer, was in debt, a difficulty he attributed to mortgages on his house Backwood in Wake Green Road. He assigned his furniture and the equity of redemption in the Moseley house to his wife, Mary, aged fifty-five, to secure the family home.

Household heads

The generally recognised household head of the middle-class home was the eldest male, the husband or father, or, in their absence, the brother, brother-in-law or eldest son. Most household heads in the Moseley sample were men (78 per cent). This leaves a significant number of female household heads, which undermines the traditional view of the Victorian household. All the case-study families had male household heads except for two, Ann Cook, a widow in 1891, and Sarah Powell in 1901, single, both in Queenswood Road. Female household heads generally inherited their position from husbands or fathers.

A well-remunerated occupation was required for middle-class men to marry and set up and maintain a household consistent with middle-class standards. Most heads were in work (70 per cent) and of these most were men (95 per cent). For a man, providing for his wife and children was considered a demonstration of affection, nurture and devotion and a compensation for his absence at work. Female heads in work were few – none in 1891 in any road analysed and none in Queenswood Road across the period – suggesting that enhanced job opportunities for women were not significantly taken up by female household heads. Many female household heads may not have needed to work and, in any case, 28 per cent of the female heads in the survey were over sixty years of age and the average age was fifty-two years. Female heads in work included two school principals (at Woodrough and Greenhill Schools), several school mistresses, a manufacturer, a manager of a food provisions company and a matron in a private hospital.

Moseley household heads in work in 1891 and 1901 were engaged in three occupational groups, 'commerce', 'industry' and 'professions', with most commercial occupations associated with manufacturing and industry, for which Birmingham was renowned. The occupational profile changed over time. Commercial occupations dominated overall in 1891 (43 per cent), followed by industrial occupations (32 per cent) and then professionals (25 per cent). Industrial occupations dominated in 1901 (46 per cent), though commercial occupations followed closely (42 per cent), leaving nine professionals (12 per cent). The occupational profile differed between roads. In 1891 and 1901 Church Road was dominated by household heads in industrial occupations and Ascot Road by commercial occupations. In 1891 commercial and professional occupations dominated in Queenswood Road, but in 1901 industrial occupations dominated. Chantry Road had household heads largely involved in commercial activities.

Position in the work hierarchy was particularly important to social status and the character of Moseley. In 1891 household heads who were employers or employed were the same proportion in the households accessed (42 per cent), leaving thirteen (16 per cent) who were engaged in independent work situations, such as doctors. In 1901, however, workers dominated overall, even when Chantry Road, with its many employers, is also taken into account (46 per cent). This reflected the increase in lower-middle-class residents. Employers were well-represented too (37 per cent), but there were only twenty independent heads (17 per cent). The situation varied in the different roads. In 1891 and 1901 workers dominated in Church Road and employers in Ascot Road. In 1901 workers dominated in Queenswood Road and employers in the new Chantry Road, showing that the well-to-do were still moving to Moseley even though the suburb was becoming built-up. Female heads in work were employers, except for the hospital matron in Chantry Road in 1901, designated a worker. Employers, workers and professionals living alongside each other brought a degree of social mixing.

The occupations of the case-study household heads reflect this mixed picture of occupational type and associated status. In 1891 Charles Tanner was a local scale and weight manufacturer: an employer. Three case-study male household heads were commercial travellers – in 1881 James Barston and William Genge in drapery and in 1901 William Crompton in iron – and they were all listed as workers. The modest semi-detached house, Mycroft, in middle-status Ascot Road, was occupied by a worker in 1881 (Genge), an employer in 1891 (Tanner) and a worker in 1901 (Crompton), showing that house type was not necessarily associated with occupation status. Occupation status could change. Althans Blackwell was firstly an employee and then later an employer, a partner with his brother-in-law in the silversmithing and jewellery factory at 186–7 Warstone Lane in the Jewellery Quarter, Birmingham.

Household heads who were not in work had other income streams. Of heads, 11 per cent had independent means, and of these 85 per cent were female, many living on inherited money; 6 per cent were retired, almost all men. The three female retired heads were widows: a retired housekeeper (1851), a retired furniture dealer (1881) and a retired book dealer (1901). John Avins was a retired timber merchant. William Adams of Sorrento (1854–1911) was retired too. He was from Sheffield. His father, a coal miner there, was a founder member of the Refuge Assurance Company. William moved to Moseley in the 1880s to become the Refuge's Midlands Manager and then later its director.

Retirement did not necessarily mean an end to involvement in business for many Moseley residents. John Avins was involved in land and property development (see Chapter 3). He also bought and sold shares in a range of firms, including steamship companies, railways, canals and tramways, but also banks, mining companies, construction firms, various manufactories and insurance companies.[7] He had important business roles, which contributed to his image as a philanthropist and brought local and national press coverage. For example, he was on a committee to promote a new railway to King's Norton (1864) and another investigating the timber accounts and the affairs of the Metropolitan Railway Carriage & Waggon Co. Ltd (1865).[8] He was director of Birmingham Financial Company (1965) and chairman of Cannock and Huntingdon Colliery Company (1873),[9] and was part of the provisional directorate launching a campaign for Sutton Coldfield Crystal Palace Aquarium and Skating Rink Co. in Cole's Royal Promenade Gardens adjoining Sutton Park (1877).[10] His business activities exemplify connections with the wider world and were typical of the middle classes with spare means and leisure time. Althans Blackwell also dabbled in stocks and shares. Between 1894 and 1897, for example, he had shares in Allday & Morris Pneumatic and Engineering Company, Lloyds Bank Ltd, Peninsular & Oriental Steam Navigation Co., Patent Nut and Bolt Company Ltd, the Metropolitan Bank and S.A. Daniell Ltd.

7 LBA, MS/1672/087/8/9/90, MS/1272 (Acc 1995/027).

8 *Birmingham Daily Post*, 23, 24 and 26 March, 5, 12, 17, 18 and 21 May 1864 and 9 August 1865.

9 *Birmingham Journal*, 25 November 1865; *Birmingham Daily Post*, 25 August 1873.

10 *Birmingham Daily Post*, 24 March 1877.

Most working heads commuted to work but some worked from home. In 1889 Fivelands, Alcester Road, had a separate dispensary and consulting room built for Dr Gosling, the household head.[11] Shops had family accommodation attached. Houses were used as schools run by men, women and couples, such as the Classical and Commercial Boarding School at Woodbridge House, Woodbridge Road, run by George Sansome and his wife, Hannah, which had two classrooms in 1850.[12] The female household heads at Woodrough and Greenhill Schools were resident in the schools they ran. Working at home also meant commissioning houses and managing property portfolios for some Moseley men and women (see Chapter 3) and, for women, work opportunities such as music and art tuition and dressmaking.

Middle-class marriage

Moseley marriages were forged through religious, family, business, social and neighbourhood connections. The middle classes in Moseley came together at a range of social, cultural, educational, sporting, fundraising and philanthropic events, in societies and clubs and at church (see Chapter 7). Thus a small set of young people met regularly together in a veritable Moseley marriage market. In 1893 Ellen Margaret Alabaster, who lived with her parents, Edward and Fanny, at 7 Park Road, married Rev. Everett James Bishop, also of Park Road.[13] Thomas Ashley Ellis, the eldest son of the late Thomas Ellis of Sorrento, married a fellow Moseley resident, Florence, fourth daughter of Thomas Hayden of Hazlewood, Moseley, in 1892 at the Baptist church, Oxford Road.[14] Althans Blackwell moved up from being an accountant clerk with the Reading Jewellery and Chain-Making business in Birmingham's jewellery quarter to become a partner in the firm when he married Agnes Reading, who, along with her brother Nathaniel Cracknell Reading, owned the business (Fig. 5.6). Marriage was important in the transmission of capital – economic, social and cultural – around and within families. It was crucial to middle-class women's futures and essential to maintaining a respectable view of themselves in society. The process from meeting to marriage offered opportunities to display wealth, status, tradition and style.

The ideal middle-class household in the second half of the nineteenth century was headed by a married couple. Most Moseley household heads in the sample were in a marital relationship on the census days in 1881, 1891

11 LBA, BPKNU, BCK/MC/7/3/1, 1586 and 459.

12 *Kelly's Directory of Birmingham with its suburbs* (1867), pp. 670–1; MSHGC, C2/D1/F10/26, Article on Schools.

13 CRL, C1/10/11, *Moseley and King's Heath Journal*, p. 7.

14 *Birmingham Daily Post*, 23 January 1892.

Figure 5.6. Agnes and Althans Blackwell. MSHGC (C3/D2/A/3).

and 1901 (70 per cent), leaving 30 per cent who were widowers, widows or singletons. Of these 58 per cent were widows, 16 per cent widowers, 15 per cent spinsters and 11 per cent single males. All the case-study male household heads were married or had been married, except for Charles Tanner, aged forty years in 1891. When John Avins died in 1891, his widow, Eliza, continued to live in their home, Highfield House, as household head. Ann Cook was a widow aged sixty-seven in 1891 and Sarah Powell, aged thirty-six years in 1901, was the only case-study example of a spinster female household head. She inherited her assets from her father.

Moseley male heads in the census survey averaged forty-nine years and just over half (55 per cent) were from thirty-one to fifty years of age, suggesting that they married later, when they were more financially secure and more able to set up an independent middle-class home. Female heads were a slightly older average – fifty-two years – and 69 per cent were over fifty. They mostly did not become heads until widowed, which accounts for their greater age compared with male heads. Of female heads, 30 per cent were over sixty years of age, compared with 13 per cent of male heads.

Of Moseley wives, 65 per cent were younger than their husbands; 53 per cent were younger by one to ten years and the others by eleven to twenty-seven years; 21 per cent were older than their husbands, including nine by six to twelve years; and 13 per cent were the same age. The age difference between case-study couples varied. John Avins was ten years older than his second wife, Eliza, and Thomas Ellis was twenty-three years older than his wife, Marion. The Blackwell and Adams couples were around the same age, but there was a five-year difference between the Barston husband and wife, six years between the Genges couple and ten years between the Crompton couple. Such differences show how widely patterns of age on marriage varied.

Widowers frequently remarried, being partially motivated by the need for someone to run the household and often to look after children. This could lead to complicated stepfamilies and half-families. John Avins' first wife Hannah died in 1847. Their son, Charles Thomas Avins, was born on 19 June 1844. Fourteen years later, on 17 June 1858, Avins married Eliza Bate at St Mary's church, Moseley, after which they moved into Highfield House, Moseley. John and Eliza's daughter, Eliza Ann Parthenia, was born four years later, in 1862, when Charles was eighteen. He was away in higher education when she was young and doesn't appear on any Moseley censuses subsequently until 1891, the year his father died. He married in 1892, settling initially in Staffordshire. Edward Holmes remarried after the death of his first wife and had a further ten children to add to the three born to his first wife. Althans Blackwell's first wife, Agnes, died in 1898, but they were childless. He remarried in 1901 and subsequently had two children. Other such examples were frequent across the suburb. For example, in 1891 a twelve-year-old stepson lived in a family in Church Road with an eleven-month-old son of the new marriage. Many Moseley widows did not remarry, because men married younger women and widows were often not an attractive prospect financially. They might also choose not to remarry if they were well provided for.

Few incidents of divorce emerged in Moseley. The *Birmingham Daily Post* of Friday 8 August 1890 reported that Kate Collins of Moseley had been granted a decree absolute on the grounds of the adultery and cruelty by her husband, a commercial traveller.[15] Divorce became possible for ordinary people after the 1857 Matrimonial Causes Act and from 1895 judicial separations and maintenance in cases of persistent cruelty could be granted. However, divorce brought disgrace and public humiliation that were exacerbated by its being discussed in open court and by salacious newspaper reports.

Of women over thirty years of age in the Moseley survey, 23 per cent were unmarried. Single women and widows were usually expected to live with a male relative – dependence on men was 'not only regarded as the norm, but as a badge of respectability, the natural and proper state of womanhood'.[16] Widows co-residing in Moseley often lived with male household heads, often their sons or sons-in-law, but this was not always the case. A widowed mother aged thirty and

15 S. Mitchell, *Daily life in Victorian England* (London, 1996), p. 142.

16 E. Gordon and G. Nair, *Public lives: women, family and society in Victorian Britain* (New Haven, CT and London, 2003), pp. 167–9.

her nine-year-old daughter lived with her own widowed mother in Church Road in 1891. Many widows were able to remain socially and financially independent. A widow in 1861 in Church Road lived with her five children, aged one to sixteen years, along with a younger brother, aged fourteen. Some unmarried women lived independently – Sarah Powell, for example. Rebecca Anderton inherited the Anderton Park estate and was independently wealthy. In 1871, at the age of eighty-two, she was living with her sister, Ann, at Mansion House, Wake Green Road, with five servants – a coachman, a footman, a housemaid, a cook and an under-housemaid. She contributed generously to Moseley's Anglican churches. Nearly half of Moseley spinsters aged thirty years and over lived with female household heads. A few widowers lived with family: in 1891 a widowed forty-two-year-old son lived with his widower father in Church Road. Men had the financial means to remain independent and such independence was socially acceptable. The possibility of men and women continuing as household heads when older depended on their resources. Having servants, for example, meant older people could stay independent for longer.

Women – particularly single women and widows – could exercise agency by working outside the home or from home. Of Moseley female heads, daughters and female relatives, visitors and boarders in the sample, 17 per cent were in work outside the home across the half-century. The number doubled between 1881 and 1901 from twenty-one to forty-four, but the proportion dropped from 21 per cent to 16 per cent, suggesting that Moseley's middle-class women were not taking up the increasing number of work opportunities for women later in the century. Many of those women who were in work were in the teaching profession or governesses, but the types of occupation broadened. By 1901 Moseley women in the census survey were in a wide variety of secretarial jobs, as well as shop-assistant roles, dressmaking and more technical and manufacturing occupations, such as a supervisor in a telegraph department and an assistant in a brass warehouse. Increasingly women were involved in occupations associated with industry and manufacturing.

The number of women listed in the commercial section of trade directories for Moseley from the 1860s to 1890s increased significantly. They were mostly schoolteachers, shopkeepers and dressmakers and many were widows, working to remain independent and support their families. Few commercial ventures run by women lasted into the following decade – only the farmers and a hosier first mentioned in the 1870s also appeared in the 1880s, which suggests a high turnover of commercial enterprises. Only seven of the women listed were unmarried and their ventures operated only in the 1890s, suggesting it took time for unmarried women to take on businesses in Moseley.

The female farmers mentioned were from the Reynolds family of Cottage Farm, Moor Green. Hannah and her husband William Reynolds had moved to this farm by 1876 with their six children, but he died in October that year and she took over the farm. In 1881 she was the household head, managing the sixty-seven-acre farm and employing two men and a boy. Her son, John Bartlam Reynolds, twenty, and her daughters, Ann, an embroiderer in 1871 and a baby-linen-maker (draper) in 1881 aged thirty, Catherine, an embroiderer in 1871 aged twenty-seven, and Hannah, aged twenty-five and a dressmaker in 1871, were living with her. Hannah's daughter, Ann Reynolds, is cited as running Cottage Farm in the 1880s trade directories and her daughter Hannah Reynolds in the 1890s, perhaps because of Hannah senior's advancing years (in 1881 she was sixty-one years of age and in 1891 seventy-one years). In the 1891 census Hannah senior, though, was still listed as the household head and described as a farmer and living with her were her daughters Annie and Catherine and a grandson, Ernest Griffin, aged nine years.[17] Ernest was the son of Hannah Sr's daughter Mary, who had married Walter Griffin and left home by 1871. Hannah Sr died in 1892 and her son, John, took over the farm. In 1901 Anne and Catherine were seamstresses and living at 89 Willows Road, Balsall Heath, with their sister, Hannah, who was married to a commercial clerk, Edward Jones.

Trade-directory entries reveal ambition and advancement in women involved in commerce in Moseley. A cow dealer in the 1880s became a milk dealer in Woodbridge Road in the 1890s. In the 1891 census Amy Julia and Jessie May Walker, aged seventeen and fifteen, lived with their parents, two sisters and a brother at 331 Ladypool Road (later Church Road) and were described as dressmakers. In the 1890s they raised their profile, styling themselves as 'costumiers' in trade directories and listing their address as 65 Woodstock Road. Mary Sparkes also advanced herself in Moseley's commercial world. In 1871 she was a young widow aged twenty-seven living with her parents and her one-year-old son in 'the village' and working as a dressmaker. In 1881 she was a draper with a shop in Woodbridge Road and living alone except for her son.

Other widows were able to support themselves and their families and live independently. In 1891 Clara Evans, aged thirty-four and a stationer, was the household head at 40 Woodbridge Road. Living with her were her mother, a widow aged seventy-five with her own means, and her niece, aged five. Clara featured in trade directories as a stationer throughout the 1890s. Harriet Day was a tobacconist in St Mary's Row. She was a widow aged thirty-one in 1881, caring for her three sons aged between eight months and six years.

---

17 Read more about the Reynolds family in an article by Edwina Rees on the Moseley Society Local History Group website <https://moseley-society.org.uk/wp-content/uploads/2022/04/Names-appearing-on-Moseley-WW2-memorials-3rdREV.pdf>, accessed 15 March 2023.

Many of the women involved in commerce in Moseley were in Woodbridge Road, which became an important shopping road. Others worked from home. Women in business at home could cultivate and maintain family life and their middle-class status while also acting as independent economic agents. Not all women working from home were listed in trade directories. Edward Holmes' daughters Mary and Margaret worked at the family home in Moseley. Mary, aged thirty-five, was a governess who taught morning pupils and Margaret, aged twenty-eight, was a music teacher.

Women were prominent as proprietors of Moseley's many small private schools. Of twenty private schools analysed, fourteen proprietors were female, eleven of whom were single and three married. The Beynon sisters (see Chapter 3) exemplify such enterprising women setting up and running private schools in Moseley. Charlotte Thrupp ran a large, successful boarding school in School Road. In 1851 she was aged twenty-seven and had the help of her sister, Mary Ann, sixteen. She employed three teachers and four servants and had twenty-four pupils aged eight to fourteen years. In 1861 a male cousin aged fifty-two and her brother aged seventeen, a clerk, lived with her and she employed five teachers and two servants and had nineteen pupils. Wives may well have had a significant role in couple-run schools. George and Hannah Sansome worked together at Sansome's Boarding School, having inherited it in 1837 when the premises were in Alcester Road. In 1852 the school moved to Woodbridge House in Ladypool Lane (later Church Road), which was specially built as a school with two large classrooms.[18] They ran it as a Classical and Commercial School. The school closed in 1882 and the house was sold.[19]

Some wives succeeded their headteacher husbands when they became widows. Mary Ann Thrupp (Charlotte Thrupp's sister) married Edward May Davis in 1859 and she ran Greenhill School after the death of her husband in 1887. The school was a family concern: in 1871 Edward May Davis was aged forty-three and Mary, his wife, forty-four. Their daughter, Gertrude Mary, aged seven, lived with them. In 1881 their son, Edward Arthur, aged nineteen, an undergraduate at Oxford, was living with them and Gertrude was a governess there. The school flourished in the 1870s and 1880s, with forty-four boarders aged between nine and thirteen in 1871 and forty-two pupils aged eight to sixteen years in 1881. Subsequently, however, it declined somewhat. In 1891 there were thirty-three boarders and in 1901 only twenty-three pupils. Mary Ann, Edward Arthur, now a teacher, and Gertrude continued to run the school after Edward's death and, when Mary died in 1904, Edward Arthur and Gertrude, neither of whom married, took over. Their pupil–boarders came

18 *Kelly's Directory of Birmingham with its suburbs* (1867), pp. 670–1; MSHGC, C2/D1/F10/26.

19 Cockel, *Moseley village walks*, p. 14.

from Birmingham, Moseley and other local suburbs and the colonies – New Zealand, Canada and India, testifying to Moseley's links with imperial Britain. Taking over a family business was one of the ways in which women could become business owners.

Women's contribution to the nineteenth-century English suburban economy, particularly the world of business, is largely unacknowledged and hidden from history, but these women and the many other women working in Moseley show that women made a significant contribution to the nineteenth-century economy.[20]

Having and raising children

After marriage and setting up a home, having and raising children was the next stage in the middle-class life-cycle. The *Birmingham Daily Post* announced the birth of a daughter to Frank Westwood and his wife at Hanover House, Trafalgar Road, on 1 February and the birth of a son (Joseph Clive Piggott) to George Thomas Piggott and his wife of Clydesdale, Park Hill, on 6 February 1892. Christenings were an important life-cycle ceremony and offered another opportunity for family to congregate, form close bonds and display status.

The middle classes moved to Moseley because it was a healthy area, but infants and young children died in surprising numbers. St Mary's church recorded the burials of 612 children under one year in the second half of the nineteenth century, 10 per cent of the 6,244 burials there.[21] The burials were recorded of 985 young children between one and five years of age, 16 per cent of total burials; 52 per cent of these were between one and two years, 29 per cent between two and three years, 11 per cent between three and four years and 8 per cent between four and five years of age. The burials of 1,597 children under five years of age, then, were recorded by St Mary's church for the half-century, 26 per cent cent of the total number of burials.

Giving birth frequently and at close intervals put a physical and mental strain on women. The gaps between births for the case-study wives varied between one and six years and were mostly one to three years. Another Moseley resident, Mary Lavinia Holmes, Edward Holmes' second wife, bore ten children over twenty years. The first six children were born more or less one per year, but the rate of births slowed down after that, with two gaps of about five years at the end. She was twenty-eight at the first birth and about forty-eight at the last one.

20 Jennifer Aston, *Female entrepreneurship in nineteenth-century England: engagement in the urban economy* (London, 2016), pp. 13, 23–4, 34, 40 and 140; Jennifer Aston, Amanda Capern and Briony McDonagh, 'More than bricks and mortar: female property ownership as economic strategy in mid-nineteenth century urban England', *Urban History*, 46/4 (2019), pp. 695–721.

21 List of burials courtesy of Rob Brown, volunteer archivist, St Mary's church.

The Victorian family is commonly associated with large numbers of offspring, but this was not borne out in the Moseley sample. Almost a third (32 per cent) of Moseley households in the survey did not have any offspring at home, while 73 per cent had between one and three offspring at home. Only fourteen had more than five offspring, though this included three with nine. The smaller families might connect to later marriages, the generally older profile of wives (54 per cent of the sample were over forty), increased access to contraception, the unfeasibility of large families given demands for increased and elaborate childcare and the costs of education.[22] It may reflect a desire to maintain a high standard of living with a limited income. Offspring may have left home or been away from home – censuses only list those at home on census day. John Avins' son from his first marriage does not appear in any census at Highfield House until 1891, when he was aged forty-six years, single, and living on his own means. He may well have been visiting, as his father died that year.

Some couples informally adopted nephews or nieces, given there was no legal adoption until 1925. Althans and Agnes Blackwell had their nephew Walter living with them towards the end of the century. One Moseley family drew attention to their 'adopted' daughter in a marriage announcement in the *Birmingham Daily Post* of 30 April 1891. It stated that George Heaven had married Mary Whitehouse (Pollie), adopted daughter of George Walker of Moseley, at St Agnes' church. Pollie was, in fact, their niece. The Walker family lived at Fairholme, Prospect Road: George Walker, a manufacturer, was seventy-one in 1891, his wife Mary sixty, and Mary Whitehouse twenty-eight. George Heaven, aged twenty-six and a manufacturer, was boarding at 11 Laburnum Grove in 1891. In 1901 he was a general commission agent, thirty-six, living with his wife, Mary, thirty-eight, their son George, eight, daughter, Helen, five, and one servant at 20 Clarence Road.

Families in the second half of the nineteenth century often included older unmarried daughters. This was not the overwhelming picture given by the Moseley sample. There was only a small proportion of daughters between twenty-six and thirty years of age at home (10 per cent) and an even smaller proportion who were over thirty (5 per cent). There were, though, higher proportions of daughters in these age groups than sons, which suggests that more sons than daughters had left the family home by the age of twenty-five. However, three sons and two daughters in their late twenties and thirties were still living at home with their parents, Edward and Mary Lavinia Holmes, in School Road, Moseley, in 1901. Unmarried daughters living at home could be of significant domestic help.

22 Mitchell, *Daily life in Victorian England*, pp. 142–3.

The offspring of the case-study families reflect the variety in families in Moseley. In 1881 the three Genge children at Maycroft were four to eight years old, the four Ellis children at Sorrento between seven and twelve years old, the three Barston sons in Queenswood Road seven to ten and Eliza Parthenia Avins in Church Road was eighteen. In 1891 the four Adams children were between one and ten years, the two Cook sons twenty-seven and thirty-one and the two daughters eighteen and twenty-one. In Queenswood Road in 1901 the Crompton sons were twenty-two and twenty-three years old.

The home was considered an important site for educating children. Samuel Smiles (1812–1904) wrote: 'The Home is the crystal of society – the nucleus of national character and from that source […] issue the habits, principles and maxims which govern public as well as private life.'[23] Women had a crucial role in transmitting cultural capital through educating the next generation in middle-class codes and competences.[24] However, more formal education was not the same for girls as it was for boys. A few Moseley girls did go away to school: Edward Holmes' daughter, Elizabeth, boarded at a girls' school in Spring Hill, Yardley, in 1871. Some girls attended day schools, of which there were several in Moseley, including The Vale, Wake Green Road, and the Misses Beynon's Ladies College at 37 Woodstock Road.[25]

Middle-class boys, on the other hand, were mostly schooled outside the home from around six years of age. Moseley had several private schools, including Greenhill School, off School and Ascot Roads. In 1891, aged sixteen, Walter Reading (Althans and Agnes Blackwell's nephew) was a boarder at Greenhill School. Previously he had attended Oakfield House School, a Moseley 'Preparatory School for Young Gentlemen', where in 1888 his report put him ninth in the class. The school was run by Principal E. Badcock and had many referees from Moseley, including Rev. William Harrison Colmore of St Mary's church.[26] Wintersloe, 17 Wake Green Road, was a private day and boarding school that opened in 1896 and was run by Sampson Howard Fisher until his death in 1931.[27]

The difference between schools run for boys and girls is clear from the curriculum on offer. Advertisements for Moseley's schools for girls highlighted languages and music, whereas those for Moseley boys' schools emphasised the quality of staff, the curriculum, facilities, moral training, exams, the classics and preparation for public

23 Quoted in D.A. Cordea, 'The Victorian household and its mistresses: social stereotypes and responsibilities', *Journal of Humanistic and Social Studies*, II/4 (2011), p. 14.

24 Gunn, 'Translating Bourdieu', p. 55.

25 *Birmingham Daily Post*, 15 September 1888.

26 MSHGC, C3/D2/A/7BRB/6–7.

27 See <https://moseley-society.org.uk/local-history>, accessed 15 March 2023.

schools and Cambridge and Oxford universities.[28] Going away to school could be stressful. Walter Reading wrote that 'Charles' was starting at Bishop Stortford College (founded in 1868 by a group of prominent Nonconformists) and 'facing it bravely'.[29] After schooling boys were trained as apprentices or worked in the family business. Some went on to university, especially in an ambitious family. High educational qualifications were forms of cultural inheritance to be passed on to the next generation.[30] A.B. Bradford, for example, after attending 'a well-known Moseley private school', went on to King Edward's School and then achieved a double first at Oxford.[31]

Of offspring in the survey of four Moseley roads across the half-century, 22 per cent were in work. This included more sons (34 per cent) than daughters (13 per cent). More sons were employers than daughters and they increased from seventeen in 1881 to twenty-seven in 1891. None of the daughters in work were employers, but by 1901 four daughters in the sample were operating on their own account, which suggests that daughters were beginning to establish themselves independently in work situations. These included a single thirty-four-year-old music teacher and a single thirty-two-year-old painting teacher in Church Road, a single twenty-seven-year-old 'masseuse' in Ascot Road, and a single forty-year-old flower painter in Queenswood Road. Most sons and daughters in work were twenty-five years of age and over. Sons were in commercial and industrial occupations, but daughters were mostly in educational, artistic and secretarial roles, reflecting contemporary gender attitudes.

All the sons in the case-study families were in work and were both employers and workers. Employers included William Crompton, a manufacturer of cardboard boxes aged twenty-two, and William Cook, a shoe manufacturer aged thirty-one. Workers included James Crompton, an insurance clerk aged twenty-three and Thomas Cook, a wholesale hosier's assistant aged twenty-seven. None of the case-study daughters were in work.

No examples of mental or physical disabilities among children and adults in Moseley were listed in the censuses. Middle-class families were likely to keep such problems secret. Many physicians came to believe that 'feeble-mindedness' was hereditary, which introduced shame and embarrassment as it reflected badly on the family's genetic stock.[32] During the second half of the nineteenth century there was a dramatic shift to purpose-built institutions for the treatment or management of such conditions. One such, the Midland

28 *Birmingham Daily Post*, 16 June 1884 and 15 September 1888.

29 MSHGC, C3/D2/A/F10/2-4.

30 Gunn, 'Translating Bourdieu', p. 56.

31 *The Dart*, 'University Honours for a Moseley Gentleman', 5 July 1889.

32 D. Cohen, *Family secrets: the things we tried to hide* (London, 2013), pp. 84 and 93.

Counties Asylum for Idiots at Knowle, catered for middle-class children and adults. Moseley residents of standing, such as Thomas Clement Sneyd-Kynnersley, William Henry Dawes and Frederick Elkington, supported it, which suggests that Moseley families might have used its facilities.

Maintaining middle-class standards was sometimes difficult and led to suicides and attempted suicides. In 1881 Birmingham-born Walter J. Harrison, a thirty-four-year-old wine merchant, was boarding with Clara and Cornish Breedon in Sandford Road, Moseley.[33] In 1883 he committed suicide by ingesting prussic acid in a field near Moseley. He had told John Arnold, a solicitor of Moor Green Lane and an acquaintance of twenty-five years, that he was 'very hard pressed' and that 'they are all round me for money'. He had 3¼d in his pocket when found dead. On 15 September 1900 the *Coventry Evening Telegraph* reported that Charles Burge, a hairdresser of St Mary's Row, attempted suicide by placing himself on the railway line in the Moseley tunnel. He was brought before King's Heath Bench, where he said, 'Life's not worth living.' His manner in court was strange and he was remanded to see how he went on. The possibility of bankruptcy and dropping out of the middle class was an ever-present one for many.

Others in suburban households

The census analysis also explored the range of other people who made up Moseley households – servants, relatives, visitors and boarders. Servants were crucial to the middle classes as a status symbol necessary to good housekeeping, self-respect and social dignity. Live-in servants helped shape the character of households and the suburb by bringing working-classes people into the middle-class home and community. This picture of help in the home does not include non-residential servants: these are absent from the record. In a period when work was being defined as something done outside the home, the number of people employed within the home was expanding, with more being employed in the domestic sector than in factories or elsewhere.[34] In 1851, 13.3 per cent of the employed population was in domestic service.[35] In 1881 this had risen to 15.9 per cent and by the 1890s one-third of all girls aged between fifteen and twenty years worked in domestic service.[36] Domestic service was one of the few respectable occupations available to working-class women. Residential servants were 22 per cent of household members over the half-century in the Moseley roads analysed. Of these, 97 per cent were female. Male servants were

33 *Birmingham Daily Post*, 27 April 1883.

34 I. Bryden and J. Floyd (eds), *Domestic space: reading the nineteenth-century interior* (Manchester, 1999), p. 104.

35 Mitchell, *Daily life in Victorian England*, p. 56.

36 *Ibid.*

higher status but more expensive and were mostly associated with the carriage class and gardening. Having servants brought middle-class women face-to-face with working-class men and women, along with the need to manage a workforce and mediate class differences.

How many residential servants a family had located them on the social scale. One servant was supposedly necessary to be considered middle class; three meant a 'standard' establishment and four a 'well-to-do' establishment.[37] The number of servants employed was related to income and various estimates have been proposed.[38] An annual income of £1,000 or more might allow four servants to be employed – probably a cook, housemaid, nursemaid and a male servant such as a coachman or stable boy; £750 meant three to four servants might be afforded, such as a cook, housemaid, nursemaid and perhaps a boy; £400–500 meant two to three servants, possibly a cook, housemaid and nursemaid; £300 allowed for a maid-of-all-work and a nurse; and £150 meant only a maid-of-all-work could be afforded. Combinations of servants, such as the governess, housemaid, cook and nurse in Church Road in 1871, the parlour maid, cook and three housemaids in Ascot Road in 1891, and the lady's companion, nurse, parlour maid, cook and housemaid in Chantry Road in 1901, indicated well-to-do homes. The number of servants could change over time, because of the birth of children, illness and old age.

Of Moseley households in the census sample 79 per cent had one or more resident servant, leaving 21 per cent without resident domestic help, a surprising outcome given that having a residential servant was such a key marker of middle-class status. Of those with servants just over half (57 per cent) had one servant and just over a third (35 per cent) had two servants. Those with more than two servants were few: 8 per cent had between three and five servants – these were clearly higher-status middle-class families. The number of houses with servants in a road highlighted its social status. Only just over half of households in Queenswood Road had servants (55 per cent), highlighting this road as lower status. In Church, Ascot and Chantry Roads over 80 per cent of households had at least one servant. Large houses such as Uffculme employed larger numbers of servants and often offered separate accommodation for married couples. In 1891 at Moseley Hall, Richard Cadbury employed George Minzies, sixty-five, as a gardener and housed him with his wife, Elizabeth, thirty-two, in one of the lodges. John Allsopp, forty-

37 D. Branca, *Silent sisterhood: middle-class women in the Victorian home* (London, 1977), pp. 43–4; John Tosh, *A man's place: masculinity and the middle-class home in Victorian England* (New Haven, CT and London, 1999), p. 19; Barrett and Phillips, *Suburban style*, p. 24.

38 Mitchell, *Daily life in Victorian England*, p. 32; M. Lochhead, *The Victorian household* (London, 1964); Branca, *Silent sisterhood*, pp. 43–4; D. Gorham, *The Victorian girl and the feminine ideal* (London and Canberra, 1982), p. 10.

nine, a gardener, and his wife Charlotte, forty-two, lived in another Moseley Hall Lodge at the same time.

The most common female residential servant was the general servant (41 per cent). Cooks were the second most popular (20 per cent), closely followed by housemaids (18 per cent). Other female servants included nurses (8 per cent), domestics (5 per cent) and undefined 'servants' (2 per cent). The rest (6 per cent) were sewing ladies, governesses, housekeepers, parlour maids and lady's or mother's helps, kitchen maids and a lady's companion. Men listed as servants in the Moseley sample (seventeen) included four coachmen, farm workers and gardeners, two stable boys and one errand boy, a page and a valet. The number and type of servants employed in the home carried important messages about middle-class suburban households and the number of servants employed had serious implications for the workload and leisure time of the mistress of the home.

Almost all Moseley servants were unmarried, but a few widows, often young, took up this role to support themselves. For example, in 1881 in Church Road three widows were employed as servants – a sewing lady aged forty-one, a general servant aged forty-four and a domestic aged thirty-eight. Few married servants appeared in the sample. Three married servants were listed in the census in Church Road in 1891 without any mention of a spouse. Thomas Harper is listed as a sixty-year-old married valet at Altadore along with Emma Marsh, a married cook aged forty-three. Annie Bradford, a forty-eight-year-old nurse, was in the employ of Mary Jane Tolkien, aged fifty-five, at 15 Church Road. Mary Tolkien was the grandmother of J.R.R. Tolkein, the writer of *The Hobbit* and *The Lord of the Rings*.

Moseley servants in the census survey varied in age. Male servants ranged from fifteen to thirty-eight years and averaged twenty-four years, while female servants ranged from fifteen to over fifty years and averaged twenty-three years. Fifty-three per cent of the seventeen male servants identified in the Moseley survey across the second half of the nineteenth century were between fifteen and twenty, 41 per cent were between twenty-one and thirty and 6 per cent were over thirty. Of the 491 female servants identified 42 per cent were between fifteen and twenty years and 33 per cent were between twenty-one and twenty-five, making three-quarters of female servants twenty-five and under – a young group; 15 per cent were between twenty-six and thirty and 10 per cent were over thirty, including six over fifties, revealing many older female servants in Moseley.

Most of the case-study families had servants. The numbers of servants varied but not necessarily in relation to the economic status or size of families. The Avins family mostly had three family members at home – John Avins until he died in 1891, Eliza, his wife, from 1858 on and Eliza, their daughter, from her birth in 1863. The number of servants they employed marked John and Eliza Avins out socially as well-to-do, living in a large house and belonging to the 'carriage class'. They had three servants in 1861, four in 1871–91 and five in 1901. Life events brought some change: by 1871 they were employing a governess for their daughter Eliza and, following John Avins' death, a companion for his wife. The Ellis family also lived in a large house, Sorrento. They were a larger unit of six, but they had only two servants in 1881, both labelled simply as 'servants' in the census. The Adams family also had six members living in the same house in 1891, but they had three servants, including a housekeeper, which was the sign of a more refined and well-to-do household. The two Blackwells at Brackley Dene had two servants in 1901, a cook and housemaid. The Maycroft household of five in Ascot Road had two servants in 1881, a governess and a general servant, but the smaller family of three there in 1891 also had two, a cook and housemaid, whereas the family of four in 1901 had only one, a general servant. The Barston and the Powell households, of five and three members respectively, in the lower-middle-class Queenswood Road, had only one servant each in 1881 and 1901, but Ann Cook and her two sisters in 1891 had none, reflecting their lower social status. These case-study servants were aged from fourteen to thirty-nine years old.

Keeping servants for any length of time was often a problem and one that could be disruptive for the family and a source of anxiety for the mistress of the house. The Hawthorns, Ascot Road, advertised for servants three times within three years.[39] The language of newspaper adverts shows that attracting servants was difficult. The adverts often used terms that implied that the workload was not heavy, including 'small family', 'family of four', 'family of three', 'girl kept' and 'nurse kept'. The comment that only 'plain cooking' was required assured prospective servants that elaborate dishes were not expected. Another enticement was 'good wages'. One advert, though, states sternly that 'only steady girls who know their work need apply', which suggests negative experiences.[40] Though the relationship between mistress and servant could be intimate and intense, servants could also feel socially isolated within the household and suffer a sense of isolation from their families.

Most Moseley servants were born in Birmingham and nearby counties, including Staffordshire, Worcestershire, Warwickshire, Gloucestershire and Shropshire. There were two Irish servants: Irish women coming over to England were mostly in low-income jobs like this.[41] In Chantry Road in 1901 there

39 *Birmingham Daily Post*, 14 May 1884, 3 February 1890 and 1 November 1893.

40 *Ibid.*

41 Clare Midgley, 'Ethnicity, "race" and empire', in Purvis, Jane (ed.), *Women's history: Britain, 1850–1945* (London, 1995), p. 253.

was a general servant born in Peshawar, India, working for Thomas Carter, a Presbyterian minister. The case-study family servants were born in the West Midlands area and local counties, but also Nottinghamshire and London.

An interaction between rising incomes making families more able to support kin, rising life expectancy, which meant there were more relatives surviving, and a cultural preference for living with extended kin gave rise to the idea of the high Victorian period as the golden age of the extended family among the middle classes. Relatives living in the home other than the core family of father, mother, sons and daughters were fewer than expected in Moseley, however, at 6 per cent of household members. There were more female than male co-residing relatives in the home across the decades (64 per cent were females and 36 per cent males), testament to contemporary ideas about the necessity of families supporting women. Most lived with married household heads (49 per cent), but some widows had the resources to support family (22 per cent).

All types of co-residing relative were represented in the survey, except for uncles and male cousins. The most frequent male relatives were brothers (fifteen), nephews (nine), grandsons (eight) and brothers-in-law (seven) (83 per cent). The most frequent female co-residing relatives were sisters (twenty-eight), nieces (eighteen), granddaughters (nine) and sisters-in-law (nine) (75 per cent). Other male relatives included three fathers, four sons-in-law and one father-in-law (17 per cent of male relatives). Other female relatives included six aunts, six mothers-in-law, five mothers, two female cousins, one grandmother and one daughter-in-law (25 per cent of female relatives).

In Moseley nieces, nephews and grandchildren under fifteen years accounted for 21 per cent of co-residing relatives in the home. Older granddaughters and nieces often acted as helpers and companions, enabling elderly family members to remain independent. In Chantry Road in 1901 an unmarried granddaughter, aged twenty, lived with her grandmother, Anne Green, a widow and household head aged seventy-two. Sisters helped out their siblings. Emily Harris, fifty-seven, was housekeeper to her brother, Joseph Harris, forty-nine, in Church Road in 1891. In the same year, Emma Fielder was housekeeper to her sister, Henty Chambers, thirty-eight, and brother-in-law, Caleb Chambers, thirty-nine. He was a ladies' outfitter and he and Henty had three sons aged two to eleven years and one servant at 1 Woodhurst Road.

Brothers took in sisters and their husbands. In Church Road in 1851, a sister aged thirty-one and her husband aged forty-seven, a provisions dealer, lived with her brother. Families took in sons and daughters and their families when the need arose. In Church Road in 1891 a daughter, aged forty-eight and her husband, fifty-three, lived with her parents along with their children, a son, seven, and two daughters, six and nine years. In 1901 William and Sarah Ward of Montrose, Queenswood Road, both aged sixty-seven, had their daughter,

Eliza, forty, their son, James, twenty-eight, his wife, Minnie, aged twenty-eight, and their one-year-old son James living with them. William Ward was an artist, an oil and colour painter, Eliza Ward a land and flower painter and James a chartered accountant.

Children were often sent to family during difficult times. In 1871 Gertrude Fanny, aged ten, the daughter of Edward Holmes and his first wife Mary Ann, who died in 1861, was living with her dead mother's parents, Samuel and Elizabeth Briggs, at 352 Moseley Road. Two daughters of Holmes' second marriage to Mary Lavinia were also living away from home in 1871: Mary Elise Georgina, aged five years, was living as a visitor with William T. Henning (aged sixty-four), a bookseller, stationer and printer, Elizabeth A. Henning (aged thirty) and Albert F. Henning (aged twenty-five) at 87 Prospect Hill, Tardebigge, Redditch; Alice Annie, aged four years, was living with her uncle and aunt, William and Elizabeth Shaw (aged sixty-seven and fifty-seven), and Ellen Shaw (thirty-four) in Chebsey, Ecceshall, Stone, Lichfield. The children were probably living away from home because Mary Lavinia had given birth to children in 1869, 1870 and 1871, which meant there was a newborn and two very young children at home.

Co-residing relatives in the home in Moseley covered a wide age span: one to eighty years for male relatives and two to seventy-seven years for female relatives. Male relatives averaged twenty-five years and females thirty-one years. Of all relatives, 30 per cent were aged up to fifteen years, a time when young relatives or their parents might need help; 30 per cent were between sixteen and thirty, a time when they might offer older relatives help or need accommodation near work opportunities; 17 per cent were between thirty-one and fifty; and 22 per cent were over fifty years of age, the age when many, particularly women, might need the support of their family.

These relatives in the home could be of economic support to the host family. A third across the decades were in work. There were more male co-residing relatives (64 per cent) in work than female relatives (36 per cent), which supports the view that male relatives often lived with family to enable access to jobs, while female relatives were more likely to be domestic support. Relatives might be a financial burden on lower-middle-class homes. Only eight of the twenty relatives in Queenswood Road in 1901 were in work and none of the others had their own means. In 1881 in Ascot Road five of the six relatives were neither in work nor had independent means but Ascot Road families were better able to support relatives.

The case-study households represented many of these patterns of kin co-residency. Althans Blackwell, a widower in 1901, gave a home to his nephew, Walter Reading, aged twenty-six, while he worked in the family firm. In 1891 Charles Tanner, a single household head, had his widower brother, Ernest, aged thirty-seven years, Ernest's daughter Ernestine, aged eight years, and Charles's unmarried sister, Fanny, aged thirty-four, living with him. However, both Ernest and Fanny were financially independent: he was a wholesale jeweller of gold, an 'employer', and she had her own income. Lone parents were more likely to appear as secondary families within households, like Ernest and Ernestine, than to have their own household. Sarah Powell, a single household head, had her two unmarried sisters, Emily and Rose, aged thirty-four and twenty-eight, living with her in 1901 in Queenswood Road. They did not work but had their own means.

Visitors were another group associated with middle-class homes. Of the sixty-eight visitors in the Moseley survey across the half-century 76 per cent (52) were women. The term 'visitor' in censuses included women with paid domestic roles who were socially above servants, such as housekeepers (Ascot Road, 1901) and lady's companions (Ascot Road, 1881 and Chantry Road, 1901). Governesses were often listed as visitors, such as the governess in 1901 in Chantry Road, who was looking after four children aged between one and ten years for a married couple. Schools often listed their staff as visitors, as at Greenhill School, where there were two male tutors and two female governesses so listed in 1891. Of the female visitors in the survey, 25 per cent were paid domestic workers, along with the two male tutors. Of female visitors, 14 per cent worked in other occupations outside the home as milliners, 'assistants' and a shop assistant, and six other men were in work – a farmer, two clerks, a brass founder, an agent and a confectioner. In contrast, 61 per cent of female visitors and 50 per cent of male visitors were not in work and fulfilling the role usually described as 'visitor'. Four of these had their own means and might have contributed to the family finances.

Most visitors were single. Two male visitors and one female visitor were married and four female visitors were widows. 75 per cent of visitors were spread singly, and the rest in twos and threes. In smaller houses, larger numbers may have been difficult to accommodate comfortably. Married household heads in Moseley were most likely to welcome visitors (63 per cent), but 27 per cent were staying with widows, 7 per cent with singletons and 3 per cent with widowers.

Boarders were a third group of 'Others' in the middle-class home. They usually paid for a room and meals, whereas lodgers usually paid for a room only, though these terms were often used interchangeably. The *Birmingham Daily Post* published 'Apartments to Let' columns, some of which related to Moseley.[42] There were various lets on offer. Some offered a sitting room and

42 *Birmingham Daily Post*: examples include 10 and 11 January, 14 and 19 March, 11 April, 11 September, 2, 17 and 17 October, 8, 13 and 14 November and 8, 12 and 15 December.

bedroom, others board or 'board if required', but many adverts were directed at 'gentlemen dining out'. Most adverts were directed at men, such as 'city gentleman or two friends', but some offered to take 'a married couple' or a 'lady or gentleman'. Descriptors used to tempt lodgers or boarders included 'private house', a 'small private family', 'no other lodgers', 'superior', 'well-furnished sitting room', 'quiet and comfortable', 'home comforts', 'modern conveniences', 'bath (hot/cold)' and 'use of piano and bathroom'. Terms were frequently described as 'moderate'. Newspaper adverts for these apartments in Moseley were few and mostly associated with roads near to Balsall Heath.

Taking in boarders and lodgers and living as such was considered socially lowering. It did not fit with the 'new notions of domestic decorum', was seen as an 'invasion of privacy' and suggested a family not coping financially.[43] It was considered acceptable only for the young, the genteel poor, relations or respectable widows in straitened circumstances. Others were 'less than full members of middle-class society'.[44] Boarders were associated with those taking up job opportunities locally and in Birmingham, but having boarders still carried the stigma of a family in reduced financial circumstances. However, taking in boarders or lodgers was essential to relieve the financial strains of maintaining a household for some. For singletons, widows or widowers, being a boarder or lodger was a practical option compared to maintaining an independent home or living with family.

Boarders and lodgers were few in Moseley – only forty-three across the period, which highlights the suburb as well-to-do. Most boarders were male (70 per cent). Most of these were single (87 per cent), but two were married men living away from their families and two were widowers. Two female boarders were widows and the rest, eleven, were singletons. Almost all boarders lived singly in households. The average age of the male boarders was twenty-nine and of the female boarders thirty-four years. Most male and female boarders were between sixteen and thirty years of age, which included scholars and apprentices, at a stage in life when many did not have their own home. Church Road in the 1891 census sample had most boarders (thirteen), closely followed by Queenswood Road in 1901 with ten. Boarders increased steadily over the period from three in 1881 to eighteen in 1901, a response to more job opportunities in Birmingham.

Most Moseley boarders were in work (63 per cent), 44 per cent of whom were men. Female boarders in 1881 and 1891 were teachers, but by 1901 they included a dressmaker's assistant, aged sixteen, an assistant warehouse worker, aged twenty-two, and a manufacturing clerk, aged twenty-five, showing how

43 Tosh, *A man's place*, p. 19.

44 *Ibid.*

jobs for women were changing. Eight boarders had their own means, but the census does not indicate either an occupation or own means for eight boarders, which suggests a possible overlap between boarder and visitor. All the Queenswood Road case-study householders had boarders, indicating a lower-status road. The Barston family in 1881 had two, a single schoolmistress aged twenty-three years and a single assistant schoolmistress aged twenty. Ann Cook in 1891 had a single male lodger aged twenty-five years who worked as a provisions agent and broker. Sarah Powell in 1901 had a single female boarder, Rebecca Weavell, aged twenty-five years, a manufacturer's clerk.

Characteristic Moseley households

Moseley households (excluding servants and the 'others' – co-residing relatives, visitors and boarders) were generally smaller than expected. They averaged three, four and six over the different decades and roads assessed and four over the half-century overall. This suggests that Moseley was moving towards a nuclear family structure, especially towards the end of the century. However, families designated as not extended were not necessarily the traditional nuclear families of two parents and offspring. Many were single-parent families. There were more stem units (vertically extended – three or four generations) than composite units (horizontal extensions – wider kin of the same generation) in 1881, but stem and composite units were more evenly spread in 1891.[45] This undermines the theory that horizontally extended family forms were characteristic of middle-class families, but also suggests that the social profile of Moseley was changing.

The world of suburban living was said to be dominated – particularly in the daytime, when men were mostly out at work – by women and women's work. When servants are included, women far outnumbered men in the Moseley survey (65 per cent). When servants are excluded, there were still more females than men in Moseley households (55 per cent).

Death

Death was an ever-present part of life, although a meeting in 1877 about a proposed Local Board for Moseley and King's Heath (see Chapter 4) claimed that 'they would not find a district in the United Kingdom which was more healthy than Moseley'.[46] Mr Ross-Jordan, a surgeon of Manor House, Moseley, confirmed at that meeting that a good state of health prevailed in

45 See Anthony Howe, *The cotton masters, 1830–1860* (Oxford, 1984); Stephen Ruggles, *Prolonged connections: the rise of the extended family in nineteenth-century England and America* (London, 1987); and Gordon and Nair, *Public lives*, p. 35.

46 *Birmingham Daily Post*, 5 February 1877.

Moseley, since over the course of one day he had visited eleven patients each over eighty years of age. The meeting reported thirty-four deaths in Moseley village for 1876, seventeen of whom were over sixty years of age. A survey of St Mary's burials reveals that between 1851 and 1900 nearly 4 per cent of all deaths were people aged eighty and over.[47] More women than men survived to these ages (140 women and seventy-seven men). Of these men, seventy-five reached their eighties and two their nineties. Of the women, 124 reached their eighties, thirteen their nineties and three lived on into their 100s.

In the Victorian period there were numerous important rituals for the middle classes around death. Black-edged mourning cards and letters were sent out and death announcements, obituaries and 'In Memoriam' columns appeared in the press, marking and evaluating the life of important residents and 'transmitting reputation'.[48] Moseley mourning cards show that Joseph Piggott (George Thomas Piggott's father) died aged thirty-four years and Edward Holmes' wife, Mary Anne, died in 1861 at thirty-one years of age, leaving three young children – Elizabeth, aged three, Edward Briggs, aged two, and a ten-day-old baby – with only two servants to help in the home, a general domestic and a nursemaid.[49] The death of George Piggott (Joseph Piggott's brother and George Thomas Piggott's uncle) of The Lions, Park Hill at the age of thirty-eight years was in the 'In Memoriam' column of the *Birmingham Post* of 19 September 1871. These were typical of early deaths in Moseley, which often left young families without a parent.

Queen Victoria proved a long-term model of the widow in mourning. The 'right' clothing was important and specialist shops opened to provide it. On 12 October 1893 Agnes Blackwell bought a 'Black Plush Mantle' and a 'trimmed felt bonnet' costing £5 15s 6d and £1 9s 3d respectively from Birmingham General Mourning Warehouse, 42 New Street, Birmingham. In April 1893 Althans Blackwell bought a grey mourning coat and vest in 'Best Fancy Cheviot Coating' (£3 13s 6d) from J.R. Currell. Popular mourning jewellery included lockets containing the hair of the deceased and brooches and other items of Whitby jet, as advertised by James Cargory, 41 Bull Street, Birmingham.

Funerals were important as a public display of mourning, social and economic status, respectability and gentility. Neighbours watched the funeral cortège and family and associates joined the procession. The funeral of Thomas Clement Sneyd-Kynnersley of Moor Green House, aged eighty-eight

47 List courtesy of PCRB.

48 M. Dick, 'The death of Matthew Boulton, 1809: ceremony, controversy and commemoration', in Quickenden, K., Baggott, S. and Dick, M. (eds), *Matthew Boulton: enterprising industrialist of the Enlightenment* (Farnham, 2013), p. 253.

49 LBLH, MS/559.

Figure 5.7. John Avins' memorial, St Mary's churchyard. Author's own collection.

years, J.P. and stipendiary magistrate for Birmingham, was described in the *Moseley and King's Heath Journal* in 1892.[50] The obituary gave the reason for his death (following an operation for a strangulated hernia) and detailed his family, education, achievements, titles and interests. The report listed all the important mourners, including his servants, two of whom were bearers. The numbers of participants and the size of the audience indicated civic worth and the presence of important attendees revealed status. The undertaking trade and the funeral industry grew enormously. Birmingham became the centre for the manufacture of decorative coffin plates and handles at, for example, Newman Brothers, 13–15 Fleet Street, Birmingham, established in 1882.

Gravestones were expensive status items, important in 'preserving, celebrating and enhancing memory'.[51] John Avins died in 1891 at Highfield House. His memorial in St Mary's churchyard is large, alongside the main path and in red granite, a very long-lasting material (Fig. 5.7). The monument was raised by the trust he set up in his will to manage his affairs and the inscription notes his contribution to the community and society, showing that they wanted him to be remembered as an important local benefactor.

Many well-to-do Moseley residents commemorated their family dead in stained-glass windows, publicising their family name, raising their status and ensuring that the deceased's reputation was carried forward. John Avins left £500 to St Mary's church and £200 to the recently erected Moseley Baptist church for stained-glass windows. Unfortunately, the St Mary's window, *Moses in the Bulrushes*, was destroyed by bombing in the Second World War and only a fragment survives (Fig. 5.8).[52] Other stained-glass windows in St Mary's church commemorate figures from Moseley who were well known in the second half of the nineteenth century, including Rebecca Anderton (1877), Thomas Clement Sneyd-Kynnersley (1893) and Caroline Assinder (1898).[53]

The well-to-do middle classes of Moseley also demonstrated their status and wealth through their wills – documents that shed light on how the deceased wanted to be seen by others. They highlighted the social importance of the family and concern for its continuity in passing on possessions. John Avins left an estate valued at £80,000 and, after securing his immediate family's financial security, left money legacies to the wider family.[54] He bequeathed jewellery, clothes, furniture, decorative objects, horses, carriages and their paraphernalia, stock, wines, liquors and provisions. These possessions illustrate the standard

50 CRL, JC6/7/1–173.

51 Dick, 'The Death of Matthew Boulton', p. 249.

52 Bold, *Architectural history of St Mary's church*, p. 25.

53 Fairn, *History of Moseley*, pp. 61 and 65; Bold, *Architectural history of St Mary's church*, p. 25.

54 LBA, MS/1672 (Add l) (Acc 1991/137).

Figure 5.8. Fragment, the Avins window, *Moses in the Bulrushes*, St Mary's church. Author's own collection.

of living and lifestyle of a gentleman and his household and the position and power of a wealthy male household head.

John Avins perpetuated his name and that of his family and established their social status by donating significant monies in his will to voluntary hospitals and by setting up the John Avins Trust to distribute money annually to medical and quasi-medical charities, a trust that continues to this day. He also left money to other causes that advertised his name locally and nationally. For example, he left £50 to Birmingham University for a John Avins Science Scholarship and £50 for an Eliza Avins Music Scholarship for girls, both of which continue still. He left £1,000 to the Royal National Lifeboat Institution, sponsoring two named boats, the 'John Avins' and the 'Eliza Avins'.[55] The 'John Avins' (1895–1905) was a thirty-four-foot, ten-oared, self-righting lifeboat, the first RNLI lifeboat for winter service in Wick, while the 'Eliza Avins' was stationed at Plymouth (1888–1920).[56] He also left money to various clubs and £200 to Moseley Medical Institute for a Provident Medical Institute for the poor of Moseley and surrounding districts. Eliza Avins sat on the board of the John Avins Trust and played a key role in the execution of her husband's will and his trust.

The Moseley middle class was a very diverse group. Some findings challenge perceptions – the number of residents born across Great Britain and abroad, the many small families, the number of homes without servants, the relatively small number of 'others' in the home, the women involved in business and the increasing proportion of middle-class residents designated by censuses as workers. The focus on individuals, families and personal experiences provides a human face, bringing the suburb to life. The next chapter moves inside Moseley's middle-class homes to reveal how residents lived in their homes, the decorating and furnishing choices they made and what influenced their decisions about their lifestyles.

---

55 LBA, MS/1672 (Add 1) (Acc 1991/137), the John Avins Trust Minute Book 1, Meeting 60, pp. 140–2, 1897; D. Owen, *English philanthropy 1660–1960* (London, 1965), p. 176; <https://sites.google.com/site/wicklifeboat02/thejohnavins>, accessed 2012.

56 By email from Elise Chainey, RNLI Heritage Support Coordinator.

6

Keeping up appearances: the middle class at home

In the second half of the nineteenth century most middle-class suburban men commuted to work, while most middle-class suburban women focused on the home. This promoted the notion of separate spheres in which the domestic and private became particularly associated with women and the public with men. The home took on considerable importance, making how homes were divided up, architectural features and fittings, decorating, furnishing and facilities, including WCs and bathrooms, significant markers of the many subtle layers within the middle classes.

Surviving photographs of Moseley interiors and bills are crucial sources of evidence. The images offer a glimpse into the homes of some of the Moseley middle classes in the last decade of the nineteenth century, including the super-elite detached Uffculme, Moor Green, built by Richard Cadbury in 1892; the elite Sorrento, a large detached house on Wake Green Road, built in the 1870s; the smaller detached Brackley Dene, Chantry Road, the home of Althans and Agnes Blackwell, built in 1892; and three semi-detached houses in Park Hill from the 1880s and early 1890s. No images have been located of Moseley interiors further down the middle-class hierarchy. The bills relate to purchases made by Agnes and Althans Blackwell for Brackley Dene and reveal what such well-to-do suburbanites bought for their home, the commercial enterprises they patronised and the costs involved.

Interior house design

Vestibules and halls were the first spaces accessed and thus important in forming initial impressions of the wealth, status and taste of the home's residents. They formed a cordon sanitaire between the noise, dirt, heat, cold and stress of the world and the safety, seclusion and warmth of the home. Only one house in the building-plan sample did not have a hall, a terraced house in Trafalgar Road.[1] The size, shape and layout of halls varied, highlighting differentiation within the middle classes. Narrow passages with staircases showed a 'want of ease and ample means on the part of the occupant', according to Robert Kerr, a contemporary writer on houses and homes, while 'the entrance at once to a large hall has a good effect, and immediately stamps the house as the abode of

1 LBA, BPKNU, BCK/MC/7/3/1, 1458.

Figure 6.1. Entrance hall, Uffculme. BCT.

gentility'.[2] Super-elite halls, such as that at Uffculme, were huge (Fig. 6.1). The hall at Sorrento was more modest, but still spacious and large enough for an occasional table and seating (Fig. 6.2). Its layout prevented glimpses of what lay beyond, providing privacy. Similarly, the stairs in a large semi-detached house in Chantry Road were tucked away to the side, whereas in most semi-detached and terraced houses stairs led up directly from the entrance.[3] Smaller halls might accommodate a table with a drawer for visitors' cards and a hard chair, a coat-and-hatstand or pegs for coats and hats. Thus, on entering a middle-class house, visitors could easily place the family's position in the social hierarchy.

2 Kerr, *The English gentleman's house*, p. 109.

3 LBA, BPKNU, BCK/MC/7/3/1, 1456.

Figure 6.2. Entrance hall, Sorrento, 1899. Historic England, BL 155542.

Drawing and dining rooms were key public spaces and having separate drawing and dining rooms was a social marker. Of Moseley building plans analysed, 78 per cent identified separate drawing and dining rooms, while 22 per cent, all located near Balsall Heath, a less salubrious area, used the working-class terms 'parlour', 'sitting room' and 'living room'.[4] For example, a semi-detached house on the corner of Church and Kingswood Roads had a parlour and sitting room identified and ten terraced houses in Kingswood Road each had a parlour and living room.

The size of rooms was also a marker of status, particularly in the case of rooms accessed by visitors, such as drawing and dining rooms. The images of drawing rooms reveal a size hierarchy – Uffculme followed by Sorrento and then Glaisdale and The Dell, Park Hill (Figs 6.3–6.6). The size of drawing and dining rooms varied, but house type was not necessarily significant. Those in two detached houses in Wake Green Road in 1882 were about 114 and 156 square yards.[5] Those in some semi-detached houses in Chantry Road ranged from twenty-eight to forty square yards, while those in three detached houses

4 A total of 111 building plans (407 dwellings) covering sixteen central Moseley roads.

5 LBA, BPKNU, BCK/MC/7/3/1, 527 and 550.

there were about twenty-five to twenty-seven square yards.[6] Those in terraced houses were generally smaller, but not always by much – those of four terraced houses in Coppice Road were almost twenty-two square yards.

Most drawing rooms in the building plans were located at the rear of the property, to give views of the garden. In the Sorrento drawing room there are tantalising glimpses of foliage in a large conservatory accessed through elegant doorways on either side of the drawing room fireplace (Fig. 6.4). Conservatories were status additions that bridged the inside and outside. Available in different sizes, they were accessible to all levels of the middle classes, and could impress visitors with their décor and their plants and fruits from around the world. Iron tracery, highly decorative floor tiles, rugs, stained and etched windows, wicker furniture, statues, urns, rock gardens and caged songbirds featured in conservatories, making them exotic spaces. Conservatories were spaces where people could socialise informally and be photographed in winter.

The size of the house placed the home in a subtle social hierarchy and determined how many different rooms could be accommodated. Building plans labelled the function of rooms, but, of course, a family might change room-use to suit their own inclinations. Only 10 per cent of the houses in building plans accessed had a breakfast room and these were almost equally spread between detached and semi-detached houses (nine detached and ten semi-detached). These included a detached house in Oxford Road and a semi-detached house in Park Hill. No terraced houses had a breakfast room, cementing their position at the bottom of the middle-class social hierarchy. Of the houses in Chantry Road, 48 per cent had breakfast rooms, raising its status, while Church Road had only one and Queenswood and Kingswood Roads none. Breakfast rooms featured more frequently in 1891 newspaper adverts than in those from 1881, suggesting that they became more popular over time. A semi-detached house in Oxford Road had a consulting room with separate entrance and two semi-detached houses had morning rooms.[7] A detached house in Chantry Road had a study on the ground floor and another in Wake Green Road had a billiard room.[8]

The number of upper-floor rooms dictated the number of bedrooms, other specialist rooms and servants' rooms, which contributed to status and differentiation within the middle classes. Most detached houses had seven bedrooms, most semi-detached houses five or six and most terraced houses three or four. House type did not necessarily denote the number of bedrooms: building plans show terraced houses with more bedrooms than semi-detached

6 *Ibid.*, 374, 514 1535, 2264 and 2340.

7 *Ibid.*, 1586 and 1456.

8 *Ibid.*, 374 and 18.

Figure 6.3. Drawing room, Uffculme. BCT.

Figure 6.4. Drawing room, Sorrento, 1899. Historic England, BL 155545.

Figure 6.5. Drawing room, Glaisdale, 1891. Historic England, BL 10873.

Figure 6.6. Drawing room, The Dell, 1891. Historic England, BL 11015.

houses and semi-detached houses with more bedrooms than detached houses. The number of upper rooms highlighted the social status of roads: twelve houses in Kingswood Road had only four bedrooms while houses in Wake Green Road had eight to eleven upper rooms.

Some Moseley homes, both detached and semi-detached, had specialist rooms on upper floors. Of the detached houses in the building plans accessed 68 per cent had dressing rooms, including one in Oakland Road. A slightly greater proportion of semi-detached houses (72 per cent) had dressing rooms, such as Clovelly, 22 Chantry Road.[9] Kerr wrote that 'In every instance of what we call a Gentleman's House, however small, there will surely be at least one of the chief bedrooms which has a Gentleman's Dressing Room attached.'[10] Monaco, 36 Chantry Road, a detached house built in 1876, had two dressing rooms, which, Kerr says, marked 'a point of very considerable advance in dignity'.[11] Higher-status roads such as Chantry Road had a large proportion of homes with dressing rooms (65 per cent) as did Anderton Park Road (58 per cent). However, lower-status roads also had dressing rooms: in Queenswood Road 52 per cent of houses had dressing rooms. On the other hand, only 27 per cent of the houses in Church Road and one of 143 houses in Trafalgar Road did.

Specialist children's rooms were infrequent in the Moseley building plans accessed. Monaco, 36 Chantry Road, had two nurseries, while four semi-detached houses, two in Oxford Road and two in Park Hill, each had a nursery.[12] Another, Chantry Glen, 12 Chantry Road, a detached house, had a playroom and day and night nurseries.[13] Kerr wrote that 'In every house, however small ... the special provision of appropriate Nursery Accommodation is a vital point', while Lord Shaftesbury claimed that 'no decent family could possibly be accommodated with fewer than three bedrooms – one for the parents, one for the boys and one for the girls'.[14] Ideally, children slept in separate rooms and beds or in same-sex rooms, with older children separated from babies. Many middle-class houses were too small for such segregation, but a lower-middle class aspirational family might call the children's bedroom a 'nursery'.

Larger houses might have other specialist rooms, on either the ground or upper floors. The more specialist rooms you had, the higher up the middle-

---

9 LBA, BPKNU, BCK/MC/7/3/1, 1435.

10 Kerr, *The English gentleman's house*, p. 151.

11 *Ibid.*; LBA, BPKNU, BCK/MC/7/3/1, 1976.

12 LBA, BPKNU, BCK/MC/7/3/1, 2682, 2686 and 2070.

13 *Ibid.*, 1652.

14 Kerr, *The English gentleman's house*, p. 159.

Figure 6.7. Billiard room, Sorrento, 1899. PCRC.

Figure 6.8. Smoking room, Sorrento, 1899. PCRC.

Figure 6.9. Library, Sorrento, 1899. Historic England, BL 155544.

Figure 6.10. Boudoir, Sorrento, 1899. Historic England, BL 15550.

class social scale you were. A detached house in Anderton Park Road had a 'Book Room' in the attic.[15] Monaco had a billiard room on the first floor, as did a detached Wake Green Road house, while another detached house in Wake Green Road had a 'boudoir', a small private room for a woman, on an upper floor.[16] Sales catalogues advertised a billiard room and library divided by sliding doors in Woodbridge House and a billiard room in Woodfield Cottage, Stoney Lane, lit by '7 skylights and 5 windows' and approached by separate stairs – clearly a significant status symbol.[17] Very large houses, such as Uffculme, had the space for a wide range of specialist rooms and the images of Sorrento include billiard and smoking rooms, a library and a boudoir (Figs 6.7–6.10). Brackley Dene had a breakfast room, study, library, billiard room, more than one dressing room and a boudoir. Of houses in building plans, 10 per cent had more than one specialist room and of these eighteen had two specialist rooms, one had three and one had six. Only eleven were detached houses. House size was the crucial factor in the range of rooms houses accommodated, but not necessarily house type. However, few homes in Moseley had other than breakfast and dressing rooms.

Photographs of the three smaller semi-detached houses in Park Hill show that, where specialist rooms were absent or limited, drawing and dining rooms were multi-purpose and multi-occupational. The books in the Glaisdale drawing room suggest that the families read in these rooms in the absence of a library (Fig. 6.5). The books, the chenille table cover and the comfortable armchair and chaise longue in the Greengate dining room show this was a room for reading and relaxation, not simply for dining, as in the case of the Sorrento dining room (Figs 6.11–6.12). The mistress of The Dell had her writing desk in the drawing room, whereas the mistress of Sorrento had hers in her boudoir (Figs 6.6 and 6.10). On the other hand, there are books in the Sorrento drawing room even though the house had a library, which suggests that some members of the family read in there too (Fig. 6.4).

Drawing rooms were used at different times as female, parental, family and entertaining spaces for visitors and guests – social, intellectual and creative spaces for both men and women. They may well have been used more by women during the day, given that many men were out at work. The social and family nature of drawing rooms is shown by the range of seating and the family photographs in the Uffculme drawing room and the pianos at Uffculme, Glaisdale and, glimpsed through the arch from the drawing room, at The Dell (Figs 6.3 and 6.5–6.6). The Sorrento dining table is set for a party of people,

---

15 LBA, BPKNU, BCK/MC/7/3/1, 1821.

16 *Ibid.*, 1976, 18 and 358.

17 LBA, Bham/Sc 890 and 1890.

Figure 6.11. Dining room, Greengate, 1891. Historic England, BL 10874.

Figure 6.12. Dining room, Sorrento, 1899. PCRC.

which probably included both men and women (Fig. 6.12). The Victorian home was 'an ocean of sociability', but it was 'private socialisation' – entertaining was mainly limited to family, friends and acquaintances.[18] Entertaining in the home displayed interior decoration and furnishing, affirming status. The suburban middle-class home was thus far from a confined and confining private or gendered arena.

Some rooms, though, appear more defined by gender. Where there was one dressing room this was mostly intended for the husband, and billiard and smoking rooms were more often occupied by men. Advice writers such as Jane Panton argued strongly that the breakfast or morning room should 'be set aside emphatically for the mistress', which suggests that these were contested spaces.[19] When colonised by women, such rooms contributed to female freedom as important sites for female work, but they were often rooms where the family came together, for example, for the morning meal and as sitting rooms later in the day.[20] The boudoir was the domain of the lady of the house, sometimes accessed from the main shared bedroom, as at Sorrento (Figs 6.10 and 6.13 a–b). Libraries have sometimes been identified as male spaces, but the Blackwell library contained items attractive to many women, including *Cassell's household guide*, *Cassell's family magazine* (1881–5), *Weldon's encyclopaedia of needlework* and *Mrs Beeton's everyday cookery book*. The middle-class home certainly involved much negotiation, given that rigid social and spatial rules did not necessarily prevail.

In very wealthy middle-class families children spent a considerable amount of time in designated spaces on the upper floors, where they were looked after by governesses, nannies, nurses or nursemaids. Most middle-class Moseley children, however, had to make do with their bedrooms and minimal servant supervision. There were only seventeen governesses in the Moseley census analysis for 1851–1901 (under 1 per cent). Nurses were more frequent (8 per cent), but most were young, untrained and uneducated, and did not stay long. In houses with only one or no servants children were often left to their own devices.

Servants usually slept in attic rooms, separating them vertically from the family and making the third floor of the home a social marker. Wealthy establishments had separate wings for servants and some servants had their own designated work, living or bedroom accommodation, signalling a social hierarchy among servants. Detached houses named a 'Housekeeper's Room' (Penlee, 34 Chantry Road) and 'Man's Room' (Church Road) and some

18 Gordon and Nair, *Public lives*, pp. 131–2.

19 Panton, *From kitchen to garret*, p. 69.

20 Jane Hamlett, *Material relations: domestic interiors and middle-class families in England, 1850–1910* (Manchester, 2010), pp. 49–50.

Figure 6.13a–b. Main bedroom, Sorrento, 1899. PCRC.

houses, such as Kingsway House, had a 'Gardener's Cottage'.[21] Servants had little privacy and had to negotiate space throughout the house, but in service they might have their own bedroom, which was unlikely in their own home.

Status was visible in the architectural fixtures and fittings of middle-class interiors, but new technology and mass production meant the less well-off were more able to emulate their social superiors. The Uffculme drawing room and Sorrento hall had elaborate ornamental plasterwork cornices and ceilings and Brackley Dene a 'beautiful moulded ceiling' in the drawing room, whereas the cornices and ceilings in the less well-to-do Park Hill homes were much simpler (Figs 6.3, 6.5–6.6 and 6.11).[22] The invention of fibrous plaster enabled the mass production of lengths of cornice, bringing fancy cornicing within the budget of the lower middle class, and new lightweight anaglypta wallpapers gave the impression of plasterwork. Scrolled plasterwork, such as embellishments and arches, added interest to confined hallways, raising their status. The wood panelling below the dado in the hall and library at Sorrento was expensive but could be substituted by cheaper heavyweight wallpapers (Figs 6.2 and 6.9). Improvements in wallpaper manufacture, along with the removal of excise taxes on paper, made patterned wallpaper inexpensive and widely available. Chemical dyes enabled the production of colour-patterned and flocked wallpapers and richer colours from the 1850s. Glass techniques improved, bringing stained glass to a middle-class mass market. The removal of tax on glass helped stained-glass elements come within the reach of the lower middle classes. Chance Brothers & Co. of Birmingham was a popular producer of stained glass. They focused on 'Modern Glass', a more lightly tinted glass that reflected a change in public taste.

Being in fashion was important to status. Fashionable occasional tables are evident in the hall at Sorrento and in the drawing rooms of Glaisdale, Sorrento and The Dell, showing fashion permeating different layers of the middle class (Figs 6.2 and 6.4–6.6). However, some Moseley residents held on to approaches they liked regardless of fashion. The five sections of skirting, dado, filling, frieze and cornice were popular from the 1880s and at the time considered essential in any house with a pretension to artistic and aesthetic taste. They were still present in 1891 in the drawing rooms at Glaisdale and The Dell and in 1899 in the hall, library and billiard and smoking rooms at Sorrento, even though by then they were considered old-fashioned (Figs 6.2 and 6.5–6.9). This sectioning was absent in the Sorrento drawing and dining rooms and in the Greengate dining room, suggesting these rooms had been redecorated and the fashion abandoned (Figs 6.4 and 6.11–6.12). Dado rails

21 LBA, BPKNU, BCK/MC/7/3/1, 527 and 1749; *Birmingham Daily Post*, May and June 1881.

22 MSHGC, C3/D2/A/F10/1.

protected walls from chairs arranged around the edge of the room but became redundant as people began to arrange furniture in conversational groups. Possessing antique furniture was no longer seen as 'eccentric', but signalled a taste for the old and exotic – an interest that spread to silver, pewter and other items of bric-à-brac.[23] It fostered 'Chinamania' from the 1860s, evident in the china collection in the Greengate dining room (Fig. 6.11). The new enthusiasm for antiques replaced the much-derided obsession with handmade objects and wealthy homemakers imported objects that were assessed and guaranteed by experts and connoisseurs.[24]

Fireplaces and over-mantels became fashionable from the 1870s and were the focus of rooms, making them status fixtures. They could impress with their size, design, materials, decorative features and intricacy, all of which contributed to the subtle social hierarchy. Some were ostentatious features that highlighted an assumed upper-middle-class status, including Uffculme's huge drawing-room fireplace and Sorrento's white ensemble featuring a marble neo-classical fireplace, tall mirrored over-mantel and door architraves (Figs 6.3–6.4). Contemporary advice writers criticised pretentious fireplaces, which suggests that middle-class householders overstepped contemporary bounds of good taste. Park Hill fireplaces were smaller and in keeping with room size, while those in Glaisdale and The Dell acquired status through their delicate carving (Figs 6.5–6.6 and 6.11). Jane Panton preferred simple unobtrusive wooden mantelpieces rather than 'staring white marble', especially in smaller homes, particularly disliked fireplaces aping stone or 'the aesthetic of the Stately Home', and recommended covering fireplace mantelshelves with decorative fabric as in the Sorrento boudoir (Fig. 6.10).[25] She strongly criticised fake finishes – the fireplaces made to look like marble, for instance, signalling an inherent snobbery on her part and the necessity for middle-class residents of 'knowing their place'.

Few villa halls were large enough for a fireplace the size of the one in the hall at Sorrento (Fig. 6.2). Bedroom fireplaces were smaller, as at Sorrento, and those in servants' rooms smaller still, possibly with a painted wooden surround, highlighting class differentiation (Figs 6.13a–b). In 1892 a hierarchy of fireplaces was installed in the Blackwells' new home, Brackley Dene, at a cost of £97 13s 3d. They ranged from iron ones in the attics to an Ashburton marble one in the study and a large carved oak chimneypiece in the dining room. A 'typical' middle-class family would burn about a ton of coal per

23 D. Cohen, *Household gods: the British and their possessions* (London and New Haven, CT, 2006), pp. 133, 150 and 154.

24 Bilston, *Promise of the suburbs*, pp. 99 and 111.

25 Panton, *From kitchen to garret*, p. 65.

month. The Blackwells spent £42 14s 8d in 1893 on coal, coke and slack from a local coal merchant.

Fireplace mantels and overmantels were 'shrines' to middle-class culture, displaying, as seen in the photographs, chinaware, glassware, candlesticks, clocks, plates, figurines and bronzes that were intended to reveal the owners' artistic erudition, taste and style and their skills in the arrangement of ornaments. Integrated mirrors visually doubled room contents, extending the impression of material wealth. Such displays of material goods signal conspicuous middle-class consumption.

New technology facilitated new services that changed middle-class homes. Gas fires supplanted coal fires for some and brought new lighting to many. Gas was more widely used by the late 1880s and considered more reliable as lighting by the 1890s, when incandescent gas mantles, which produced a brighter light, were developed. The Sorrento hall was lit by an elegant stained-glass lantern and the Uffculme drawing room featured splendid central gas lighting, while the Sorrento drawing room had gas brackets alongside the fireplace, wall-mounted because of the necessary piping (Figs 6.3–6.4). Gas table lamps became possible later, joined to gas taps by tubes. Better lighting led to the use of rich dark colours on walls, such as the popular hall colours Prussian blue, sage green and burgundy. It multiplied possessions in the polished surfaces and mirrors, enhancing impressions of wealth, and lengthened the day for leisure, allowing time to be spent with the family after dark. Althans Blackwell had gas tubes fitted to fifty locations at a cost of £25 10s 6d in 1892. However, gas lighting created dirt and dust. Electric lighting became available in 1899. Central heating developed towards the end of the century and cast-iron radiators, highlighting social status and technical innovation, are visible in the Sorrento drawing and billiard rooms (Figs 6.4 and 6.7). These were much cleaner than coal fires, which produced mess, smoke and smells.

Domestic material culture

The home displayed the family to the outside world, conveying social, economic and cultural status, a significant factor that made how the home was decorated and furnished hugely important. It needed to impress the extended family, neighbours, visitors and servants and was a means of expressing the self and of assessing others.[26] A beautiful home was considered a counterweight to the problems and difficult conditions of the public sphere, with beauty and good taste promoting a moral, self-denying and self-disciplined character.[27] In

26 Cohen, *Household gods*, pp. x, 13 and 24.

27 Bilston, *Promise of the suburbs*, pp. 82–3.

the 1890s writers such as Jane Panton urged readers to display individuality.[28] Mrs Talbot Coke wrote: 'the house is one's mind, the home of one's soul: one's ego', while in 1898 columnist Penelope declared: 'Show me your room and I will tell you who you are'.[29] Acquiring and displaying good taste was especially important in marking middle-class artistic identity: it was considered a trait that could be cultivated and was available to all. Certain objects, such as the Japanese fan in the drawing room of The Dell, communicated artistic flair (Fig. 6.6). Thus, 'things' became important as a way of expressing the self and assessing others and as an influence on the individual. They conferred membership of the middle classes, irrespective of education and income, which made how people spent money more important than how they earned it. These ideas underpinned conspicuous consumption, made women arbiters of taste and helped the private sphere become an effective indicator of status in the public sphere, which gave women an important role. The increasingly affluent middle classes had more disposable income and mass-manufactured goods were more readily available, especially so given Moseley's close proximity to Birmingham and its industrial and manufacturing success.

Displaying contemporary design styles in one's home was important to status and Moseley residents took up different styles and expressed new ideas about taste and individuality in various ways. The Queen Anne Revival and the Arts and Crafts Movement dominated architecture in Moseley in the late nineteenth century and these are reflected in the photographs reproduced here. The Uffculme, Sorrento and Glaisdale drawing rooms suggest the Queen Anne Revival and the drawing room of The Dell and the Greengate dining room the Arts and Crafts Movement (Figs 6.3–6.6 and 6.11). Nevertheless, these rooms also display striking differences in taste and style. Moseley residents often followed their own instincts rather than relying exclusively on contemporary fashions, and the differences do not necessarily relate to economic status. The Uffculme and Glaisdale drawing rooms appear similarly heavily patterned, crowded and busy, but also have the feel of relaxed family and entertainment rooms (Figs 6.3 and 6.5). This is shown at Uffculme in the numerous family photographs, the casual arrangement of furniture and the piano. The more formal character of the Sorrento drawing room and its antique ambience contrasts with the other drawing rooms (Fig. 6.4).

Displaying wealth was an important part of decorating and furnishing middle-class homes. This became acceptable in the second half of the nineteenth century because wealth was seen as a sign of just rewards for a productive life. Wealth was shown in the costly fitted carpet in the hall at

---

28 Panton, *From kitchen to garret*, p. 154.

29 Cohen, *Household gods*, p. 137.

Sorrento (Fig. 6.2) and the expensive 'heavy, solid wood floors', in which a decorative pattern was set at Brackley Dene.[30] The Blackwells paid £49 18s 1d to have pitch-pine and deal block-and-parquet flooring laid in July 1892, a cost beyond many. Few could afford fitted carpets. Most key rooms in better-off homes had large Turkish, Persian and Axminster rugs, as in the drawing rooms at Glaisdale and The Dell, but new technology brought cheaper mass-produced carpets within the reach of most villa dwellers (Figs 6.5–6.6). Small long-haired rugs became popular. They were recommended by contemporary style experts to give a 'homely' feel and can be seen in the homes even of the wealthy – in the Uffculme drawing room and the hall at Sorrento (Figs 6.2–6.3). The less affluent opted for plain wooden floors and drugget or oilcloth, while alternative hall flooring materials included stone, slate, tiles, wood and linoleum. However, it was important to spend money wisely and get the balance right between ostentation and parsimony. Kerr emphasised that 'the effect to be aimed at must be that of solid value for the money spent, nothing more, but certainly nothing less'.[31] This was especially significant given that outfitting the home was expensive, costing possibly up to a year's salary. The Blackwells displayed their moderation by having Royal Axminster carpets and an old velvet-pile carpet cleaned and remade as bordered squares.

Wealth, but also erudition, refinement and artistic identity were signalled by displaying art works. Middle-class residents sought material confirmation of their social attainments and aspirations through art and the staggering growth of the art market was a response to this attempt to emulate the aristocracy.[32] This can be seen in the hall at Sorrento and the area immediately beyond (Fig. 6.2). Glaisdale, Greengate and The Dell also displayed art works, though these were smaller and fewer than at Sorrento (Figs 6.5–6.6 and 6.11). The better-off invested in oils, while prints and engravings were a cheaper alternative for the less well-to-do. In 1893 while in Florence the Blackwells bought an important original figure group of a young man and girl, 'Mi vuoi bene' or 'Declaration of Love'. It was carved in best Carrara marble inset with jasper, stood on a revolving column and cost £2,100, £700 of which was paid on account, with the balance paid on delivery. The Blackwells bought many pictures, including, in 1895, an oil painting by the American artist Walter Blackman (£16) and, in 1897, a watercolour by Helena Maguire (£20) and a painting by A. Glendenning (£11), all from Frank Kendrick, who had two showrooms in Birmingham.

30 MSHGC, C3/D2/A/F10/1.

31 Kerr, *The English gentleman's house*, pp. 97–8.

32 Elizabeth C. Mansfield, 'Women, art history and the public sphere: Emilia Dilke's eighteenth century', in Balducci, T. and Belnap-Jensen, H. (eds), *Women, femininity and public space in European visual culture, 1789–1914* (London and New York, 2014), p. 193.

The Blackwells favoured pictures of rural, domestic, middle-class, cottage and foreign scenes. Thomas Ellis' valuable collection of oil paintings and watercolours was described as 'formed with great care and judgement' when his possessions at Sorrento were sold following his death in 1890.[33] In his will in 1891 John Avins left family portraits, ten oil paintings, two bronzes of Columbus and Galileo and a timepiece with a figure of Lucretia to the mayor and aldermen and the City Art Gallery for the citizens of Birmingham. However, they were refused, because they were not of sufficient merit to justify taking up any of the gallery's limited storage space.[34] This refusal highlights the existence of an artistic hierarchy and showed that even the Moseley well-to-do could be found wanting.

Other cultural activities in the home were similarly important if one aspired to gentility. Owning and displaying the right books signalled an educated family interested in a wide range of subjects. In 1896 Althans Blackwell bought *The days of auld lang syne* by Ian Maclaren, *The pleasures of life* by Sir John Lubbock, *The beauties of nature* by the same author and *A knight of the white cross* by G.A. Henty.[35] Blackwell's book collection included classic novels and volumes on history, travel, politics and art. Musical accomplishment and performance were part of the home life of many suburban middle-class residents. Althans Blackwell had an inlaid music cabinet with shelves for 'Songs', 'Sacred' and 'Operas'. Among the possessions of Thomas Ellis of Sorrento sold following his death in 1890 were a grand piano by Brinsmead and Sons, a London firm, and two cottage pianofortes by Kirkman.[36] Jane Panton described pianos as 'very ugly pieces of furniture' and recommended draping material over them.[37] Over the years at Brackley Dene, the Blackwells paid around £2 per term to E.W. Rickett for piano lessons for their nephew Walter, who was living with them.

Industrialisation and technological innovation made the production of material goods possible on an unprecedented scale and in a wide range of qualities and prices to suit all pockets, which fostered conspicuous consumption. Designs came to market regularly, promoting rapid changes in fashion, and the desire for newness further intensified consumerism. The development of new manufacturing techniques produced numerous furniture styles in many different materials, making up-to-date furniture accessible to a wider group.

33 *Birmingham Daily Post*, 1 May 1890.

34 LBA, MS/1672 (Add l) (Acc 1991/137).

35 Ian Maclaren, *The days of Auld Lang Syne* (London, 1895); Sir John Lubbock, *The pleasure of life* (New York, 1887) and *The beauties of nature* (London, 1892); G.A. Henty, *A knight of the white cross* (London, 1896).

36 *Birmingham Daily Post*, 1 May 1890.

37 Panton, *From kitchen to garret*, pp. 86–87.

Decorative objects came in different qualities, highlighting the social hierarchy. Porcelain and French bronze figures, for example, were at the upper end of the market, while at the lower end were coloured overglaze and parianware, 'marble substitute for the masses'.[38] Seating comfort was enhanced by the technical development from the 1850s of deep buttoning and coil springs. Such 'patterned, padded and puffed out' seating is evident in the photographs of the hall, library, billiard and smoking rooms at Sorrento and in the Glaisdale drawing room and Greengate dining room (Figs 6.2, 6.5, 6.7–6.9 and 6.11).[39]

The Blackwells were part of the conspicuous-consumption trend. In March 1893 they bought an American walnut side table with mirror, carved legs and a shelf under for £8 15s 0d. They bought two Satsuma vases (£1 17s 6d and £3 10s 0d) and a bronze pot (£2 0s 0d) in 1895 from Liberty & Co., Regent Street, London. The bedroom items they acquired in 1895 included a suite in fine pollard oak – a wardrobe and dressing table – a washstand, towel rail and four cane chairs (£100), an all-brass Parisian bedstead and, for the bed, handsome drapery in figured silk tapestry with an upholstered trimmed headboard (ten guineas). They bought a large settee 'covered in best English velvet and stuffed with hair' for £15 and a round settee upholstered in silks and wool tapestry and silk trimmings for ten guineas.

Some furnishings suggest a concern for privacy. Kerr proclaimed privacy 'a first principle with the better classes of English people' and that 'Family Rooms' should be 'essentially private' and 'as much as possible the family thoroughfares too'.[40] Portières (curtains across doorways) and screens helped separate rooms, preserve privacy and protect from draughts. They are visible in the drawing rooms at Uffculme and The Dell and in the Sorrento rooms (Figs 6.2–6.4, 6.6–6.10 and 6.12–6.13a–b). The Dell portières were much simpler than those in Sorrento, signalling a lower social level. In boudoirs and bedrooms portières covered doors leading into corridors to protect the privacy of the master and mistress from servants. In large establishments servants had their own stairs: The Vale, Wake Green Road, was advertised as having a best and second staircases.[41] The presence of servants meant the middle-class home was never wholly private. Warmth and intimacy were possible between the family and servants, especially, though not necessarily, where there was only one servant. Those in paid domestic roles such as companions and governesses might more easily develop close relationships with family members because they were socially superior to servants.

---

38 T. Logan, *The Victorian parlour: a cultural study* (Cambridge, 2003), pp. 127–128.

39 S. Lasdun, *Victorians at home* (London, 1985), p. 10.

40 Kerr, *The English gentleman's house*, p. 74.

41 *Birmingham Daily Mail*, adverts: 8 March, 19, 22 and 24 February and Saturday 6 September 1890.

Window treatments prioritised privacy too. The large bay windows in the Sorrento drawing room had three rich-looking layers, including a ruched blind, probably muslin and known as the 'glass curtain', a lace curtain and elaborate, highly patterned velvet drapes (Fig. 6.4). This popular layering provided privacy, but also guarded against draughts and prevented direct light fading precious hardwoods, 'grained' finishes or wallpapers. Faded finishes were 'down at heel' and signalled a failure to keep up middle-class standards, as well as hinting at possible economic difficulties. The curtains in the hall at Sorrento were elaborately draped, tasselled, ruched and festooned and had an ornamental scalloped valance (a lambrequin), suggesting the high standard of furnishings in the rest of the house (Fig. 6.2). Excessively ornate curtain arrangements drew criticism: they were 'symptomatic of the desire for everything in one's villa to be just a little more than it seemed', wrote Charles Locke Eastlake (1836–1906), a British architect and furniture designer, in *Hints on household taste* in 1869.[42] His concerns about excess imply the risk of an insecure seeking after status, but such window treatments were fashionable among the middle classes in the Victorian era.[43] In July 1892, just before moving into their new home, Brackley Dene, the Blackwells bought thirty-three Holland blinds finished with lace edging and insertion and five Holland blinds finished plain and complete with fittings, all of which came to £24 12s 0d, together with twenty-two full madras muslin curtains costing £7 4s 3d.

Many middle-class residents 'paraded and displayed' their homes to show superiority and gain status in the public world, which undermined any concept of the home as a wholly private domain.[44] The family silver and glassware laid out on a sparkling white linen tablecloth ready for a dinner party at Sorrento in Fig. 6.12 shows how the family displayed its wealth and taste. A presentation such as this would have been costly: in September 1892 the Blackwells bought a dining-room suite in the finest pollard oak consisting of six stuffed back chairs and two made higher for carving, which were upholstered in best-quality green buffalo hide with plain seats and backs. In March 1893 they bought a damask tablecloth (£1 14s 0d) and a chenille table cover (£2 14s 0d). Such table covers can be seen in various rooms in homes of differing status, such as the Sorrento library, the Greengate dining room and the drawing room of The Dell (Figs 6.6, 6.9 and 6.11). In July 1895 the Blackwells spent £15 18s 4d on fine electro-plated bone-handled cutlery.

---

42 Charles Locke Eastlake, *Hints on household taste in furniture, upholstery and other details* (London, 1869).

43 Barrett and Phillips, *Suburban style*, p. 68.

44 Gordon and Nair, *Public lives*, pp. 108 and 132; S. Gunn, *The public culture of the Victorian middle class: ritual and authority and the English industrial city, 1840–1914* (Manchester, 2000), p. 26.

The privacy of the home was also challenged by connections to the outside world. Many items were the result of industrialisation, mass production, new technology and science, and the home was important in expressing modernity through these. Material culture brought the outside inside through natural materials, such as marble, slate, cut flowers, potted plants, designs on wallpaper, textiles, china and ornaments and in the subjects of paintings and prints. The exotic was brought to Britain via the empire and overseas trade in the form of plants such as palms, natural materials, including bamboo, man-made items such as carpets from the Far East and decorative items such as oriental porcelain, Japanese fans and Moorish room designs. The stag's heads in the Sorrento and Uffculme halls and stuffed birds and animals elsewhere brought in the wild (Fig. 6.2). Conservatories were the sites of material culture that spoke to the exotic outside world through plants, furnishings and caged songbirds.

This material culture suggests a desire to connect with the natural or public world while safely within the privacy of one's own home. It provided an avenue of escape from Victorian taste and, for women, afforded 'imaginative access to realms of experience otherwise closed off and an opening into a wider world'.[45] Furthermore, colonial goods in the home conveyed the idea of a benign relationship to colonisation, effacing or sublimating the violence and threats of violence that characterised British foreign policy. The Great Exhibition, museums, global products in department stores and post-Grand-Tour middle-class tourism were important influences. Bringing items from all round the world into the home, though, removed them from their context and absorbed them into middle-class culture, making them safe and acceptable and different from what they were in their original environment.

Gender impacted on decoration and furnishing. Kerr associated drawing rooms with the feminine, writing that they, 'like other female spaces', needed 'cheerfulness, refinement of elegance, lightness' and 'comparatively delicate' decoration, a commonly held contemporary view.[46] The Moseley drawing rooms were indeed generally lighter both in the shades of colour used and in the impression of weight or ornateness of the material goods. They featured floral wallpapers and textiles and more delicate furniture, but these rooms were used by both men and women. Uffculme's drawing-room fireplace and over-mantel were large and dark, but this did not necessarily reflect male taste: the contents of the room, such as the family photographs, show this was a family room (Fig. 6.3). The Sorrento dining room was more heavily patterned, with darker, more imposing furniture, a dark fireplace and large paintings sporting heavy frames, while the Uffculme dining-room fireplace and its surround were dark, but these

45 Logan, *The Victorian parlour*, pp. 124 and 195–9.

46 Kerr, *The English gentleman's house*, p. 119.

Figure 6.14. The dining room fireplace, Uffculme. BCT.

rooms were used by both men and women, making how they were decorated and furnished more about taste than gender (Figs 6.12 and 6.14). The décor of the Greengate dining room was much lighter, showing that decorative schemes for dining rooms varied (Fig. 6.11). The Moseley drawing and dining rooms, then, were not conclusively different in terms of what might be considered male or female decoration and furnishing, which suggests that style was a more important factor in many decisions about decorating and furnishing.

How some specialist rooms in Moseley were decorated and furnished, though, suggests male influences and male spaces. The stag's head hung above the fireplace

Figure 6.15. The study, Uffculme. BCT.

in the hall at Sorrento bespoke 'the country gentleman' and similar features furnished the Uffculme hall (Figs 6.1–6.2). The Uffculme study was dark with heavy leather seating and a sturdy desk (Fig. 6.15). The Sorrento library had dark, varnished wood panelling below the dado rail, a dark fireplace and mantel, a dark table cover, padded seating, highly decorative cornice and landscape paintings in large gilt frames (Fig. 6.9). There was specific furniture for men: in 1890 the Blackwells bought 'gents chairs' with pillow seats upholstered in tapestry and silk trimmings for £7 7s 0d. Wardrobes for men were monumental, the most desirable being the 'winged' type – a double wardrobe with a central mirrored section.

The Moorish design of the Sorrento billiard and smoking rooms, popular from the 1880s, was considered rakish and was typical of male spaces (Figs 6.7–6.8). The design involved geometric patterns on the carpet, upholstery, portières and walls, velvet coverings (thought to absorb smoke), inlaid mother-of-pearl, fretted decoration, eastern arched alcoves and fashionable *trompe l'oeil* wallpaper. *The Lady's Companion* of 1897 noted that oriental-style rooms could be created for less than £50.[47] Painted wooden fretwork arches were a cheap and easy way to achieve this Moorish design style as they could be bought as a single piece. The light sources in the Sorrento billiard room were particularly impressive – natural light came from a stained-glass atrium and artificial light from an elaborate brass overhead light fixture that could be raised and lowered and which was testament to new lighting technology (Fig. 6.7).

Smoking rooms were considered male spaces; they protected others from cigar and cigarette smells. Cheap cigarettes were available from the 1880s and, with the expansion of smoking towards the end of the nineteenth century, the smoking room became common in larger houses. Jane Panton was opposed to smoking, describing it as 'a habit that … has not one merit to recommend it', and asked if men ever reflected 'on what their smoke costs them'.[48] She strongly objected to women having to retreat to other rooms to avoid the smell and having to deal with stale smoke. Over the course of 1895 Althans Blackwell bought 325 cigars at a total cost of £7 4s 6d. In 1895 he bought two smoking chairs 'with stuffed seats and backs covered with best English velvet and stuffed with hair' for £9, two smoking chairs with 'stuffed rail and wood seats' for £8 and a smoking or card table in oak for £2 10s 6, a total of £19 10s 6d. Smoking and billiard rooms were also sites for drinking. Althans Blackwell bought barrels of beer in 1892 at £3 12s 0d and whisky and wine in 1893 at £14 8s 0d. Smoking and billiard rooms were more clearly gendered spaces than other rooms and were areas to which men supposedly 'fled' to escape domesticity.[49]

Some other rooms and furnishings appear more directed at women. The shawl thrown over the back of a chair in the drawing room of The Dell and the *chaise longues* in the Greengate dining room and Sorrento bedroom suggest the presence of women (Figs 6.6, 6.11 and 6.13a–b). The Sorrento boudoir has a small writing desk, frills to the door and fireplace drapes, light and airy wall treatments, small and dainty furniture, flower arrangements and numerous personal photographs, all of which suggest a feminine space (Fig. 6.10). In 1890 the Blackwells bought a 'lady's chair' with a 'soft pillow seat upholstered

47 Cohen, *Household gods*, pp. 6, 128–130 and 135.

48 Panton, *From kitchen to garret*, p. 60.

49 Tosh, *A man's place*, pp. 179 and 182.

in rich silks and tapestry ensuite with trimmings' for £9 9s 0d and a 'Boudoir overmantel with panelled centre painted' for £3 8s 6d. The main Sorrento bedroom was decorated and furnished in a style that was considered feminine – light wallpaper, white furniture and water jugs decorated with floral designs (Fig 6.13a–b). Althans Blackwell bought a 'white painted wardrobe with hanging space and shaped and bevelled mirror' in 1890 for £27 16s 5½d and a bedroom overmantel in pine with shaped mirror to a special design at £37 15s 0d. Small armless chairs were considered more appropriate for women's skirts and crinolines, as in the Uffculme and Glaisdale drawing rooms (Figs 6.3 and 6.5).

There is, however, no evidence in the photographs of the creative activities associated with middle-class women at the time. Such evidence may, of course, have been tidied away when the rooms were photographed, in the interests of presenting a 'show home'. Moseley women were involved in sewing: the Middlemore Charity Home Annual Reports show that Eliza Avins and her daughter, Eliza Parthenia, donated 270 items sewn by them between 1894 and 1904.[50] Two developments might have deterred some middle-class women from engaging in home handicrafts: the emerging Arts and Crafts culture increasingly derided home handicrafts, which meant that such activities became unfashionable, and items that had once been crafted at home were readily available on the market in a range of designs, encouraging women to buy rather than make them.[51]

However, manuals, 'ladies' journals', specialist craft departments, shops and mail order firms show that domestic handicrafts were flourishing.[52] The homes photographed had servants, so the question of leisure time was not an issue. Women with little help in the home would not have had much spare time to qualify as 'a lady of leisure', so much part of the stereotype of Victorian middle-class womanhood.

Robert Kerr, writing in 1864, considered women best suited to decision-making about decorating and furnishing:

> It must be acknowledged, certainly, that the more graceful sex are generally better qualified, both as respects taste and leisure, to appreciate the decorative element in whatever form of development; and it is, perhaps, frequently the case in these days of universal hard work, that the master of the house finds a relief in relinquishing to the hands of his wife the control of all that is artistic.[53]

50 LBA, L41.31/19–45 222, Middlemore Charity Home Annual Reports, 1892–1902.

51 Bilston, *Promise of the suburbs*, p. 74.

52 *Ibid.*; Logan, *The Victorian parlour*, p. 163.

53 Kerr, *The English gentleman's house*, p. 96.

However, men appear to have had total financial responsibility for home furnishing until the 1880s, with a collaborative approach operating thereafter in which men continued to retain overall control of the finances.[54] Some of the Blackwell purchases were made while the couple were travelling, which suggests a collaborative approach. Most of the other Blackwell bills were directed to Mr Blackwell, with about a quarter – specifically household goods (for example, furniture, fittings, ornaments, china, lights and blinds) directed to Agnes Blackwell. She may have ordered on credit in her husband's name and been responsible for the actual shopping.

Decorating, furnishing and conspicuous consumption were facilitated by a retail revolution that brought new ways of buying and selling through department stores, emporia, catalogues and mail order, and new systems of store credit. By the last decade of the nineteenth century Birmingham had well-developed retail areas: its streets were renovated into sites of consumption and display with department stores and distinct shopping districts, such as arcades. The House of Fraser, for example, opened a drapery shop in 1851 at 78 Bull Street, Birmingham, which in 1898 was extended into the North-Western Arcade. Department stores gave women new freedoms, which were also facilitated by the development of transport. Such stores were public spaces in the city, but safely enclosed and respectable, and they were central to women's shopping and social life. Increased employment for women brought more women onto city streets with new buying power, stimulating the development of such stores. Such commercial activity connected the middle-class home to the public realm and took women into the public sphere, making them an important part of the English economy.

The Blackwells shopped mostly in Birmingham (72 per cent of their bills), but also, though to a much lesser extent, in the immediate local area, as well as throughout the West Midlands, in London and further afield in Europe. Moseley residents could shop locally at such shops as James Williams, General Furnishing Ironmonger, St Mary's Row, Thomas Hadley & Sons, Grocers and General Provisions Merchants, Moseley House, and Matthias Watts, Art Dealer and Framer, 15–17 St Mary's Row, near the Bull's Head. They could engage a range of services locally, including housepainters, decorators, carpenters and cabinet makers, such as Henry Hooper, Plumber, Glazier, Paper Hanger, Gas Fitter, House Sign and Decorative Painter, Bankside, Alcester Road.

Many families took on the challenge of decorating and furnishing their home with confidence or, failing that, with the aid of a design consultant. For others it was fraught with insecurity and anxiety, particularly first-time buyers, those new to the middle classes, marriage and the suburb and those living

54 Cohen, *Household gods*, pp. 90 and 92.

away from their birth-family support networks. Many were concerned about getting it right, displaying good taste, not overstepping the bounds of good taste, keeping up with fashions, fitting in, making the right impression and keeping up appearances. Familiarity with the codes and being able to take new ideas on board was essential. The ever-present danger that one's middle-class lifestyle might not be able to be maintained went together with anxieties over expectations that décor would be upgraded when one's prosperity increased. A powerful advice lobby grew up. Jane Panton, in her book *From kitchen to garret*, told her readers what colours and materials to use in different rooms, what furniture and material goods to buy and where to buy them. Design ideas were also absorbed from the wider culture – from catalogues, guides, periodicals, lectures, family, friends and neighbours.

The decoration and furnishing of the suburban middle-class home brought many advantages and opportunities. In creating an appropriate domestic environment and dealing with many of the practicalities – buying and ordering items, supervising and managing contractors, taking deliveries and arranging and maintaining the material goods – women ensured the private sphere of the home was an effective indicator of the family's status in the public sphere. This gave women an important role. The decorative arts were a powerful form of self-expression and self-fashioning that could bring women power, praise, satisfaction and self-fulfilment. Women wrote about the 'pleasure' involved.[55] Jane Panton was a paid design consultant who saw women architects as crucial to better-designed homes that met the needs of the family, but it wasn't until 1898 that the first woman, Ethel Charles (1871–1962), gained entry to the Royal Institute of British Architects.[56] Interior design brought suburban women together in new interest groups, reading the same advice books and shopping together. These relationships helped forge shared values and new communities.

Consumerism helped shape the evolving suburb and provide a sense of connection with the modern world. Suburbs facilitated conspicuous consumption not only in the initial setting up of a home but also in the redecoration of the home that followed the frequent moves and the need to 'keep up appearances' and respond to changing design fashions. Other factors, too, underpinned conspicuous consumption. Income per head doubled between 1851 and 1901, giving the increasingly affluent middle classes more disposable income, while the cost of necessaries, especially food, fell, leaving more people with even more to spend on luxuries.[57] Mass-manufactured

55 Logan, *The Victorian parlour*, p. 98.

56 Panton, *From kitchen to garret*, p. 4; Royal Institute of British Architects: <https://www.architecture.com/ethel>, accessed 2023.

57 Cohen, *Household gods*, p. 13.

goods were more readily available. The middle classes expanded, increasing from 12.5 per cent of the population in 1851 to 25 per cent in 1901, bringing new middle-class purchasing power.[58]

Health and hygiene

The provision of facilities within the home became increasingly important and was also indicative of financial status. In the later nineteenth century WCs, along with bathrooms with hot and cold running water, were being rapidly included inside middle-class homes. In adverts in the *Birmingham Daily Post* the proportion of Moseley houses where an internal WC was noted increased significantly, from 17 per cent in 1881 to 53 per cent in 1891, showing how standards in the suburb were improving. However, they were initially not freestanding and required a wooden enclosure, which was also added to baths and sinks.[59] This prevented efficient cleaning. From the early 1880s freestanding sanitary appliances that could be more easily kept clean were being advocated for indoors, such as Doulton's 'Combination' and Twyford's 'Unitas'.[60] The quality of WCs ranged from 'cane and white' fireclay to highly ornate models complete with decoration in relief or colour, or a combination of both, with mahogany seats polished to a high sheen for the family and inexpensive untreated scrubbable white pine for servants.

Of Moseley houses in the sixty-five fully unfoldable building plans accessed, 80 per cent had an indoor WC. Forty houses in nine building plans did not. Of those that did not, two were detached houses, twelve semi-detached and twenty-six terraced, which suggests that house type was a factor. Eleven of these houses were built in the 1870s, when indoor WCs were less common, but twenty-nine were built in the 1890s, when an indoor WC might be expected in a middle-class house. Here house size and type are again significant: only one was a detached house, four were semi-detached and twenty-four were terraced houses. The social status of the roads might be a factor too: the houses without indoor WCs were mostly located in less well-to-do roads, where houses were smaller.

Indoor WCs were usually on the first floor and in a larger house there might be a ground-floor WC too. Two substantial houses, a detached house on the corner of Anderton Park and Forest Roads and a detached house in Park Hill, had an additional downstairs WC and another is noted in a catalogue.[61] Where there were two WCs, men and women used separate facilities. Outside WCs were used by servants always and by men if there was only one internal

58 *Ibid.*

59 Eveleigh, *Privies and water closets*, p. 47.

60 *Ibid.*

61 LBA, BPKNU, BCK/MC/7/3/1, 1821 and 1826; LBA, Bham/Sc R1.

WC. Woodbridge House had an internal WC just for servants, which was unusual.[62] Plan documentation in the 1890s specifies 'Twyford's Water Closet', 'Flush-out closets' and 'Earthenware with flushing system', showing that Moseley was introducing the latest models.[63] Five plans (eleven semi-detached houses) from 1891 to 1897 for houses in higher-status Chantry Road and Park Hill included 'lavatory', a lower-status term, suggesting the term was still in circulation among higher social groups. Status also came from having WCs separate from or partitioned off from bathrooms to prevent 'the sound of apparatus being transmitted'.[64] Of WCs in the Moseley building-plan survey, 78 per cent were separate or partitioned off, and in a pair of semi-detached houses on the corner of Anderton Park and Woodstock Roads the WC in the bathroom was screened off.[65]

Bathrooms were status symbols. 'No house of any pretensions will be devoid of a bathroom', wrote Kerr, while John Loudon concluded that bathrooms were 'a cheap and useful luxury, which would be considered by many persons an indispensable requisite for a perfect villa'.[66] By the 1870s houses with an annual rent above £35 usually had a bathroom with running hot water and flush toilets.[67] Installing hot-water pipes cost about £50–£60 in the 1880s, but this outlay was easily recouped in rents.[68] Geysers – water heaters mostly powered by gas – were installed in bathrooms in the 1860s to heat water just before it was used. This was cheaper for landlords than hot-water pipes, but disliked by tenants as the running costs fell to them and geysers were noisy and sometimes dangerous.

Nearly 60 per cent of the houses in Moseley's extant building plans accessed had bathrooms. Again, this leaves a surprising number that did not. Only sixteen homes without bathrooms were built in the 1870s, the rest being constructed in the 1880s and 1890s, when bathrooms might be expected in a reputable middle-class suburb, which suggests that the date of building was not a significant factor. All the detached houses had bathrooms, but 57 per cent of the semi-detached houses, such as fourteen houses on the corner of Church and Woodstock Roads and four on the corner of Church and Queenswood Roads, did not.[69] The terraced houses, many of which were in Trafalgar and

62 LBA, Bham/Sc 890.

63 LBA, BPKNU, BCK/MC/7/3/1, 1821, 1484 and 2331.

64 J. Flanders, *The Victorian house: domestic life from childbirth to deathbed* (London, 2003), p. 286.

65 LBA, BPKNU, BCK/MC/7/3/1, 1586.

66 Kerr, *The English gentleman's house*, p. 168; Loudon, *Encyclopaedia*, p. 803.

67 Flanders, *The Victorian house*, p. 91.

68 *Ibid.*, pp. 287–8.

69 LBA, BPKNU, BCK/MC/7/3/1, 738 and 627.

Woodstock Roads, did not either.[70] This suggests that house size, type and location were significant. The provision increased over time: the 1890s plans had 57 per cent more bathrooms than plans from the 1880s and 58 per cent more adverts mentioned bathrooms in 1891 than in 1881. All the bathrooms identified on building plans were on the first floor.

The Brackley Dene bath was described as superior because of its surrounding polished wooden seat.[71] However, like many larger homes, Brackley Dene, with eleven bedrooms, had only one bathroom, which highlights the necessity of the toilet set: a toilet pail, two water sets and two water jugs that the Blackwells bought in 1893 for £7 16s 0d. A washstand, jugs and bowls and towels are visible in the Sorrento bedroom, suggesting that use of the bathroom was limited in that home too (Fig. 6.13a). Concerns for health led to the ceramic tiling of bathrooms and WCs, frequently in rich colours. Wall tiles were mass-produced from the 1870s, making them more widely available. New technology not only improved health and hygiene for the suburban middle classes but also brought colour and design to bathrooms and the 'smallest room'.

Health and hygiene were particularly pertinent in the service areas – the kitchen, scullery, pantry and larder. These were separated from the family areas to protect people, particularly visitors, from the sights, sounds and especially the smells of cooking and cleaning. The Blackwells' domestic areas were divided from the hall by swinging doors with two round glazed insets.[72] Segregation in the service areas was also important. Kitchens were for cooking, sculleries for activities that involved water and larders and pantries separated meats from other foodstuffs. All Moseley building plans accessed had separate kitchens and sculleries, including two semi-detached houses in Church Road and one detached property on the corner of Church and Coppice Roads;[73] 46 per cent had pantries and three houses had two pantries; 24 per cent had a larder and 5 per cent, such as the eight semi-detached houses on the corner of Anderton Park and Forest Roads, had both pantry and larder.[74] The service areas in many houses, though, were not large enough for much segregation.

Storage facilities were important to the smooth running of the home, an impression crucial to the family's public image. Two houses had a knife room: a detached house on the corner of Wake Green Road and Wakefield Road and John Padmore's house on Wake Green Road.[75] Special provision for china

70 *Ibid.*, 1473,1438, 3 and 130.

71 MSHGC, C3/D2/A/F10/16.

72 MSHGC, C3/D2/A/F10/16.

73 LBA, BPKNU, BCK/MC/7/3/1, 1616 and 1816.

74 *Ibid.*, 169/70.

75 LBA, BPKNU, BCK/MC/7/3/1, 358 and 18.

and other linen cupboards, work and storerooms and closets for clothes were provided in 29 per cent, while Woodbridge House also had a boot store and 'excellently fitted wardrobes'.[76] Nearly a quarter of sales particulars in the sales catalogues accessed mentioning cellars identified wine and beer cellars and one had 'enclosed bins and vaults for storage and ventilation'.[77] Later in the century concern about the damp and smells in cellars meant that many houses were built without them, but they did not go totally out of fashion.[78]

Health and hygiene were important in bedrooms too. The beds in the main Sorrento bedroom were brass, which was considered healthier than wood, and the arched recess there replaced half testers because of concerns about dust and the circulation of fresh air during sleep (Fig. 6.13a–b). Bedstead making developed into 'one of Birmingham's most profitable trades with a worldwide export market'.[79] Brass bedsteads were 'stocked by all the leading home-furnishers and coveted … as a tangible sign of affluence'.[80] Hoskins and Sewell of Bordesley, founded in 1846, was a 'pioneer bedstead firm' and 'one of the largest in the world'.[81]

Most Moseley homes were too small for much segregation and key rooms were multi-functional. Interior architectural features, decoration, furnishing and material goods were crucial to status in the public arena and women's role in managing these was important. Gender influenced the decoration and furnishing of some rooms, particularly specialist rooms, but style, taste, fashion and wealth were major factors in many choices made. New technology helped the less well-off to emulate their social superiors, and the number of internal WCs and bathrooms increased significantly. The next chapter takes the family outside the home to discover how Moseley's middle classes, including women, operated in the public realm.

76 LBA, Bham/Sc 890, 1260 and 456.

77 *Ibid.*, 890.

78 Barrett and Phillips, *Suburban style*, p. 54.

79 <https://www.bedbazaar.co.uk/metal-bedsteads-for-prince-and-peasant/>, accessed 2022.

80 *Ibid.*

81 *Ibid.*

7

The Moseley middle classes in the public sphere

The Victorian period became a philanthropic Golden Age and an era of civic and religious endeavour made possible by the comparative financial security of middle-class incomes and increased leisure time. A wider public culture developed that was integral to the formation of the middle classes and men and women engaged with public life in meaningful ways in the context of a complex and rapidly changing world.[1] Moseley's middle classes involved themselves in volunteerism and philanthropy associated with politics, civic endeavour, religious and educational institutions, Birmingham's voluntary hospitals, charity schools and disabled children's institutions, and local social, cultural and sporting clubs and societies.

Many motives underpinned the involvement of the Moseley middle classes in volunteerism and philanthropy. The Victorians valued 'morally exemplary actions, especially service to others', and altruism was framed as 'not only preferable but necessary if one was to conceive of oneself as a good person'.[2] Involvement, though, also displayed and enhanced status, established identity both professional and personal, demonstrated religious credentials, enabled networking and memorialised individuals and family. It offered opportunities to interact socially with others and people of higher status, exercise power, use and develop skills and achieve a sense of independence and satisfaction. Women could take part legitimately in public service, new residents could make connections and young people could find marriage partners.

Political and civic endeavour

Political and civic endeavour was central to middle-class identity, inspired by a desire for improvement. It brought power, influence and prestige locally and nationally and drew local people into the orbit of important personages. Moseley was at the heart of national and local politics because of Joseph Chamberlain (1836–1914), who lived at Highbury, Moor Green, a house he

---

1 Jeffrey Auerbach, 'Review of Simon Gunn. *The public culture of the Victorian middle class: ritual and authority and the English industrial city 1840–1914* (New York, 2000)', *The American Historical Review*, 107/3 (2002), p. 937; Temma Balducci and Heather Belnap-Jensen (eds), *Women, femininity and public space in European visual culture, 1789–1914* (London and New York, 2014), p. 6.

2 Bilston, *Promise of the suburbs*, p. 152.

Figure 7.1. Celebrating Joseph Chamberlain's 70th birthday, 1906. Author's own collection.

built in 1878 and occupied until his death in 1914. He was elected to the town council in 1869, was mayor between 1873 and 1876 and became an MP in 1876. Highbury was the hub of Chamberlain's political career. Important members of the national and local elites were welcomed there and rallies, fundraising events and other large social gatherings, such as receptions, dances, horticultural shows and the annual garden parties for his West Birmingham constituents and West Birmingham Liberal Union, were held there. Moseley people were 'justly proud of him' and there were 'not many people in the neighbourhood who have not on some occasion or other had a glimpse of the interior of Highbury'.[3]

Highbury is one of the images on a souvenir postcard issued for Joseph Chamberlain's seventieth birthday in 1906 (Fig. 7.1). It depicts it as one of Chamberlain's four local spheres of influence, along with his Birmingham civic building programme, improvement schemes and his lengthy political representation. It confidently expresses and confirms the public culture that symbolised the middle classes in the second half of the nineteenth century. Moseley's association with the Chamberlain family brought national attention and local prestige to the suburb.

Chamberlain's presence and the activities and involvements of his sons, Austen Chamberlain (1863–1937), elected MP for East Worcestershire in

3 CRL, C1/10/11, *Moseley and King's Heath Journal*, 'Our Public Men', No. 10, March 1893, pp. 237–44.

1892, and Arthur (more often referred to as Neville (1869–1940), drew local people into politics. A Moseley Liberal Association was formed at the Trafalgar Hotel in Moseley in 1874.[4] The three Chamberlains were leading lights in the Moseley branch of the East Worcestershire Liberal Unionist Association, formed following Joseph Chamberlain's split from the Liberals in 1886.[5] The East Worcestershire Liberal Unionist Association subscription list for 1900 shows that key members lived in Moseley: the chairman was Councillor John Skinner of The Grove, the honorary secretary was William Lord of Glenholme, Oxford Road, and the assistant honorary secretary was William Arundel of Jesmond Dene, 6 Park Hill.[6] There were twenty-six Moseley representatives on the Divisional Council, including the Chamberlains and Alderman John Bowen JP, Councillor Arthur Ellaway, Councillor Nathaniel Cracknell Reading and Althans Blackwell.

Nathaniel Cracknell Reading (1849–1924) of Inglewood, Wake Green Road, Moseley, where he lived until his death, was the Association's first honorary secretary.[7] He was a manufacturer of 'watch alberts, necklets, pendants and guards in rolled gold, best gilt and white metal' at 186 and 187 Warstone Lane in the Jewellery Quarter, Birmingham, and was a founder member and later honorary treasurer and vice-president of the Birmingham Jewellers' and Silversmiths' Association. He took over the family's jewellery firm with his sister Agnes on the death of his father and Althans Blackwell became his partner on marrying Agnes. Nathaniel Reading served as honorary secretary to Austen Chamberlain in 1892 and became a familiar figure for his political and civic activities (Fig. 7.2). Other Moseley men were involved too: John Padmore, Samuel Clarke, Lister Lea and Hubert Bewlay were assentors for Moseley, endorsing the nomination of Austen Chamberlain that resulted in his unopposed return to parliament.[8] Althans Blackwell supported the East Worcestershire Liberal Unionist Association by subscribing one guinea per annum between 1895 and 1897. Associations with the Chamberlain family and the Liberal movement fostered political awareness and personal involvement, raising the profile of Moseley individuals and the suburb.

Conservatives were also well represented in Moseley. John Arnold of Moor Green presided over a meeting at the Fighting Cocks on 22 April 1874 to establish a Conservative Association for Moseley, King's Heath and Balsall

4 LBA, MS/579/4 Acc 71aE.

5 *Some Moseley personalities*, Vol. II (Birmingham, 1994), pp. 37–40.

6 MSHGC, C3/D1/F8/1, The East Worcestershire Liberal Unionist Association Subscription List, 1900.

7 *Ibid.*

8 *Birmingham Daily Post*, 31 March 1892.

Cartoon of N C Reading:
No. 104 of "Familiar Figures" from the
Birmingham Despatch

Figure 7.2. Nathaniel Cracknell Reading. *Some Moseley Personalities*, Vol. II, p. 39 (Birmingham: Moseley Local History Society, 1994).

Heath, and the Rev. William Harrison Colmore became its president.[9] No evidence has survived that reflects on any conflict between the Rev. Colmore's role as vicar of St Mary's church and his involvement in politics. He was also to the fore in local civic, cultural and social arenas.

The Moseley suburban middle classes were active in a range of civic endeavours. Sir John Charles Holder (1838–1923), a pronounced Conservative,

9 LBA, MS/579/4 Acc 71aE; Fairn, *History of Moseley*, p. 62.

served on the councils of Balsall Heath and King's Heath for a short time.[10] He bought John Arnold's estate in Moor Green on his death and built Pitmaston there in the 1870s, the same year he became a baronet. He was a wealthy maltster and brewer who owned the Midland Brewery in Nova Scotia Street, close to Curzon Street Station, Birmingham, and was a JP in both Worcester and Birmingham, High Sheriff of Worcestershire (1903), Deputy Lieutenant of the county and a Knight of Grace of St John of Jerusalem.[11] In 1894 the Rev. William Harrison Colmore pressed for district councillors for Moseley following the 1894 Local Government Act and from 1894 three councillors represented Moseley on the King's Norton Rural District Council: 'a farmer, an accountant and a gentleman'.[12] Nathaniel Cracknell Reading was one of the original members of King's Norton parish council when it was created in 1894 and its vice-chairman from 1896 to 1899.[13] Other Moseley men served as councillors from 1890, including Arthur George Ellaway, John Skinner and Walter George Lyndon. The 1894 Act allowed women to become councillors, but no Moseley women took on the role in the nineteenth century. James Smith, an iron-bedstead-maker of The Dingle, Wake Green Road, was the mayor of Birmingham for 1895 and 1896.[14]

Many other Moseley residents held civic and legal positions. Thomas Clement Sneyd-Kynnersley (1803–92) of Moor Green Hall was a barrister, the stipendiary magistrate of the borough of Birmingham for thirty-five years, recorder for Newcastle-under-Lyme, a JP for Worcestershire and Staffordshire and deputy lieutenant for Warwickshire.[15] He was particularly interested in criminal reform, especially juvenile crime, and popular education. Frederick Elkington was one of several JPs, along with Neville Chamberlain and George Frederick Lyndon, who held their sessions at the Fighting Cocks.[16] William Adams of Sorrento was a JP for Warwickshire and a member of the county council. James Guest of Elmhurst, the large house visible in Figure 1.1, was the registrar of Birmingham County Court. The Rev. Colmore was on the King's Norton School Board from 1877 and became its chairman in 1895.[17] In 1892

10 MSHGC, C3/D1/F7/5, pp. 11–12.

11 *Some Moseley personalities*, Vol. I (Birmingham, 1994), pp. 11–12; *Worcestershire Chronicle*, 6 April 1870; *Birmingham Gazette*, 7 April 1866; *Birmingham Daily Post*, 3 April 1868 and 8 April 1872; LBA, MS/39/1/2/3.

12 Fairn, *History of Moseley*, pp. 56 and 62.

13 *Some Moseley personalities*, Vol. II, pp. 37–40.

14 Fairn, *History of Moseley*, p. 51.

15 LBLH, B.COL 08.2;96586, *Birmingham Faces and Places*, Vol. 1, pp. 71–3.

16 Gilbert, *The Moseley trail*, pp. 9–10.

17 CRL, JC6/7/1–173, *Moseley and King's Heath Journal*, No. 1, June 1892, p. 19; CRL, C1/10/11, *Moseley and King's Heath Journal*, No. 10, March 1893, p. 268.

its members were the Rev. Colmore, chairman; James Carr (gun manufacturer, Carlton House); Rev. George Type (Congregational minister, Trafalgar Road); Alfred Coley (solicitor, Woodstock Road); Arthur Pass (auctioneer, Trafalgar Road); and Arthur James Hutchinson (confectioner, Trafalgar Road). James Botteley (gentleman, Park Hill) joined them in 1893.

John Avins of Highfield House was guardian to King's Norton Union Parish, surveyor for King's Norton, on the Grand Jury at King's Norton and overseer and surveyor at King's Heath Petty Session.[18] Edward Holmes of Wyndcliffe, School Road, was a member of the King's Norton Board of Surveyors and chairman for a period, when 'he filled the important capacity of chairman with an impartiality and success which is truly enviable'.[19] He was very interested in the working of the Local Government Act of 1891 and took great interest in labour disputes, especially those connected with the building trades, acting often as a very successful arbitrator.[20] William John Davis of Trafalgar Road was the first general secretary of the Amalgamated Society of Brass Workers, founded in 1872, while William Adams of Sorrento was associated with Joseph Arch, the founder in 1872 of the National Agricultural Labourers' Union and a fellow Methodist.[21] Moseley individuals contributed significantly to local civic endeavour, providing an army of unpaid volunteers who upheld the status quo and the interests of ratepayers and kept the machinery of local government working smoothly. Their efforts also impacted on the wider community.

Many residents were involved in improving Moseley's facilities, as previous chapters have shown. They were instrumental in improving the sanitary situation in Moseley following the outbreak of typhoid in the 1870s and in sorting out street lighting. They set up and served on various committees and established pressure groups, such as the Moseley and District Property-Owners' Protection Association, the Ratepayers' Protection Association and the Anti-Steam Tram Nuisance Society. Edward Holmes was instrumental in widening Woodbridge Road and making improvements to Moseley Station.[22] John Avins persuaded the Midland Railway Company to provide more trains to Moseley and sat on the Committee for Moseley Public Lighting and on the Moseley Village Green Trust.[23]

---

18 *Birmingham Gazette*, 7 April 1866; *Birmingham Daily Post*, 3 April 1868 and 8 April 1872.

19 *Some Moseley personalities*, Vol. II, pp. 27–9; MSHGC, C3/D2/F1/36, *Moseley Society Journal*, I/10 (November 1894).

20 MSHGC, C3/D2/F1/36, *Moseley Society Journal*, I/10 (November 1894).

21 *Some Moseley personalities*, Vol. II, pp. 2–3.

22 *Ibid.*, pp. 27–9.

23 LBLH, B.COL 08.2, *Birmingham Faces and Places*, I/8 (1 December 1889), p. 123; *Birmingham Daily Post*, 5 July 1883.

On 23 June 1897 Moseley village green was gifted to King's Norton parish council to be dedicated 'for the use and benefit of the inhabitants of Moseley as open space'.[24] Fifteen years previously, in 1882, a meeting at the Moseley National Schools presided over by John Arnold considered what should be done about the village green, given residents' fears that it might be built on. The meeting passed a resolution that the green be purchased by Moseley inhabitants to become 'their property forever'.[25] This move was complicated by the need to identify the rightful owner of the green. Some at the meeting thought the Blayney family were the owners and some that William Dyke Wilkinson owned it, while others maintained the green already belonged to the public – that it was common land and inhabitants ought not to be asked 'to buy their own property'. Some wanted residents to buy the green and hand it over to the Highway Board, given that it was a small area bounded by roads. Solicitors investigated the deeds and found that Mr Wilkinson's claim to the land was a 'just and good one', and in 1883 a move for residents to buy the green went ahead. Canvassers soon had promises of £350, enabling Mr Wilkinson to be paid a deposit of £25 on the purchase money, with the remainder to be paid 'with as little delay as possible'. The Village Green Trust was set up to oversee this and to improve and maintain the village green.

Two years later, in early 1885, the parish magazine declared that 'our readers may rest assured that the green will become a thing of beauty and a joy forever', which suggests there was some concern about its state.[26] In September 1885 the *Birmingham Gazette* stated that the green was 'still a wilderness' and inhabitants were 'hinting that the committee have lost heart and despair of beautifying a spot which is so hopelessly disfigured by those hideous tall Scotch railings'. Eight years later, at a meeting of the trustees on 19 January 1893, the chair, the Rev. Colmore, reported that there was no fund for keeping the green in order and £7 was owing for work done.[27] An appeal for funds brought in £11 13s 0d in nine contributions, including £2 from Richard Cadbury and two guineas from the Holt Brewery Company. However, £5 was still needed to pay for laying out the green and the vicar hoped that someone would get up a subscription for painting the railings 'as they sadly want a coat of paint'.[28] The financial struggle to improve and maintain the village green continued over the next four years and ultimately proved too much for the trust, which led to the gifting of the green to King's Norton parish council. In the context of a well-

24 *Victorian Moseley* (Birmingham, 2013), p. 21.

25 *Birmingham Daily Post*, 5 September 1882.

26 SMCA, *Canon Colmore's log book*, p. 234.

27 *Ibid.*, pp. 439 and 445.

28 *Ibid.*, p. 445.

Figure 7.3. St Mary's church, *c.*1871–80. MSHGC, Clive Gilbert Photographs (MC/D1/F12/6).

to-do, status-obsessed suburb, this failure of local philanthropy is surprising and reflects a move towards local government intervention.[29] The trustees' action in passing on the responsibility for the green, though, ultimately secured the area for the future.

The number of Moseley people involved in local political and civic endeavour was significant, but they were all men. This suggests that Moseley women had little political power, but many middling women were engaged in the 'politics of everyday', in which their political choices, strategies and decisions were related to, for example, religious worship, education or sport and were part of the process by which women became politicised.[30]

St Mary's church

The Victorian period witnessed a 'religious boom', an overwhelmingly middle-class phenomenon, in which the church had a social, political and philanthropic role and exercised a pervasive influence. Membership of a religious community conferred position and identity, gave personal comfort and security in a rapidly changing and unstable world, and offered opportunities to help the less

29 *Victorian Moseley*, p. 21.

30 Kathryn Gleadle, *Borderline citizens: women, gender and political culture in Britain, 1815–1867* (London, 2009); June Hannam, 'Women and politics', in Purvis, Jane (ed.), *Women's history: Britain, 1850–1945: an introduction* (London, 1995), pp. 217–18.

fortunate, to meet contacts outside kin and to form networks and marriage ties. The church linked members with a wider religious network, both locally and across England, and even overseas.

In 1853 St Mary's became a district or parish church, raising its status (previously it had been a chapelry). The building dated from the fifteenth century and had an imposing location on a rise close to the village green, as Figure 7.3 shows. The cottages that stood in front of the church in earlier years (Fig. 1.9) have gone in this image and a white picket fence and gate signal the entrance to the railway station. Oxford Road, formed in the early 1870s, is now evident in the foreground. The view to the village green, Moseley Hall grounds and beyond remains open and rural.

Extensions and additions to the church included the first chancel (1872), the north aisle and the arcade of columns (1885), the parish vestry (1891) and an extended chancel and the lady chapel (1897).[31] These added 326 sittings, of which 150 were free. In 1851 just over half of the seats in St Mary's were privately rented. Having a private pew brought social visibility and status, but created a sense of social inferiority among the working classes and was a factor in keeping them away. St Mary's was originally the only place of worship in Moseley. Two sister churches were subsequently built, St Anne's and St Agnes', contributing more sittings for the expanding suburb. The middle classes built many churches, inspired by 'piety and local attachments – benevolence and longing for perpetual remembrance – principally, doubtless a sincere desire to honour God and a natural desire to raise a lasting monument to themselves'.[32]

A Baptist church was built in 1888 in Oxford Road and a Presbyterian church in 1898 on the corner of Alcester and Chantry Roads, but other denominations had to go elsewhere to worship. Althans Blackwell had worshipped at King's Heath Baptist Chapel, paying 6s per quarter in 1876 for the rent of two sittings. There was a substantial Methodist group in Moseley, including William Adams of Sorrento, Wake Green Road. Forty-one Moseley families and a further twenty-seven individuals, 214 people in all, donated money to the Central Methodist Hall between 1898 and 1904.[33] Joseph Chamberlain was a Unitarian. When he came to Birmingham he joined the congregation of the New Meeting, which later became the Church of the Messiah. While there he became part of a network of people who wielded

31 *St Mary's Moseley*.

32 *Census of Great Britain 1851, Religious Worship in England and Wales*, abridged from the official report by Horace Manners to George Graham Esq, Registrar-General (London, 1854), 'Spiritual Provision and Destitution', p. 63.

33 <www.mywesleyanmethodists.org.uk>, accessed 2015. *Wesleyan Methodist Historic Roll*, 'Birmingham Moseley Road Circuit'.

power and influence within the city. Another important member of Moseley society, Richard Cadbury, was a Quaker.

Attending church was an important marker of the respectable middle classes and provided opportunities to see and be seen. On the morning of the 1851 religious census 282 people attended St Mary's church, plus sixty-five scholars from Moseley National School and 190 in the afternoon, together with forty-three scholars.[34] The lack of lighting meant there were no evening services in 1851.

Members of St Mary's church were extensively involved in volunteering and philanthropy through the church, but the experiences of men and women differed. Men took on more public and leadership roles. They served as wardens, overseeing church finances, managing investments and representing the church in the diocese: for example, on the Ruridecanal Chapter to the Diocesan Conference in 1893.[35] The wardens were very committed. Twenty-two men served as church wardens and fifteen as parish or people's wardens from the 1850s to the 1890s. Four men served more than twenty times between 1850 and 1890, six between ten and nineteen times, sixteen between five and nine times and twenty-nine between one and four times. John Avins served for six years (1862–8), Francis Willmot eight years (1869–77) and John Arnold fourteen years. Attendance at vestry meetings was high. John Avins was mentioned forty-eight times in the vestry minutes between 1862 and 1887.

Enhancing the church was important at a time when Moseley was expanding and there was competition from other denominations and dissenting churches. Men dominated improvements and extensions to the facilities and fabric. They supervised the laying on of gas and lighting (1866), fencing footpaths (1869) and building a new access roadway alongside the Bull's Head (1878).[36] They raised money through voluntary subscriptions in 1870 to meet a liability of £70 and invested £360 15s 1d from the burial fees fund in the East India Railway Stock in 1873 and 1874. They purchased land from William Dyke Wilkinson for the extension of the graveyard in 1878 and negotiated with Thomas Hadley about further graveyard extensions in 1882.[37] From 1872 a committee of men solicited subscriptions for church extensions and, as part of this, Thomas Clement Sneyd-Kynnersley made a loan to St Mary's, which was paid back at the rate of £170 per annum.[38] In 1884 a committee of men

34 John Aitken (ed.), 'Census of Religious Worship, 1851: The Returns for Worcestershire', Worcestershire Historical Society (Worcester, 2000), Entry 486, p. 100.

35 LBA, EP77/5/2/1 (Acc. 92/92) DRO 77/39.

36 LBA, L14.51, *Moseley Parish Magazine*, 1893, p. 6.

37 *Ibid.*; *St Mary's Moseley*, 2018, p. 15.

38 LBA, EP 77/5/2/1 (Acc. 92/92) DRO 77/39.

received the tender for the addition of the north aisle, designed by Julius Alfred Chatwin and built in 1885. Men were more frequently named as subscribers, representing their families as household heads who controlled family finances.

Men dominated in other areas too. Between 1886 and 1888 far more men (forty) than women (seventeen) subscribed to the parish organ fund, raising £800. Only 11 per cent of subscribers to the new vestry fund between 1890 and 1892, which raised just over £750, were women. Men were also more likely to donate gifts to St Mary's. In 1874 Sir John Charles Holder contributed a ring of steel bells from Sheffield.[39] Mr Thomas Walker gave a small organ in 1887 and Edmund Mackenzie Sneyd-Kynnersley, the son of Thomas Clement Sneyd-Kynnersley, provided hymn books in 1888 and in 1891 a piano and a print of the late Walter Farquhar Hook, perpetual curate at St Mary's between 1826 and 1828. In 1892 John Charles Holder gave a cheque for £500 for rebuilding the parish church.

Men took a prominent role in the establishment and furnishing of the new churches, St Anne's, St Agnes' and the temporary church set up for parishioners while St Agnes' was being built. The land for St Anne's was donated by William Francis Taylor of Moseley Hall, and Francis Willmot, a prominent member of St Mary's church, gave the land for St Agnes'. Wealthy women had an important place here, though. Rebecca Anderton bore the building costs of St Anne's in 1872 and donated several windows, four bells, the communion vessels and the 1737 silver alms dish.[40] Miss Sarah Taylor of Moor Green Hall donated a new barrel-organ.[41] In 1879 and 1882 thirty-seven women organised new surplices, a contribution that highlights the 'domestic' nature of much of women's involvement.

In fact, women gave gifts to St Agnes' Church in 1879, 1884 and 1885 in equal numbers with men (ten men and ten women along with two couples), but their gifts were different in nature. The women mostly gave smaller items that were more domestic in nature, such as altar cloths, kneelers, vases, candlesticks, book markers, offertory bags and bible and prayer books. Men gave architectural fittings, including the stone fence wall, gates and tile paving in the chancel, the chancel screen railing, a stone pulpit, the altar and an altar desk.

The money for the new churches came from St Mary's membership, but men dominated. Ninety-four men and seventeen women subscribed to the fund for the building of the temporary church in 1878. The St Agnes' church committee in 1881 and 1885 were all male, as were its trustees in 1883 and those giving further subscriptions in 1884 and bank loans in 1885. Twenty-

39 Bold, *Architectural history of St Mary's church*, p. 26.

40 *Ibid.*, p. 25.

41 Fairn, *History of Moseley*, p. 65.

seven men were involved between 1879 and 1880 and 103 men and thirty-two women subscribed to the new church between 1885 and 1889, when they raised just over £640. In 1892 only men were listed as attending a meeting about extending St Agnes', and more men than women ultimately contributed financially to the extensions, with 161 men and fifty-three women giving £1,575 between 1892 and 1893.

Money was also raised through collection boxes and this was done primarily by women. Standing on a mantelpiece, these boxes signalled the individual's commitment to service to the church and community. The social interactions and the home-centred nature of this type of fundraising might have made this method more acceptable for women, but it enabled women to make a place for themselves in the public arena. In 1886 five men and eight women raised £153 15s 6d in amounts ranging from 17s 6d to £73 16s 6d for the St Agnes' church organ fund through collecting boxes. A total of £168 was collected for the Newfoundland Mission, the Additional Curates' Society and the Home and Foreign Missions through collection boxes between 1879 and 1893.

Women were significantly involved in fundraising events. Amelia Milton James, wife of John Milton James, and other ladies held a sale of work in Moseley in 1873 and many other such events followed.[42] The stalls in 1885 were run by thirty-nine ladies. In 1887 a fifteen-strong ladies' committee was formed specifically to raise funds for the new organ alongside a men's committee, and they raised £150 6s 5d in May and June 1887. Also in 1887, a meeting called on 'ladies' to help run a large bazaar: 'we feared Moseley would have, sooner or later, to appeal to the ladies to get the parish out of debt by means of a large bazaar', reported the *Parish Magazine* in November 1887. For these men women's contribution was their domestic and consumer skills, but there is a reluctance in recognising women's ability to raise funds and the parish's dependence on them for this. About forty ladies were invited by the Rev. Colmore to the home of Mr and Mrs Francis Willmot, Wake Green House, to discuss this bazaar and about thirty attended. However, two men were appointed honorary secretaries of the bazaar – the Rev. John Henry Jones and William Fowler. The bazaar took place on 11–14 April 1888 at the Moseley and Balsall Heath Institute. Women planned the stalls and men managed the printing, decorating and amusements, an allocation of responsibilities highlighting male expectations of women. Stalls were named after holders' favourite flowers and goods included babies' shoes, antimacassars, dog biscuits and strawberries.

Women sometimes received publicity for their efforts. A bazaar that ran over three days in 1894 was held at the Moseley and Balsall Heath Institute and

42 *Birmingham Daily Post*, 3 December 1873.

all thirty-two 'ardent saleswomen' were named in the *Birmingham Daily Post* on 22 November 1894. The bazaar was opened by 'Mrs Smith-Ryland', making this very much a women's affair. The money raised was for the church and the National School. There were six main stalls and a refreshment stall, all draped in delicate artistic fabrics of white and amber, and fancy goods and knick-knacks were on sale. A total of £487 16s was raised. Women were 'ever to the front in well-doing' at a 'Sale of Work' in 1900 to raise money for the Indian Famine Fund, which demonstrates a philanthropic relationship to empire.[43] 'Theatricals', 'dramatics' and a 'conversazione'[44] that attracted some 350 people were other money-raising events.

Between 1879 and 1893 St Mary's church gave through their offertories and special collections nearly £800 to the National School, nearly £1,000 to hospitals, £357 to the poor and £50 to the Indian Famine Fund. Church members acted independently too: John Avins contributed to three cheap-dinner schemes for poorer children and gave two guineas to the 'Chicago Fire Daily Post Fund' in 1871 and £10 to the 'Special Fund for the Unemployed' in 1886.[45]

Moseley residents from other religious denominations also gave extensively to secular charities. Children's charities were important to the Blackwells, including Middlemore Children's Emigration Homes, Moseley Hall Children's Convalescent Home, the National Society for the Prevention of Cruelty to Children and the Police-Aided Association for Clothing for the Destitute Children of Birmingham. Two other charities they supported were for ladies – the Ladies Association for the Care of Friendless Girls and the Birmingham Ladies' Negro's Friend Society, which campaigned for the welfare of emancipated slaves and universal abolition after the 1834 Slavery Abolition Act. These highlight women's initiative in organising independent charity associations.

St Mary's church continued to support Moseley National School in the second half of the nineteenth century (Fig. 1.10).[46] Poorer children paid 2d and the rest 3d weekly, along with ½d paid into a club for schoolbooks, among other items: costs that excluded the destitute. Fluctuating attendance impacted on this income: seventeen attended in February 1862, seventy-four in March 1862 and 105 in May 1865. In 1890 the grants from the Education Department totalled £226 6s 3d, subscriptions and donations £92 17s 2d,

---

43 LBA, MS/579/6/71aE, Programmes and Posters.

44 A social gathering held by a learned or art society for conversation and discussion, especially about the arts, literature, medicine and science.

45 LBA, L14.51, *Moseley Parish Magazine*, 1890; *Birmingham Daily Post*, 10 March 1886, 14 and 17 October 1871 and 18 September 1889.

46 Price, *Moseley Church of England National School.*

offertories £57 14s 0 and the School Pence from pupils' weekly payments £93 18s 1d. This left the school with a deficit of £19 7s 11d. Fees were abolished in 1891 and substituted by 10s a head for voluntary schools paid for by the state, an amount that was equivalent only to a pupil paying 3d for forty weeks. It was not until the 1902 Education Act that the maintenance of voluntary schools was finally placed on the rates. The financial contributions made by Moseley churches and local people, then, were crucial to the survival of the school. The aims of the school continued as before – to encourage good habits, such as church attendance, economy, decency and cleanliness, and to reduce drinking, crime, strikes and riots. Contributors were stimulated by faith and belief in the transformative capacity of schooling, but changing the behaviour of the working classes was part of the purpose of the initiative.

The Moseley National School continued to develop under the aegis of the church.[47] In 1873 the managers were John Arnold (chair), the Rev. Colmore (secretary) and Thomas Clement Sneyd-Kynnersley (treasurer). There were improvements to the building (1854), extensions to the playground (1864), the installation of gas lighting (1872), a new classroom (1876), a new infant classroom (1883) and extensions to the infant classroom (1895) when £129 was raised by a bazaar and donations. The extra classroom space was made necessary by the extension of the school leaving age to ten years by the 1881 Education Act and, later, to eleven and twelve years. Following the 1870 Education Act the syllabus broadened in most elementary schools to include singing, elementary science, cookery, woodwork, 'military' drill, which led to organised sports and games, and outings to exhibitions and places of interest. After the 1881 Act an increasing range of subjects were required to receive grants, including metalwork. Attendance figures were crucial to the amount of grant awarded. In 1862 there were 109 on roll (sixty-five boys and forty-four girls) and in 1883 the accommodation provided for 411 pupils (170 boys, 158 girls and eighty-three mixed infants). The ladies of St Mary's church organised halfpenny dinners during harsh winter days to save children walking home and back, thus helping to ensure the school was well attended even in inclement weather. In March 1890 1,666 dinners were produced and in 1891 the dinners commenced in January and continued for eight weeks, during which 2,910 dinners were provided, 357 of which were free.[48]

These were major acts of hands-on philanthropy, and there were others too. In 1878 Edmund Mackenzie Sneyd-Kynnersley restarted the school library, contributing many books, and started a school museum by donating a glass-fronted cabinet containing specimens that would form the nucleus of

47 *Ibid.*

48 SMCA, *Canon Colmore's log book*, pp. 334, 358, 381, 385 and 419.

a collection. Miss Harriet Kynnersley, Edmund's sister, brought in specimens for the museum, objects illustrating cocoa manufacture were donated by the Cadburys and items illustrating pin- and needle-making were also donated. Edmund arranged a magic-lantern show and gave a prize for the best essay on the magic lantern. He paid for rebuilding the 'outhouses' and for putting the drains in order, and arranged for the draining and filling in of a stagnant pond. Miss F. Willmot took the 6th Standard in darning and the Misses Kynnersley (Anna and Harriet) often visited the Girls' School and helped in the afternoons. The Reverend John Robert Davison also helped regularly with drawing, singing and scripture, and his wife, Elizabeth Davison, with drawing, singing, scripture and needlework at the Girls' School. In 1880, when a certified cookery mistress was appointed to the Girls' School, Mr Willmot gave a gas stove. Ladies were admitted by 5s tickets to cookery lectures on Friday afternoons to witness 'Miss Boot's cooking skills'.

School treats were special occasions organised and funded by St Mary's members. James Bullock and Charles Miles took the infants to venues in their carts. Mr and Mrs Francis Willmot opened their gardens and adjoining field in the 1880s to the school pupils. The chief attraction was the ascent of balloons accompanied by the strains of King's Heath Band. One balloon, representing an elephant, was of immense size. In 1889 the balloons included 'Baldwin and his Parachute', which referenced an 1888 balloon flight at Villa Park by Professor T.S. Baldwin, an American, who had ascended rapidly into the air by balloon and then dropped from a harness and parachuted back to earth.[49] In 1891 Mrs Hannah Heaven of Wake Green Road 'rendered signal service as did several other ladies'.[50]

Concerts performed by Moseley residents and held at the National School were regular events to raise money for the school and the church.[51] In 1879 a concert raised money to buy a bookcase and books for the school library. A miscellany concert, also in 1879, raised money for psalters and hymn books for the temporary church. Church members put on dramatic performances at the National School on two consecutive evenings (Friday and Saturday evenings) at the end of October, November and December 1882, as well as in January and February 1883. The final evening included a performance by the Moseley handbell ringers, the singing of glees by the temporary church choir, impersonations, ventriloquism and dramatic pieces. Mr Charles Cotterill was thanked for his 'unflagging zeal and able management'. A concert in 1890

49 *Ibid.*; <www.avfc.co.uk>, accessed 15 March 2023; Simon Inglis, *Villa Park – 100 Years* (Warley, 1997).

50 SMCA, *Canon Colmore's log book*, p. 396.

51 *Ibid.*, pp. 58, 60 and 160.

involving singing and the violin was 'excellent in every way'.[52] Cultural events such as concerts were a significant aspect of middle-class identity – public rites for the well-to-do and 'a place to be seen'.[53]

St Mary's members organised and funded local events. Annual parish tea parties ran from 1879 and provided tea and entertainment for 200 to 400 people. They were held in early January each year at Moseley National School until 1891 and subsequently, because of increased numbers, at King's Heath Institute, where 'gas lights glittered on tea urns'.[54] The 1883 report noted 'the kindly faces of several ladies who, as ever, were ready to give their services at the tea urns'.[55] In 1887 there was 'a bountiful fare of buns, scones and cakes', cards and crackers, as usual, and 'files of young lady waitresses flitted with radiant zeal up and down the rows or hovered round, ready with smiling alacrity to anticipate the wants of one and all'.[56] Entertainments followed, including songs, a new feature in 1882 in the form of 'graceful dancing little Miss Thomas', theatricals, recitations, the Moseley parish handbell ringers, readings and operettas. In 1890 an eminent conjuror, 'Herr Blitz', 'astonished and amused', in 1891 there were also glees, violin and banjo, and in 1892 the church choir.[57] These entertainments, which were very well received, were described as 'diversified entertainment' in 1887 and 'first class' in 1891.

St Mary's members collaborated with others in organising and financing special celebrations for Moseley. The eighteen men listed on the circular as organising Queen Victoria's golden jubilee celebrations on 21 June 1887 were described as Moseley's 'great and good'.[58] They included Richard Cadbury, Joseph Chamberlain, the Rev. William Harrison Colmore, John Charles Holder, Thomas Clement Sneyd-Kynnersley, George Frederick Lyndon, John Padmore, James Smith and Francis Willmot. The day was 'ushered in by the ringing of joyous peals on the church bells repeated at intervals throughout the day'. Every cottager was provided with beef and plum pudding to eat at home. At 3pm 400 school children assembled at the National Schools. They each received a Jubilee Medal and then marched to the grounds of Moseley Hall, lent by Richard Cadbury, where the national anthem was sung to the accompaniment of a string band, which played throughout the afternoon. Tea for all followed, served from a large marquee. Amusements included races with

52 *Ibid.*, p. 377.

53 Gunn, 'Translating Bourdieu', p. 52.

54 SMCA, *Canon Colmore's log book*, p. 381.

55 *Ibid.*, p. 158.

56 *Ibid.*, p. 270.

57 *Ibid.*, pp. 354 and 381.

58 *Ibid.*, pp. 277, 279 and 281.

prizes and presents were freely distributed to all children. Balloons were sent up, including another inflated elephant and later a colossal policeman. Next came a greasy pole, which gave rise to much amusement, and the festivities concluded with fireworks. The 'Queen's weather prevailed and it was the brightest day of an unusually bright and glorious June'.[59]

Queen Victoria lived on to enjoy her diamond jubilee ten years later in 1897. The celebrations organised by Moseley's middle classes cost £250.[60] Six hundred children from the National School and local Sunday schools marched in procession to the village green, where festoons and bunting decorated shops and the church. The National Anthem was sung, after which the procession went to a large meadow at Moor Green belonging to Richard Cadbury. There they enjoyed sporting activities and a tea, while the elderly ate their meal at home. The children at Moseley Hall Convalescent Home decorated the interior of the hall with flags and 'two fine trees were planted in the gardens' by the youngest and eldest child and the National Anthem sung. A special tea was supplied by the ladies and the Amusement Committee and Hannah Heaven was once again to the fore, as at the annual parish tea parties, giving each child a medal. Coloured fires were lit and balloons sent up in the evening and each child was given a toy. There was enough money left to pay for the water trough and fountain on the village green and to help Moseley's Working Men's Club obtain premises of their own.

St Mary's church was behind movements in Moseley to curb alcohol consumption, drunkenness and disruptive behaviour among the working classes. The Rev. Colmore decided a hut was needed for the Moseley village cabmen to keep them out of the pubs.[61] During 1884 ladies were to the front in collecting and giving additional subscriptions for the hut and, after the vicar had obtained permission to erect the shelter in 1886, two ladies volunteered to collect more subscriptions.[62] The shelter was erected the week before Christmas and the cabmen asked the vicar to thank all contributors and said they had 'found it a very great boon in the wintry weather'.[63] £28 2s had been collected, which did not quite make up the sum required, but by 1887 the hut had been paid for and permission was given by the Sanitary Authority for it to remain on the green.[64] The process took at least three years and subscriptions were slow coming in, which suggests concern for the cabmen

59 *Ibid.*

60 Hewston, *History of Moseley village*, pp. 39–40; Fairn, *History of Moseley*, p. 60.

61 SMCA, *Canon Colmore's log book*, p. 185.

62 *Ibid.*, p. 225.

63 *Ibid.*, p. 269.

64 *Ibid.*, p. 270.

was not significant. This hut was replaced in 1902 by a cab shelter donated by Joseph Lucas, manufacturer of electrical equipment and father of Harry Lucas, who lived at Hilver, St Agnes Road, Moseley, at a cost of £250. This formed part of a programme of cab shelters organised by the Town Mission, an interdenominational temperance movement in Birmingham.[65]

In 1870 nine members of the twenty-one-strong ladies committee of the Town Mission at Tindal Street, Balsall Heath, came from Moseley, including Mrs Padmore of the Lindens, Mrs T. Wilcox, Park Road, and Mrs Hawkes, The Grove, Wake Green Road.[66] A Temperance Society was set up in Moseley in 1882 and on 2 August 1889 *The Dart* announced a 'Temperance Demonstration, on a large scale' to take place in the grounds of Moseley Hall on bank holiday Monday under the auspices of the Birmingham Temperance Mission and the patronage of the mayor, Alderman Barrow. The Blackwells subscribed to the Birmingham Town Mission in the 1890s.

On 24 January 1898 the *Birmingham Mail* and the *Birmingham Daily Post* reported on the laying of the foundation stone for the 'Moseley Social Club' for working men and youths in Alcester Road by Richard Cadbury's wife, Emma, which was to be run on temperance lines. The Cadburys were Quakers, many of whom took an active role in the temperance movement. Moseley residents were in attendance, including the Rev. Colmore, Henry Heaven, Hannah Heaven's husband, and Thomas Hadley. Richard Cadbury promised £100 conditionally on £500 being raised. The club was intended to provide reading, chess and billiard and bagatelle rooms, but was also a means of keeping young men off the streets and out of the pubs. There was an appeal for further financial support for the building, which, when completed, would cost about £700. A bowling green was planned for the rear.

Concern for young people was expressed in the establishment of other clubs in Moseley.[67] On 20 January 1885 a well-attended meeting at the Moseley National School chaired by Edmund Mackenzie Sneyd-Kynnersley decided to set up a club – Moseley Social and Recreation Club – not just for young men, but for all men above the age of sixteen years in Moseley. The Rev. Colmore was elected president and Frank Halward honorary treasurer, and a sub-committee was appointed to draw up the rules and enquire about a ground. Funds were raised on, for example, 8 October 1885, at a concert held at Moseley and Balsall Heath Institute. In October 1886 the general meeting of the club decided that a debating class be formed to 'develop local talent'. The

65 LBA, L41.2/82356, Annual Report of the Birmingham Town Mission, 1903. Courtesy Michael Dillon, PhD student, Birmingham University.

66 *Ibid.*

67 SMCA, *Canon Colmore's log book*, pp. 213, 215, 232, 243, 334, 338, 343, 373 and 452.

subjects of debates included 'Free Trade', 'Free Education', 'Abolishing the House of Lords', 'Instinct versus Reason' and 'Colonisation', an adventurous and political agenda that appears quite radical and highlights Moseley as an open community questioning the status quo. The classes met fortnightly on Monday evenings.

Subsequently the club lapsed somewhat. In May 1889 it was about to be revived and the use of two 'very suitable and central' rooms belonging to Charles Miles, the cab and car company proprietor, near the village green (Fig. 3.4), had been procured. In August 1889 an Ambulance class was begun – a rather more conservative initiative that was open to men only and was conducted by Dr Francis Underhill of Altadore, Church Road. He was described as lecturing in a 'very popular and lucid style'. In November 1889 certificates were presented to successful candidates in the Ambulance examinations, showing that this was a popular and successful venture. A pair of brass candlesticks was presented to Francis Underhill for the 'kindness he had shown in acting as lecturer'. In September 1889 a lending library was formed and, according to the honorary secretary Frank Greenhill, 'donors of books or money for this object will be conferring a great boon upon the working men and youths of Moseley'. He requested the works of Sir Walter Scott, Charles Dickens, Edward Bulwer-Lytton, George Eliot, Charles Kingsley, Edna Lyall, James Fenimore Cooper and Miss Mulock, all popular authors. In September 1890 lectures were given by Mr Bernard Badger (an Oxford University extension lecturer) at the Moseley National Schools on 'Physiography' (physical geography), including sessions on 'Springs and Rivers' and 'Ice'. Non-members were admitted on payment of a small fee.

In 1891 ladies of St Mary's church 'expressed a wish to start a Working Girls' Club'.[68] Women were becoming much more independent in the 1890s and mixed gender clubs acceptable. Perhaps this move for a club for girls was stimulated by the revival of the men's club, which was still men only. Subscriptions were requested from any parishioners 'who are willing to help forward this good work'. Those wishing to be members were to apply to Florence Charlton, The Limes, Alcester Road, for a ticket to the opening tea at the Moseley National Schools, when the object of the club 'will be explained'. This first meeting was attended by nearly forty girls. The club opened weekly at first on Wednesdays, running from 7pm to 9pm. Subscriptions cost 1d per week. Thirty-eight girls were present on the second Wednesday, showing 'a real desire to enjoy the advantages of the club'.[69] In February 1892 Moseley Girls' Club was thriving, with 476 attendances. In its first two years £11 7s

68 *Ibid.*, pp. 398, 400, 415 and 428.

69 *Ibid.*, p. 400.

5d was spent on a piano, room hire, printing and advertising, music, books, stationery, games and room cleaning, leaving 3s in hand. In the summer of 1893 Moseley Girls Club was open only one evening a month, but an August report states that it was to reopen on Wednesday 5 October for the winter quarter with a tea at 7pm and tickets costing 3d. The committee reminded the 'kind friends who helped them last year with subscriptions, that ... they cannot continue their work without assistance'. Books to start a library were also needed. No evidence has been located to reveal what took place at club meetings or who joined other than the names of fifteen women, including Hannah Kynnersley, who volunteered to help and who appear to have been from Moseley's middle classes.

St Mary's church and its members made a significant impact on Moseley in the second half of the nineteenth century. The church was the centre of social life, philanthropy, volunteering and community care. It supported the Moseley National School, the first National School in Birmingham and one of many such schools that were forerunners of primary education, financially, organisationally and in practical ways. St Mary's was extended, two new sister churches built and all three beautified. The church gave to a range of charities, published the parish magazine, introduced annual parish teas, set up clubs and, along with other Moseley residents, organised celebrations. It raised the necessary funding through subscriptions, bazaars and performances, and brought people together to help form a community.

Moseley and Balsall Heath Institute

The idea of an institute for the locality was stimulated by the Mechanics' Institute movement, which emerged in the early nineteenth century. The Moseley and Balsall Heath Institute originated as a debating society.[70] Some members met in late autumn 1876 at the house of Walter Bach in Moseley and founded a new society, Moseley and Balsall Heath Literary Association. The group held lectures in Lime Grove Schools, then the largest hall in the district. The membership increased rapidly, signalling that the new society was answering to local interests.

In 1878, with a membership of over 400, the Institute moved to Clifton Road Board Schools, Balsall Heath. There were evening classes, a programme of lectures and choral and dramatic societies. The first conversazione was held in the same year at Highgate Board Schools. There were impressive exhibitions focusing on technological innovations such as pen making, electro-motor

70 Alfred Wiseman, *Moseley and Balsall Heath Institute, 1876–1926, 'The Institute – a souvenir'* (Birmingham, 1926). This book underpins most of the information on the Moseley and Balsall Heath Institute here.

Figure 7.4. Moseley and Balsall Heath Institute. LBA, WPS/WK/M6/313, by permission of the Library of Birmingham.

sewing machines, glass engraving, microscopes and chemical experiments.[71] Moseley men contributed exhibits, including 'Electro-plating' by Frederick Elkington of Moseley Hall and 'Cases of Butterflies and Birds' by Samuel Blakemore Allport of Pymore Cottage, Alcester Road. A complete telephone system – the first recorded exhibition of the telephone in Birmingham – was set up. A printing press was installed, which printed a paper called *The Moseley Microphone News* during the evening.[72]

Two sisters, Miss Ellen and Miss Emma Lawrence, who lived at The White House on the corner of Edgbaston Road, had a crucial impact on the future development of the society. In 1878 they offered land on the Moseley Road for a purpose-built institute. Meanwhile, in 1880 the headquarters moved to the newly erected schools in Tindal Street, Balsall Heath, and a public

71 *Birmingham Daily Post*, 3 January 1878.

72 Wiseman, *Moseley and Balsall Heath Institute*, p. 5.

meeting there in 1882 tested the interest of the district in a dedicated building, during which a considerable amount of financial support was promised. Some £5,000 was needed to begin building work. A building fund was opened and realised £994 19s 6d from 126 donations. John Avins donated £50, Nathaniel Cracknell Reading £25, Joseph Chamberlain £21 and Althans Blackwell ten guineas. Many other donors were from Moseley, including John Padmore, James Smith and Francis Willmot. Mrs Reading senior was one of the women who donated in her own name; 93 per cent of the donors were men. The most common donation was five guineas (43 per cent); 19 per cent were for £10 and over, 17 per cent for two guineas and 15 per cent for one guinea.

It was some time before the building was completed (Fig. 7.4). The further sum of £1,431 7s 0d was raised by a bazaar at Birmingham Town Hall that ran over five days in October 1883. The balance was raised by a loan of £2,000 obtained on the personal guarantees of the thirty-six-strong committee, twelve of whom, including Nathaniel Cracknell Reading, undertook to pay the interest on a further £600 for two years. The names of these guarantors are inscribed on stone tablets in the vestibule. The terms of the Trust deed, signed on 18 December 1883, required that the building be used as 'a Literary and Scientific Institute'. The architect was Mr John Bowen. The large hall, the Lawrence Room, with a gymnasium underneath, opened in October 1883 and the small hall on the first floor, named after Tennyson, and two classrooms on the ground floor the following January. During this period 270 members paid a guinea annually and 290 subscribers – people from members' families – 10s annually.

In 1887 a bazaar raised £649 18s 5d, which, together with monies accumulated in the Building Fund, allowed two classrooms and an art room to be added. Women were to the fore in this bazaar and their efforts much appreciated:

> In the work of furnishing and otherwise rendering valuable assistance, over a hundred ladies were actively employed for several months before the opening and during the bazaar. They attended at stalls and displayed so much tact, energy and industry as to make the bazaar a success.[73]

A third bazaar, opened by the countess of Warwick, was held in 1896. The mayor of Birmingham arranged a civic reception at the railway station and officially accompanied her to the opening ceremony. The £531 raised meant the building, including the Masefield and Milton Rooms, could be completed.

The committee running the new Institute were all men, with Moseley men to the fore: Professor Henry Morley was the first president (1877–8) and Walter

---

73 *Ibid.*, p. 13.

Bach was honorary secretary from 1876 to 1879. Nathaniel Cracknell Reading was a committee member who also ran the Dramatic Society. Presidents included Moseley men – apart from Professor Henry Morley, there was Austen Chamberlain (1893–4), James Smith (1895–6) and John Charles Holder (1896–9).

During the first year at the dedicated site, 1883–4, the programme included lectures on geography, history, health and science, as well as dramatic recitals, entertainments and concerts. An 1883 advert in the *Birmingham Gazette* alerted readers to lectures by St John's Ambulance (a Ladies' Class and a Men's Class), French Classes, Shorthand, Gymnastics, Art Classes and a Choral Society. Conversaziones were held annually. Change was afoot, though. A paid secretary was appointed, the Institute Dramatic Society and Institute Orchestra were replaced by outside dramatic organisations and professional orchestras and new trustees were appointed. The popularity of the Institute fluctuated, but it attracted many members and subscribers over the years. There were 185 members and 174 subscribers (family of members) in 1880–1, 264 and 314 in 1886–7, 123 and 207 in 1890–1 and 217 and 364 in 1899–1900. Subscribers' tickets were reduced from 10s to 5s in 1892, following the drop in numbers in 1890–1. The Blackwells were members and paid a one-guinea member's ticket annually between 1893 and 1897.

The Moseley and Balsall Heath Institute became widely known as 'Moseley Town Hall'. John Avins offered land to the value of £1,600 in Church Road together with funds of £1,000 for a Moseley assembly rooms, but this was not taken up, despite a letter of support from Edward Holmes to the *Birmingham Mail* published on 12 April 1890. Interest in a Moseley assembly rooms was raised again in 1893 when Spurrier wrote that 'Although parts of Moseley are within easy reach of an Institute, an Assembly Room with reading rooms attached would be a great acquisition, but it must be conveniently situated – say nearly opposite the village green, or at the junction of Wake Green and Church Roads.' No Moseley assembly room was built.

Moseley residents also joined the Moseley and King's Heath Institute, of which the Rev. Colmore was honorary secretary from its foundation.[74] Activities at this institute were mostly concerts, theatricals, singing, instrumental music, recitations, conjuring and dances. Their conversazione exhibitions consisted of photographs and paintings lent by the congregation and 'some very good microscopes', a more modest enterprise compared with those of the Moseley and Balsall Heath Institute.[75] Various societies met at this institute, including a horticultural society.

---

74 Fairn, *History of Moseley*, p. 62.

75 LBLH, F/6 LF 55 4260592; SMCA, *Canon Colmore's log book*, pp. 383, 411 and 440.

The local clubs and institutes accommodated a wide range of activities in which both men and women took part. They were established and run by the middle classes and appear to have been largely enjoyed by the middle classes, but local artisans may well have benefited too. Some clubs were set up specifically for the working classes. These associations spoke to the Victorian enthusiasm for self-education and supporting the education of lower social groups, and provided further opportunities to see others and be seen. They offered Moseley residents social, educational, cultural and philanthropic opportunities and provided the more spacious rooms needed for the wide variety of events that were organised.

Birmingham voluntary hospitals, disabled children's institutions and children's charity schools

Voluntary hospitals and children's institutions opened in Birmingham before 1850. These included the General Hospital (1779), the first hospital in Birmingham, Queen's Hospital (1841), probably England's first purpose-built teaching hospital, the Orthopaedic Hospital (1817), the Birmingham and Midland Eye Hospital (1823) and the Birmingham Ear and Throat Hospital (1844). Children's institutions included the Birmingham Deaf and Dumb Institution (1814), the Birmingham Blind Institution (1848) and the Blue Coat Charity School (1722).[76]

After 1850, the Moseley middle classes continued to support these bodies through subscriptions, donations and legacies. Other hospitals were established and supported, including Birmingham Dental Hospital (1858), Birmingham Women's Hospital (1871), Birmingham Skin and Lock Hospital (1881, started by James Startin of Moseley) and the Jaffray Convalescent Hospital (1885).[77] John Throgmorton Middlemore founded the Children's Emigration Homes, known as Middlemore Homes, in 1872. They took destitute children or children recommended by the police or magistrates between the ages of ten and thirteen who were too young to be admitted to industrial schools but not obliged to go to school. Children were sent to Australia and Canada, supposedly for a better life.

Voluntary hospitals were intended for the 'deserving poor', those who were unable to pay for medical treatment but were above the level of paupers, who were treated in Poor Law establishments. Concern for the plight of the poor and disabled prompted involvement in charity schools and schools for disabled children and young people, but these were also a means of getting such children and young people off the streets with the intention of producing independent, self-supporting workpeople.

---

76 <www.thebluecoatschool.com>, accessed 15 March 2023.

77 J. Reinarz, *Health care in Birmingham: the Birmingham teaching hospitals, 1779–1939* (Woodbridge, 2009).

Annual reports listed contributors and their contributions and these were reported on in newspapers and local magazines. Such public benevolence brought donors status both locally and further afield and the possibility of finding themselves listed alongside Birmingham's great and good. People donating £10 became governors, could be part of committees administering the hospitals, had a vote at the AGM and could grant tickets of entry to clients, which enhanced their status further and gave them power, patronage and a sense of importance in the community. Manufacturers subscribing to voluntary hospitals might secure contracts for work and hospital treatment for their workers, given that many industrial accidents occurred.

An analysis of the Moseley subscriptions to nine hospitals and children's charities listed in their annual reports reveals that Moseley residents made significant contributions – a total of about £6,300 between 1851 and 1891.[78] A 'Moseley philanthropic elite' was formed by this group, including seventy individuals and four couples who gave £10 and over in any one year during the period. They contributed nearly £4,000, while those giving less than £10 in any one year contributed £2,355 between them, a significant amount. The 'top ten' Moseley philanthropists gave about £1,780 over the forty-year period. These included Rebecca and Anne Anderton, who gave around £184; John Avins, who gave around £122; Richard Cadbury, who gave around £162; Joseph, Austen, Beatrice and Clara Chamberlain, who gave around £871; William Henry Dawes, who gave around £112; Sir John Charles Holder, who gave around £163; and Thomas Clement Sneyd-Kynnersley, who gave around £166. Moseley residents also contributed to other hospitals and charity institutions, including the Jaffray Convalescent, Skin and Lock and Ear and Throat Hospitals and the Middlemore Charity School.

Of the top seventy individual contributors, 76 per cent were men. Of the elite individual contributors, men gave more than the women (approximately £2,641 compared with £1,061). Most individual elite subscribers gave between £10 and £49 in any one year. Only two subscribers, both men, gave £200 and over. Almost as many women as men, though, gave between £50 and £99 (six men and four women) and between £100 and £199 (five men and four women). The four couples gave between £25 and £100, and a total of £250 8s 0d. Of these members of the 'philanthropic elite' –

78 The subscriptions analysed in the annual reports of the hospitals, charity schools and disabled institutions included those of the General, Queen's, Women's, Orthopaedic, Ear and Throat and Eye hospitals, Blue Coat School, the Deaf and Dumb Institution and the Blind Institution. £6,300 in 1890 is equivalent to almost £517,000 in 2017, according to https://www.nationalarchives.gov.uk/currency-converter.

individuals and couples – 61 per cent supported one or two institutions, 28 per cent supported three to four and 11 per cent five to seven.

The most popular institution with Moseley subscribers was the General Hospital. The least popular overall was the Women's Hospital. By far the most popular with elite men were the Queen's and General Hospitals and the Blue Coat School and, with elite women, the Women's Hospital, signalling their special interest in women's health. The Ear and Throat and the Orthopaedic Hospitals were least popular with elite men and women. Male subscribers significantly exceeded women in subscribing to all hospitals, except for the Women's.

Before retiring to Moseley John Avins subscribed to the Institute for the Blind, Queen's Hospital, the Eye Hospital and the Blue Coat School through his family's firms at Worcester Wharf, where he lived and worked. After his move to Moseley in 1858, he continued to support the same charities, but in his own name, and added others too. Between 1858 and 1891, when he died, he subscribed to nine hospitals and institutions and donated to seven, bringing his total contributions to £239, an average of just over £7 per year. During his first decade in Moseley he added the General and Orthopaedic hospitals to his portfolio, in the 1870s the Women's Hospital and the Deaf and Dumb Institution and in the 1880s, the Jaffray Convalescent Hospital, the Middlemore and the Skin and Lock and Ear and Throat Hospitals. John Avins was not put off by the associations of the Skin and Lock Hospital with venereal patients, as many were. He gave most after moving to Moseley to the Blue Coat School, which alone received £71, followed by the Jaffray Convalescent Hospital (£39), the Orthopaedic and Children's Hospitals (£27) and the General and Queen's Hospitals (£21 each).

Some Moseley residents took on managerial roles. The Chamberlains were significantly involved with the Women's Hospital. They donated £671 to this hospital, far more than anyone else, and Joseph Chamberlain took on the role of president. Henry Rotton of Moseley, a land tax commissioner, was a visitor at the General Hospital in 1868, on the committee of the Ear and Throat Hospital and its chairman in 1869, as well as auditing subscriptions for Birmingham General Dispensary in 1882.[79] In 1873, the Dental Hospital AGM was presided over by mayor Joseph Chamberlain and in the same year William Gough was on the committee of the General Institute for the Blind. In 1877 two Moseley men were involved in the Deaf and Dumb Institution and another was a member of the Children's Hospital committee in 1889.[80]

79 *Birmingham Journal*, 18 April 1868, 20 July 1871 and 16 February 1882.

80 *Birmingham Daily Post*, 20 February 1873, 3 December 1873, 12 September 1877 and 29 January 1889.

John Avins donated £21 to the General Hospital in 1863, thereby becoming a life governor, a role he kept until his death in 1891.[81] His ten-guinea donation to the Women's Hospital also entitled him to the privileges of a life governor. In 1889 John Avins' wife, Eliza, became a life governor at the Women's and Orthopaedic Hospitals as did their daughter, Eliza Parthenia, from 1892. No records show that the family ever attended meetings or exercised any governorship rights. Men dominated voluntary management roles, but between 1892 and 1897 59 per cent of the Committee for the Election of Medical Officers at the Women's Hospital were women, as were 31 per cent at the Orthopaedic Hospital between 1894 and 1920.[82]

Single gifts and legacies were invaluable to these institutions because they provided a steady accumulation of fixed capital, enabling expansion. Men were particularly associated with posthumous philanthropy, ensuring their names were remembered after death. John Avins left £22,000 to the Orthopaedic Hospital, £2,000 of which was to establish workshops for the manufacture of instruments, with the income arising from this to go to patients. He also left £1,000 to the General Hospital Building Fund and set up a separate trust, to give money annually to medical charities, which still pays out today.[83] James Taylor left £20 to the Blind Institution in 1854.[84] Richard Cadbury left £50 to the Jaffray Hospital in 1888 and Lord John Charles Holder £107 in 1891.[85] Mrs Underhill left £50 to the Blind Institution in 1854 and Rebecca Anderton £100 in 1873 to the Blue Coat School.[86]

Many wives and daughters took over subscriptions following the death of husbands or fathers. Jane Padmore, the wife of Thomas Padmore of Wake Green Road, continued her husband's contributions to the Women's Hospital from 1879 and Emma Cadbury her husband Richard's contributions to the Eye Hospital in 1900.[87] After John Avins' death his wife Eliza subscribed and donated substantially more than her husband in her lifetime, a total of £34,178, her favourites being the General Hospital (£4,100), the Orthopaedic Hospital (£16,867) and the Women's Hospital (£12,053). Their daughter Eliza favoured the Orthopaedic Hospital (£14,594), the Women's Hospital (£101) and the Middlemore Home (£71), giving a total of £14,766.

81 LBA, GHB4/14 and HC/GH/1/3/1, General Hospital.

82 LBA, WH/1/10/4–7, Women's Hospital; LBA, HC/RO/A/13–15, Orthopaedic Hospital.

83 LBA, MS/1672 (Add l) (Acc 1991/137).

84 LBA, L.4861/7, Blind Institution.

85 LBA, L46.21, General and Jaffray Hospitals.

86 LBA, L.4861/7.

87 LBA, WH/1/10/2–3.

Social, cultural and sporting involvement

The Moseley middle classes were out and about in the public sphere not only in areas of formal public service such as politics, the church, education and philanthropy but also in more informal situations – leisure activities that offered opportunities for enjoyment, social and cultural engagement and sporting endeavour, as well as involvement in volunteerism and charity.

Moseley residents socialised locally. Mrs Adams of Sorrento, for example, arranged a private dance for seventy guests at her home in 1894.[88] Concerts in Moseley Park brought people together too. Moseley Park & Pool Consortium organised 'A Vocal and Instrumental Promenade Concert' on 26 June 1900 at 6.30pm with the Moseley Quartette & Concert Party, Gilmer's Military Band, the illumination of the pool and grounds and a fireworks display.[89] On 8 September 1900 they organised a 'Promenade and Pyrotechnics', with Willenhall Prize Band and their 'high-class' music and fireworks, which was attended by 3,000 people.[90]

Residents also advertised their status by socialising in Birmingham. Althans and Agnes Blackwell attended the Wesleyan Philharmonic Society, paying a subscription of 5s in 1878. They raised their status by subscribing to the Birmingham Central Literary Association, which cost 5s in 1879–80, and by buying their magazines at 2s 6d each. They attended the lord mayor's fancy dress ball on 22 April 1881, at which Joseph Chamberlain was dressed in a cabinet minister's court dress and 'Miss Chamberlain' as a fifteenth-century Burgundian duchess.[91] In June 1896 they attended a banquet for the lord mayor, Sir James Smith of The Dingle, Wake Green Road, at the City of Birmingham Council House. They subscribed to the 'Ladies Room' at the Birmingham Library at a cost of 2s in 1897. They went to Mr Stockley's orchestral concerts, the Birmingham Choral Society and the Birmingham Festival Choral Society annually, with tickets costing from about 14s to one guinea per person. Attending 'invitation-only' events and participating in civic occasions cemented and broadcast social standing. Attending ticketed events allowed the better-off middle-class suburbanites to assert their presence and display their wealth and importance. Living in a suburb was not just about proximity to the country, but also about participation in the opportunities of the city.

The Moseley middle classes set up and participated in an array of social and cultural clubs and societies. Moseley and King's Heath Gentlemen's Club was founded in 1893/4 in Alcester Road, Moseley. It was a licensed male-only

---

88 Fairn, *History of Moseley*, p. 56.

89 LBA, F/6 LF 55.4 LF 55.4260592.

90 *Ibid.*

91 *Birmingham Daily Post*, 22 April 1881.

establishment with a restaurant, reading room, bowls, billiards and smoking with fees (two guineas and a further annual subscription of two guineas) that excluded the working class.[92] This club suggests a 'flight from domesticity' and men seeking to escape the 'tyranny of the five o'clock tea', but the club also provided leisure opportunities for middle-class men that were not available to those living in smaller homes.[93] Smoking could be enjoyed in the club without the stale smoke and smell causing distress to the family that Jane Panton highlighted with such disapproval.[94] At Moseley, King's Heath and Balsall Heath Horticultural Society keen gardeners shared their gardening expertise, learnt from others and from lectures and mixed with the super-elite and upper middle classes, Joseph Chamberlain being a keen member. They displayed their achievements at horticultural shows in the grounds of the local elite's homes. Of the Moseley individuals belonging to this horticultural club, 70 per cent were men.[95]

Various groups provided opportunities in Moseley for cultural expression and the local display of aesthetics and erudition, including the Moseley Amateur Dramatic Society, the Moseley Shakespearean Society, the Moseley Musical Club, the Moseley Choral Society and, from the 1880s, the Photographic Society.[96] The Blackwells belonged to the Moseley Choral Society, paying George Thompson, the treasurer, of Bathurst, Chantry Road, a one-guinea subscription in 1893. In 1894 they joined the Oxford Road Literary Association at a cost of 2s. They paid two guineas to the Moseley Social Club, via the president, of Beech Cottage, Forest Road, Moseley, in 1897. These groups were open to men and women, but men largely took the lead, reflecting contemporary ideas about what was gender appropriate. The Rev. William Harrison Colmore, for example, ran the Moseley Shakespearean Society.[97] Women ran the female-orientated groups, such as the Girls' Friendly Society, and Agnes Colmore, the Rev. Colmore's wife, ran the local female-only Needlework Guild, which comprised twenty-two female members in 1885 and produced 104 garments for charity in 1900.[98]

Most sports clubs were male-orientated. Sport was seen as a solution to perceived bodily weakness in men due to their sedentary work and as a means of producing the physical power, skills and team spirit considered essential for

92 Cockel, *Moseley village walks*, p. 6.

93 Hamlett, *Material relations*, p. 95; Tosh, *A man's place*, pp. 179 and 182.

94 Panton, *From Kitchen to garret*, p. 80–1.

95 MSHGC, C3/D1/F8/3/24.

96 Gilbert, *The Moseley trail*, pp. 9–10; Fairn, *History of Moseley*, pp. 56–7.

97 *Ibid.*

98 LBA, L14.51, *Moseley Parish Magazine*, 1890–1900.

manliness.[99] Middle-class men led, managed and developed Moseley's sports clubs and supported them with donations and gifts.

Sports clubs flourished in Moseley under the aegis of the middle classes. These included Moseley and Balsall Heath Cricket Club (1855), Moseley Cricket Club (1864), Moseley Quoit and Bowling Club (1867) and Moseley Football (Rugby Union) Club (1873). Moseley Harriers Athletic Club was founded in 1881 and Moseley Park Lawn Tennis Club held its first annual tournament at The Reddings in 1886. Newton Tennis Club was sited in Belle Walk and Chantry Road Tennis Club in Moseley Park. Moseley Golf Club opened in 1892 at Billesley Hall Farm and the Moseley Ladies' Cycling Club was formed in 1896.[100] Walter Bach inspired the formation of the Ashfield Cricket Club in 1900, enlisting support from 'gentlemen of influence'.[101] Men met to form the club at his home, Beverley, Ashfield Avenue, which gave the club its name, and he was the first president and a key figure for thirty years. Such an abundance of sporting clubs provided opportunities for exercise, socialisation, the display of athletic skills and achievements and the enjoyment of delightful rural environments.

The first president of Moseley Football (Rugby Union) Club was Amos Roe. Edward Holmes was vice-president in 1894. He became a leading referee in international games and a writer on rugby union football. Nathaniel Cracknell Reading became president later and William Adams of Sorrento was a leading member. There were female members and admission for them was free in 1879. In 1888 the grounds were upgraded with a new covered stand free to all members, but 'ladies not members will be required to pay half a crown a season'.[102] Many female spectators apparently enjoyed the football experience greatly: 'Quite a large number of the fair sex graced the game with their presence, and judging by their unstinted applause when a fine bit of play came off, I should fancy they entered thoroughly into the spirit of the game'.[103] *The Dart* of 12 October 1888 stated that 'The ladies, as usual, made a brave show in spite of the keen wind'.

The only woman named as a committee member was Mrs W. Thomas, who was on the Moseley Quoit and Bowling Club committee in 1889.[104] Its

99 Joanne Begiato, *Manliness in Britain, 1760–1900: bodies, emotion and material culture* (Manchester, 2020), p. 43.

100 R.V. Mirams, *Moseley milestones: a history of the Moseley Golf Club, 1892–1992* (Birmingham, 1993), p. 2.

101 Ross Reyburn (ed.), *Life at the graveyard: Moseley Ashfield Cricket Club 1900–2000* (Birmingham, 2000), pp. 7–8.

102 *The Reddings: The Home of Moseley Football Club (Rugby). A History 1880–2000* (Birmingham), pp. 5–7.

103 *Ibid.*, p. 9.

104 MSHGA, C3/D1/F8/3/4.

Figure 7.5. Moseley Quoit and Bowling Club, 1875. MSHGC, Clive Gilbert Photographs (MC/D1/F12/18).

officers at the time, though, were all men – Mr Samuel Clarke was president, Nathaniel Cracknell Reading honorary secretary and James Milligan of Coppice Road the treasurer.[105] Nathaniel Cracknell Reading, as secretary, informed members by letter and card of the beginning of quoit and bowling play, matches and due dates for subscriptions.[106] In 1889 there were ninety-six members, of whom eleven were past presidents.[107] In May 1897 Nathaniel Cracknell Reading's brother-in-law, Althans Blackwell, paid a three-guinea entrance fee and subscription to the club.

Figure 7.5 shows the men-only Moseley Quoit and Bowling Club in 1875. They look serious, but are grouped in relaxed stances. They are bearded and dressed in quality gentry country clothing that looks something like a 'uniform' – respectable representatives of a male world, but at ease. Beards were physical markers of 'rugged, daring manliness' from the 1860s on, which is why they

105 *Some Moseley personalities*, Vol. II, pp. 37–40; MSHGA, C3/D2/A5, Moseley Quoits and Bowling Club Cards.

106 MSHGA, C3/D2/A5.

107 The past presidents were H. Bewlay, a constructional engineer and director, 76 Alcester Road, S.C. Cowen, Alcester Road, P. Gallimore, Church Road, T. Haydon, Coppice Road, H.W. Hyde, Wake Green Road, J. Milligan, Coppice Road, A. Patterson, Forest Road, W. Thomas, Oxford Road, G.J. Williams, Trafalgar Road, E. Worrall, Elm Villa, Alcester Road and J. Zair, Merle Lodge, Wake Green Road.

Figure 7.6. Early members of the Moseley Golf Club. Courtesy of Moseley Golf Club.

became popular.[108] Such team photographs were intended to record sporting events and achievements and advertise skills. They marked out individuals, raising their status: the well-known John Zair of Merle Lodge, Wake Green Road, is on the left, with Hubert Bewlay, in 1911 a constructional engineer and director living at 76 Alcester Road, on his right. Both these men were permanent members of the committee and trustees.

Moseley Golf Club started around 1892 with twelve members, all men, and averaged eight members across 1893–5.[109] Ladies provided curtains for the new Moseley Golf Clubhouse, while in 1896 men donated a bell, coat hooks and a hanging lamp. The president presented a silver cup for competition and Mr Willmot a lawn roller. In the early days male members could nominate ladies of their family to play on any day except Saturday and bank holidays. A 'Ladies Section' began in 1896 and was a breakthrough for Moseley women golfers. Miss Isabel Broughton and Mary Badger, the wife of Edward Badger, were the first women to be proposed. Women were still denied Saturday afternoon play, however. In early 1896 there were ten women members, but at the end of 1897 there were twenty-four and forty-four men. Women were

---

108 Begiato, *Manliness in Britain*, pp. 42 and 46–7.

109 Mirams, *Moseley milestones*, pp. 1–10.

Figure 7.7. Newton Tennis Club, 1899. MSHGC (MC/D3/F8/A/6a–f).

excluded from the Moseley Golf Club post-AGM dinner at the Grand Hotel in Birmingham in 1896. They had to be satisfied with a toast to them in their absence given by Hubert Bewlay (Fig. 7.6) and Ernest Bewlay, architect and first owner of the Cottage, 39 Park Hill.

Figure 7.6 shows early members of Moseley Golf Club, again all men. These men also look serious and formally dressed, but, at the same time, relaxed and companionable in the way they sit closely together. The image shows male clubbability rather than overt masculinity, but in 1899 they now sport moustaches and pipes and cigarettes that testify to changes in habits and the increased popularity of smoking. Hubert Bewlay is on the far right. Next to him, left to right, are other well-known Moseley residents proud of their involvement, including Harry Padmore, a refiner, of 20 Wake Green Road and Philip Willmot, solicitor, of 12 Wake Green Road.

Tennis clubs were quite different. Women were significantly involved and the atmosphere in the image of Newton Tennis Club (Fig. 7.7) contrasts greatly with that in the images of the golf and the quoit and bowling club. This 1899 image includes men and women – nine women and twelve men – and one child – singletons, married couples and families, according to the names listed on the rear of the image.[110] There is a casual air that is particularly evident in those sitting on the grass in the foreground but also in the informal gender mixing and the casual and varied clothing. This suggests Moseley society was more relaxed by the end of the century.

110 Mirams, *Moseley milestones*, p. 3.

Moseley, then, became a lively place where middle-class residents with money and leisure time to spare joined together in a wealth of political, civic, religious, educational, philanthropic, social, cultural and sporting environments both locally and in Birmingham. This reflected the middle-class suburban way of life and was important to middle-class identity and the social formation of the middle classes and the suburb. An 'elite' group emerged, which gave more to charity, held positions of authority and power and received public recognition. Any involvement by the lower middle classes went unmarked and the working classes were largely the recipients of patronage.

8

Conclusion

Over the course of fifty years Moseley developed from a small village just south of Birmingham to a flourishing middle-class suburb. Moseley's suburbanisation was stimulated by the growth and aspirations of the middle classes and Birmingham's industrialisation, expansion and wealth generation. Its development began in a proto-suburban phase in the first half of the nineteenth century, when wealthy industrialists and manufacturers from Birmingham made Moseley their home and the transport infrastructure – an improved toll road, a railway line and an omnibus service – was laid down. Moseley had numerous natural advantages, including its proximity to Birmingham, its rural ambience, its healthy environment, a geology ideal for building and a village green, a hall and an old Anglican church at its heart. These advantages continued to exert influence after 1850.

Development in the second half of the nineteenth century was not linear – there were fluctuations, rapid advances and setbacks. The introduction of the railway station at the heart of the village in 1868 was crucial to Moseley's suburbanisation, but the development of horse and tram omnibuses was particularly important before that, as was the later introduction and development of steam trams. The cost of owning and housing private transport and the ticket prices and timings of public transport contributed to Moseley's development as a middle-class suburb.

The role of the landowner was crucial. Moseley benefited from land being concentrated in the hands of a limited number of wealthy local families concerned to protect the environment and the middle-class character of the suburb. They ensured a more regulated expansion and a largely middle-class population by controlling land coming onto the market and designating houses on good-sized plots that were beyond the reach of lower social groups. Investors, mostly the local middle classes, were surprisingly small-scale, though some were more heavily involved. They included Moseley women as renters, owners and developers.

Moseley's domestic built environment provided a stage on which to display status and middle-class identity. It reflected changing contemporary architectural styles, which ultimately gave the suburb an eclectic physical character. Semi-detached houses dominated, but variations in the size and type of houses differentiated the middle class and created a degree of social zoning. Building controls ensured quality housing, but a typhoid outbreak in the 1870s highlighted poor sanitation. Residents formed pressure groups to hasten improvements, but concerns about sanitation continued to be expressed for some time, along with dissatisfaction with street lighting, roads and paving. These were crucial measures of a high-status suburb. Gardens were an important part of the built environment and another arena for display for the middle classes. Moseley residents took on board new ideas and plants from around the world but modified or disregarded styles to best suit their personal tastes and the space available. Their enthusiasm was stimulated by horticultural societies, the print media and the products of scientific and technological advances.

Moseley's middle-class families were very diverse. Suburbanisation is often spoken of as the middle class moving out of the city, but many Moseley residents came from areas other than Birmingham – from across Britain and abroad – all people preferring not to live in the city. Other findings about Moseley families defy popular conceptions. Many Moseley families were surprisingly small, as were the levels of co-residency of relatives, visitors and boarders, and many homes either did not have a resident servant or had only one. There was a surprising number of female household heads and they frequently offered shelter to others, including men. Most male household heads at the end of the century worked in industrial roles rather than commercial or professional positions, and many were workers, rather than employers. Many Moseley women, though, were out at work, largely in accepted female roles, such as schoolteachers, but also involved commercially in the village. Other women worked from home, as dressmakers for example, and job opportunities for women expanded towards the end of the century. Moseley families were not without problems, but most were kept secret. Infant and maternal death was high. Middle-class suburban life was bounded by life-cycle stages and associated rites and rituals, transmitting cultural capital and consolidating middle-class identity.

The size of the middle-class Moseley home decreed how the home was divided up and used. Given the lack of space, specialist rooms in smaller houses were few and key rooms were multi-occupational and multi-functional. Larger homes had a range of specialist rooms, some of which were gender orientated. In some cases the uses of the different rooms and who used them were flexible. Libraries, for example, were often not the only places where people read and were spaces where family members came together. Material culture was important in reflecting status and identity and a preoccupation of many. New technology and mass production enabled the less well-off to emulate those above them in the social hierarchy. Contemporary fashions influenced decoration and furnishing, but the style and taste of Moseley interiors differed strikingly. The impact of gender was notable in only some specialist rooms.

The home was important to male identity; it reflected the status of the family in the public realm, which also gave women an important role. For some, getting interiors 'right' and 'keeping up appearances' was a worry, though there were many advice books available. The expertise women developed as garden and interior designers provided a launching pad for professional employment. Over time facilities within the home improved and became widespread, but, even so, a surprising number of homes did not have an inside WC or bathroom and even large houses often only had one bathroom.

Privacy, a supposed concern of the middle class, was manifest in many ways – in the desire for single-family homes and gardens, in how plot boundaries were established and gardens planted up and in the designation of public spaces within the home. However, the home was never wholly private because of the desire to project status, the extent of social entertaining, the presence of servants, the commodification of the home and the items brought into the home from the outside.

Moseley became a lively environment with its residents much involved in a range of political, religious, social, cultural and sporting associations and in volunteering and philanthropy. Increased leisure time and financial stability enabled Moseley's middle classes to initiate and take part in these activities, which helped forge a new community. Their involvement in volunteering and philanthropy was motivated by genuine concern for others less fortunate than themselves, but also by other, more personal and self-seeking imperatives. Women were involved in all these public endeavours but not to the same extent as men and they were rarely to the fore. Women, though, were out and about in the world, involved in the housing market in Moseley, increasingly out at work in the public sphere or working gainfully at home, shopping, travelling on public transport – where they learnt new patterns of behaviour – gardening and entering horticultural competitions and attending events locally, in Birmingham and further afield.

The suburban middle class were a strong cultural force, possessing a distinctive way of life that became synonymous with middle-class identity and differentiated it from those both above and below. Suburbia was a new residential setting which for many Victorians 'seemed a physical manifestation of middle-class values'.[1] As the half-century progressed more members of the lower middle classes moved to Moseley, changing its social and physical character, but, while an 'elite' dominated, one of the distinctive features of suburban culture was its 'elasticity', its ability to accommodate residents from

1 Sarah Bilston, '"They Congregate … in towns and suburbs": the shape of middle-class life in John Claudius Loudon's *The Suburban Gardener*', *Victorian Review*, 36/1 (2011), p. 144.

the very wealthy to the small-villa contingent.[2] The subtly different middle-class layers had much in common that drew them together as a group and within networks. The suburb was not exclusively middle class: the working classes were crucial to building, maintaining, servicing and serving it. Different social levels and religious groups came together, which created opportunities to enhance mutual understanding and cement cohesion. Residents worked together to improve the suburb, forming pressure groups to that end: the middle class making, moulding and preserving their own environment and forming a new community with new opportunities.

Moseley was not an isolated and insular residential area. Birmingham's industrial and commercial success provided the wealth that enabled the middle classes to live in Moseley. The city centre provided the transport hub, creating a feasible commute and facilitating visits to the city for shopping, entertainment, cultural activities and onward journeys. Suburbanites could go into the city, but city dwellers could also travel outwards to take advantage of the countryside and the rural environment, though sometimes in unwelcome ways. The link with Birmingham supported the development of Moseley by bringing new services – sewerage, water and gas – and others such as postal deliveries, newspapers and a great variety of goods. Moseley also had connections to the wider world, including political links through Joseph Chamberlain with London and parliament. Some residents were from other parts of the UK and abroad, and plants and materials in the home came from across the globe, telling of empire and different ethnicities. Residents took journeys to the seaside, as well as to other parts of the UK and abroad.

Moseley became increasingly engulfed. People 'leapfrogged' over it to more rural suburbs further out. It went from 'sought-after suburb on the edge of the country to an integral part of the fully urbanised central metropolis' when it was absorbed into Birmingham in 1911 by the Greater Birmingham Act, along with large areas of Staffordshire and Warwickshire.[3] Demographical changes further into the twentieth century and Moseley's redefinition as a café and restaurant enclave and live-music venue in the twenty-first century carried the story of this exclusive suburb forward. Moseley, though, has retained its individuality and character as well as its reputation as an attractive and vibrant middle-class suburb.

Suburbanisation came at a cost to the rural and peaceful environment of the original village and, while many welcomed the suburb's modernity, convenience and lifestyle, others looked back with nostalgia to a simpler time. Moseley in the second half of the nineteenth century was indeed more than a

2 Gunn, 'Translating Bourdieu', p. 53.

3 Thompson, *The rise of suburbia*, p. 4.

collection of buildings where people lived: it was a physical, social, cultural and psychological space where people conveyed messages about who they were and how they wanted to be seen for themselves and others.

Bibliography

Primary Sources

Library of Birmingham Archives

392143, W.B. Bickley.

BCKJ/MB/6/13/1–26, Sanitary Assessments, 1873–96.

BPKNU, BCK/MC/7/3/–, King's Norton Union Building Plans.

Children's Charitable Institutions Annual Reports: L41.31/19–45 222, Middlemore Charity Home, 1892–1912; MS/622/1/5/1–39, L48.113, Blue Coat Charity School, 1857–96; L48.62, Deaf and Dumb Institute, 1836–83; L.4861, Blind Institution, 1849–97.

EP/77/2/4/1, St Mary's Church Burials, 1813–50.

EP/77/5/2/1 (Acc. 92/92) DRO 77/39, St Mary's Church, Moseley, Vestry Minutes Book, 1853–1940.

Everson, H.J., 'Directory of Moseley', 1896.

HC/BCH/1/2/4, Minutes of the Birmingham and Midland Free Hospital for Sick Children, 10 November 1890.

Hospital Annual Reports: GHB4/14 and HC/GH/1/3/1, General Hospital; HC/GH/1/3/1 and L46.21, General and Jaffray Hospitals, 1779–1843, 1885–96; HC/QU/1/8/1–15, Queen's Hospital, 1865–91; WH/1/10/1–7, Women's Hospital, 1871–1902; HC/BC/1/14/1, Children's Hospital, 1862–1901; HC/RO/A/10–15, Orthopaedic Hospital, 1874–1900; L46.315, Ear and Throat Hospital,1862–95; HC/EY/2/1/3/1, Eye Hospital, 1869–1933.

L41.2/82356, Annual Report of the Birmingham Town Mission, 1903.

MS/39/1/2/3, Will of William Congreve Russell, 1873.

MS/39/26/6, William Anderton: Will.

MS/39/26/21–2 a/3/273/17, Conveyance of Samuel Lloyd: Freehold Estate, Balsall Heath House, 1839.

MS/183, Grange Farm building estate brochure.

MS/579/4 Acc/71aE, Meeting at the Fighting Cocks, 1874.

MS/718/9, An abstract of the title of George Bayliss and his mortgages on two villa residences in Church Road in 1893.

MS/1672/087/8/9/90 (Acc 1991/137) and MS/1272 (Acc 1995/027), John Avins Trust Minute Books 1–3, John Avins Trust Ledger, John and Eliza Avins' wills and legal papers.

MS/3069/13/3/76–7, W.B. Bickley.

MS/179416, Bham/Sc, Birmingham: a collection of auctioneer's bills, Vol. 1, 1779–1875.

MS/355198, Moseley Hall.

MS/383200, Shorthouse's Greenhill Estate Plans, 1853 and 1858.

The Library of Birmingham Local History

Aris's Birmingham Gazette, Obituary Index, Vol. 1, A–B, No. 8, December 1889.

B.COL 08.2;96586, *Birmingham Faces and Places*, Vols 1–6, 1889.

L14.51, *Moseley Parish Magazine*, 1890–1900.

L50.7, *The Central Library Magazine*.

MS/559, In Memoriam Cards.

MS/579/6/71aE and F/6 LF 55.4, LF55.4260592, Programmes and Posters.

MS/355198, Newspaper Cuttings: Moseley Hall.

WPS/WK/M6/6, Image: A Steam Tram, Moseley Village Green.

WPS/WK/M6/99, Image: '"Bona-Fide Travellers" Requiring "Refreshment"', Moseley, 1873.

WPS/WK/M6/144, Image: St Mary's Chapel, 1812.

WPS/WK/M6/313, Image: Moseley and Balsall Heath Institute.

Cadbury Research Library, University of Birmingham

JC6/7/1–173 and C1/10/11, Misc., Joseph Chamberlain; *Moseley and King's Heath Journal*, 'Ourselves', No. 1, June 1892 and No. 10, March 1893.

MS/14/3, *The journal of Joseph Dixon, 1822–1828*.

MS/220/E/1/3, Letter 5, 25 May 1888, Miscellaneous Papers, Stevens and Matthews Family.

MS/447, *Travel diary of Lavinia Bartlett, 1843–1851*.

MS/804/1/2/3/2/3, Meeting of subscribers of the Queen's Hospital, 30 November 1857.

US/41/7/24, Correspondence of Dr R. Norris; Dr R. Norris–G. Dean, Springfield College, Letters 19; Dr R. Norris–Dr D.W. Simon, Letter 59.

The Moseley Society History Group, 'The Collection'

Reading-Blackwell Archive: C3/D2/Artefacts A/1–10; C3/D2/A/7/BRB/1–20; C3/D2/A/F10/1–18; *Matthew Boulton's diary, 1838–1841*; Bills and Receipts.

C1/D3/BB1/2, Thorpe, Harry, Galloway, Elizabeth, B., and Evans, Lynda, A., 'The Rationalisation of Urban Allotments Systems – A Case Study of Birmingham'.

C2/D1/F4/_, Thomas Anderson, *Memories of Moseley in the nineteenth century* (17); Isgrove, David, 'A Snapshot of Moseley', Bham13 (21); 'Old Moseley (Worcestershire)' (22); *The Dart*, 'Tittle Tattle by Mollie', July 1891, p. 27 (25).

C2/D1/F4/14, C3/D1/F11/2 and C3/D2/F1/31, Moseley Botanical Gardens.

C2/D1/F9/4/29–31, Scott, C.D., 'Birmingham 13', 'St. Mary's Row', 1995.

C2/D1/F10/_, Hart, Val, 'Joseph Balden', Balsall Heath Local History Society, undated (25); Article on Schools (26); Image: Mason Family (44/9).

C2/D3/F7/21, Image: Moseley National School.

C3/D1/F5/4, Image: Luker, the Woodbridge Road baker and confectioner, *c.*1909.

C3/D1/F7/5, Polling Card.

C3/D1/F8/_, The East Worcestershire Liberal Unionist Association Subscription List, 1900 (1); Moseley Quoit and Bowling Club (3/4); Moseley and King's Heath Horticultural Club Members (3/24).

C3/D2/A/3, Image: Agnes and Althans Blackwell.

C3/D2/A/F10/9, Image: Brackley Dene, Chantry Road, 1891.

C3/D2/A/F10/16, Contemporary comment on Chantry Road.

C3/D2/A5, Moseley Quoits and Bowling Club Cards.

C3/D2/F1/36, *Moseley Society Journal*, 1/10 (November 1894).
C3/D3/F4/12, C3/D3/F6/2, 14 and 25 and C3/D3/F7/10, The Shorthouse Family.
MC/D1/11/7, Image, Mansion House.
MC/D1/F12/_, Clive Gilbert Photographs.
MC/D3/4, Tithe Landholding, 1840 Moseley Yield.
MC/D3/F8/A/6a–f, Image, Newton Tennis Club.
MC/D5/7 and MC/D6/15–18, Image, Carriage Hire.

Historic England
BL 10873, Drawing Room, Glaisdale, 96 Park Hill, Moseley, 1891.
BL 10874, Dining Room, Greengate, 98 Park Hill, Moseley, 1891.
BL 11015, Drawing Room, The Dell, Moseley, 1891.
BL 15550, Boudoir, Sorrento, Wake Green Road, Moseley, 1899.
BL 155542, Entrance Hall, Sorrento, Wake Green Road, Moseley, 1899.
BL 155544, Library, Sorrento, Wake Green Road, Moseley, 1899.
BL 155545, Drawing Room, Sorrento, Wake Green Road, Moseley, 1899.

St Mary's Church, Moseley
Canon Colmore's log book, 1876–93.

Private Collections
Author's own.
Barrow Cadbury Trust, Kean House, 6 Kean Street, London WC2B 4AS.
Rhodes, Mike.
Volunteer archivist, St Mary's Church, Moseley: R. Brown.
Cockel, R.
Adams, F.

Printed Primary Sources

Newspapers and Journals
Birmingham Daily Post, 1850–95.
Birmingham Gazette.
Supplement to the London Gazette, 1864.
Worcestershire Chronicle, 1870.

Trade Directories
Bentley's directory of Worcestershire, 1841.
Dix & Co.'s General and Commercial Directory of the Borough of Birmingham and 6 miles around (Birmingham, 1855 and 1858).
Francis White & Co.'s Commercial and Trades Directory of Birmingham, Vol. 11 (Sheffield, 1875).
Francis White & Co.'s History and General Directory of the Borough of Birmingham (Sheffield, 1849 and 1855).
Francis White & Co.'s History, Gazetteer and Directory of Warwickshire (Sheffield, 1850).
Isaac Slater's General and Classified Directory of Birmingham and its vicinities (Manchester, 1852–3).
W. Kelly & Co.'s Directory of Birmingham with its suburbs (London, 1867, 1868, 1871, 1875).

W. Kelly & Co.'s Directory of Birmingham with Staffordshire and Worcestershire (London, 1850).
W. Kelly & Co.'s Directory of Worcestershire (London, 1850, 1876, 1878 and 1879).

Censuses

Aitken, John (ed.), 'Census of Religious Worship, 1851: The Returns for Worcestershire', Worcestershire Historical Society (Worcester, 2000), Entry 486.

Census of Great Britain 1851, Religious Worship in England and Wales, abridged from the official report by Horace Manners to George Graham Esq, Registrar-General (London, 1854).

Censuses 1851–1901: https://www.ancestry.co.uk.

Other Printed Primary Sources

Anderson, James, *The new practical gardener and modern horticulturist* (London, 1875).

Anderton, Thomas, *A tale of one city: the new Birmingham* (Birmingham, 1900).

Beeton, Mrs, *The book of garden management* (London, 1862).

Blomfield, Reginald, *The formal garden* (London, 1892).

Cartwright, Julia, 'Gardens', *The portfolio* (London, 1892).

Eastlake, Charles Locke, *Hints on household taste in furniture, upholstery and other details* (London, 1869).

Henty, G.A., *A knight of the white cross* (London, 1896).

Kerr, R., FRIBA, *The English gentleman's house or how to plan English residences* (London, 1864).

Loudon, J., *Encyclopaedia of cottage farm and village architecture*, new edn, ed. Mrs Loudon (London, 1846).

Loudon, Jane, *Gardening for ladies and companion to the flower garden*, ed. A.J. Downing (New York, 1840).

Loudon, J.C., *An encyclopaedia of cottage, farm, and villa architecture and furniture* (London, 1833).

Loudon, J.C., *The suburban gardener and villa companion* (London, 1838).

Loudon, J.C., *The villa gardener* (London, 1850).

Lubbock, Sir John, *The pleasure of life* (New York, 1887).

Lubbock, Sir John, *The beauties of nature* (London, 1892).

Maclaren, Ian, *The days of Auld Lang Syne* (London, 1895).

Panton, J.E., *From kitchen to garret: hints for young householders* (London, 1890), 7th edn, Project Gutenberg, eBook, 2016.

Robinson, William, *The wild garden* (London, 1870).

Ruskin, John, *The seven lamps of architecture* (London, 1849).

Ruskin, John, *The stones of Venice* (London, 1851–3).

Ruskin, John, 'Of Queen's Gardens', in *Sesame and lilies* (London, 1865).

Sedding, John Dando, *Garden-craft old and new* (London, 1892).

Wiseman, Alfred, *Moseley and Balsall Heath Institute, 1876–1926, 'The Institute – a souvenir'* (Birmingham, 1926).

Secondary Sources

Aston, Jennifer, *Female entrepreneurship in nineteenth-century England: engagement in the urban economy* (London, 2016).

Aston, Jennifer, Capern, Amanda and McDonagh, Briony, 'More than bricks and mortar: female property ownership as economic strategy in mid-nineteenth-century urban

England', *Urban History*, 46/4 (2019), pp. 695–721.

Auerbach, Jeffrey, 'Review of Simon Gunn. *The public culture of the Victorian middle class: ritual and authority and the English industrial city 1840–1914* (New York, 2000)', *The American Historical Review*, 107/3 (2002), pp. 937–8.

Balducci, Temma and Belnap-Jensen, Heather (eds), *Women, femininity and public space in European visual culture, 1789–1914* (London and New York, 2014).

Ballard, P. (ed.), *Birmingham's Victorian and Edwardian architects* (Wetherby, 2009).

Barrett, H. and Phillips, J., *Suburban style: the British home, 1840–1960* (Boston, Toronto, London, 1993).

Bath Postal Museum guidebook.

Baxter, M. and Drake, P., *Moseley, Balsall Heath and Highgate, the archive photographs series* (Chalford, 1996).

Begiato, Joanne, *Manliness in Britain, 1760–1900: bodies, emotion and material culture* (Manchester, 2020).

Best, G., *Mid-Victorian Britain 1851–1875* (St Albans, 1973).

Bilston, Sarah, '"They congregate ... in towns and suburbs": the shape of middle-class life in John Claudius Loudon's *The Suburban Gardener*', *Victorian Review*, 36/1 (2011), p. 144.

Bilston, Sarah, *The promise of the suburbs: a Victorian history in literature and culture* (New Haven, CT and London, 2019).

Bold, A., *An architectural history of St Mary's church 1405–2005* (Moseley, 2004).

Branca, P., *Silent sisterhood: middle-class women in the Victorian home* (London, 1977).

Bryden, I. and Floyd, J. (eds), *Domestic space: reading the nineteenth-century interior* (Manchester, 1999).

Bryson, J.R. and Lowe, P.A., 'Story-telling and history construction: rereading George Cadbury's Bournville Model Village', *Journal of Historical Geography*, 28/1 (2002), pp. 21–41.

Burke, T., *Travel in England* (London, 1945–6).

Cadbury, Helen, *Richard Cadbury of Birmingham* (London, 1906).

Calder, J., *The Victorian home* (London, 1977).

Cockel, R., *Moseley village walks from the dovecote* (Birmingham, 2006).

Cohen, D., *Household gods: the British and their possessions* (London and New Haven, CT, 2006).

Cohen, D., *Family secrets: the things we tried to hide* (London, 2013).

Constantine, Stephen, 'Amateur gardening and popular recreation in the 19th and 20th centuries', *Journal of Social History*, 14/3 (1981), pp. 387–406.

Cordea, D.A., 'The Victorian household and its mistresses: social stereotypes and responsibilities', *Journal of Humanistic and Social Studies*, II/4 (2011), pp. 9–17.

Creese, W.L., *The search for environment, the garden city: before and after*, 1st edn (Hartford, CT, 1966).

Davidoff, L. and Hall, C., *Family fortunes: men and women of the English middle class 1780–1850* (Abingdon, 2002).

Dick, M., 'The death of Matthew Boulton, 1809: ceremony, controversy and commemoration', in Quickenden, K., Baggott, S. and Dick, M. (eds), *Matthew Boulton: enterprising industrialist of the Enlightenment* (Farnham, 2013), pp. 247–66.

Dyos, H.J., *Victorian suburb: a study of the growth of Camberwell* (London, 1966).

Eveleigh, D.J., *Firegrates and kitchen ranges* (Aylesbury, 1986).

Eveleigh, D.J., *Privies and water closets* (Oxford, 2011).

Fairn, A., *A history of Moseley* (Halesowen, 1973).
Flanders, J., *The Victorian house: domestic life from childbirth to deathbed* (London, 2003).
Freeman, M.J. and Aldcroft, D.H. (eds), *Transport in Victorian Britain* (Manchester, 1988).
Gaskell, M., 'Gardens for the working class: Victorian practical pleasure', *Victorian Studies*, 23/4 (1980), pp. 479–501.
Gilbert, C., *The Moseley trail* (Birmingham, 1986).
Girouard, M., *Sweetness and light: the Queen Anne movement 1860–1890* (New Haven, CT and London, 1977).
Gleadle, Kathryn, *Borderline citizens: women, gender and political culture in Britain, 1815–1867* (London, 2009).
Gordon, E. and Nair, G., *Public lives: women, family and society in Victorian Britain* (New Haven, CT and London, 2003).
Gorham, D., *The Victorian girl and the feminine ideal* (London and Canberra, 1982).
Griffiths, A., *The history of the Ellis family: the Sorrento connection* (Studley, 2013).
Gunn, S., *The public culture of the Victorian middle class: ritual and authority and the English industrial city, 1840–1914* (Manchester, 2000).
Gunn, Simon, 'Translating Bourdieu: cultural capital and the English middle class in historical perspective', *The British Journal of Sociology*, 56/1 (2005), pp. 49–64.
Hall, P. and Ward, C., *Sociable cities: the legacy of Ebenezer Howard* (Chichester, 2000).
Hamlett, Jane, *Material relations: domestic interiors and middle-class families in England, 1850–1910* (Manchester, 2010).
Hannam, June, 'Women and politics', in Purvis, Jane (ed.), *Women's history: Britain, 1850–1945: an introduction* (London, 1995), pp. 217–45.
Hardy, D., *Utopian England: community experiments 1900–1945* (London, 2000).
Harrison, M., *Bournville: model village to garden suburb* (Chichester, 1999).
Helmreich, A., *The English garden and national identity: the competing styles of garden design, 1870–1914* (Cambridge, 2002).
Hewston, N., *The history of Moseley village* (Stroud, 2009).
Howard, E., *Garden cities of tomorrow*, 2nd edn (Rhosgoch, 1985).
Howe, Anthony, *The cotton masters, 1830–1860* (Oxford, 1984).
Inglis, Simon, *Villa Park – 100 years* (Warley, 1997).
Jenson, A.G., *Early omnibus services in Birmingham 1834–1905* (Biggleswade, 1963).
Lasdun, S., *Victorians at home* (London, 1985).
Listed buildings of Moseley (Birmingham, 1989).
Lochhead, M., *The Victorian household* (London, 1964).
Logan, T., *The Victorian parlour: a cultural study* (Cambridge, 2003).
Long, P.J. and the Reverend W.V. Audrey, *The Birmingham and Gloucester Railway* (Gloucester, 1987).
McKenna, J., *Birmingham: the building of a city* (Stroud, 2005).
Mah, A., 'Demolition for development: a critical analysis of official urban imaginaries in past and present UK cities', *Journal of Historical Sociology*, 25/1 (2012), pp. 151–76.
Mansfield, Elizabeth C., 'Women, art history and the public sphere: Emilia Dilke's eighteenth century', in Balducci, T. and Belnap-Jensen, H. (eds), *Women, femininity and public space in European visual culture, 1789–1914* (London and New York, 2014), pp. 189–203.
Marsh, Peter and Pick, Justine, *The house where the weather was made: a biography of Chamberlain's Highbury* (Alcester, 2019).

Midgley, Clare, 'Ethnicity, "race" and empire', in Purvis, Jane (ed.), *Women's history: Britain, 1850–1945* (London, 1995), pp. 247–77.

Mirams, R.V., *Moseley milestones: a history of the Moseley Golf Club, 1892–1992* (Birmingham, 1993).

Mitchell, S., *Daily life in Victorian England* (London, 1996).

Musgrove, F., 'Middle-class education and employment in the nineteenth century', *The Economic History Review*, NS, 12/1 (1959), pp. 99–111.

Owen, D., *English philanthropy 1660–1960* (London, 1965).

Paxman, J., *The Victorians: Britain through the paintings of the age* (Reading, 2009).

Perrie, Maureen, '"Almost in the country": Richard Cadbury, Joseph Chamberlain and the landscaping of south Birmingham', in Dick, Malcolm and Mitchell, Elaine (eds), *Gardens and green spaces in the West Midlands since 1700* (Hatfield, 2018), pp. 138–159.

Perrie, M., 'Hobby farming among the Birmingham bourgeoisie: the Cadburys and the Chamberlains on their suburban estates, c.1880–1914', *Agricultural History Review*, 61 (2013), pp. 111–34.

Price, F., *The Moseley Church of England National School: a history 1828–1969* (Birmingham, 1998).

The Reddings: the home of Moseley Football Club (rugby). A history 1880–2000 (Birmingham).

Reinarz, J., *Health care in Birmingham: the Birmingham teaching hospitals, 1779–1939* (Woodbridge, 2009).

Reyburn, Ross (ed.), *Life at the graveyard: Moseley Ashfield Cricket Club 1900–2000* (Birmingham, 2000).

Ruggles, Stephen, *Prolonged connections: the rise of the extended family in nineteenth-century England and America* (London, 1987).

St Mary's Moseley: guidebook and history (Moseley, 2018).

Schmucki, B., 'The machine in the city: public appropriation of the tramway in Britain and Germany, 1870–1915', *Journal of Urban History*, 38/6 (2012), pp. 1060–93.

Some Moseley personalities, Vols I–III (Birmingham, 1991, 1994 and 2014).

Thompson, F.M.L. (ed.), *The rise of suburbia* (Leicester, 1982).

Tosh, John, *A man's place: masculinity and the middle-class home in Victorian England* (New Haven, CT and London, 1999).

Turner, K., *The lost railways of Birmingham* (Studley, 1991).

Victorian Moseley (Birmingham, 2013).

Waters, Michael, *The garden in Victorian literature* (Aldershot, 1988).

Thesis

Bailey, A.R., 'Constructing a model community: institutions, paternalism and social entities in Bournville 1879–1939', PhD thesis (University of Birmingham, School of Geography, Earth and Environmental Sciences, 2002).

Index